The Illustrated Elvis

King
of
Rock an Roll

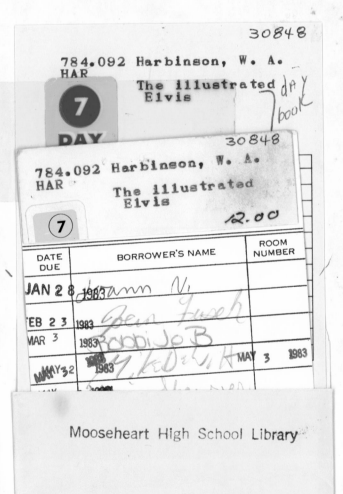

For Maxine and Glyn

The Illustrated Elvis

784.098
ILL

BY W.A. HARBINSON
DESIGNED BY STEPHEN RIDGEWAY

GROSSET & DUNLAP
Publishers New York
A Filmways Company

First published in the United States in 1976 by
Grosset & Dunlap, Inc.
51 Madison Avenue
New York, N.Y. 10010.
Copyright © W.A. Harbinson 1975
All rights reserved

Library of Congress catalog card number: 76-556
ISBN 0-448-12572-2 (hardcover)
ISBN 0-448-12461-0 (paperback)

Originally published in Great Britain
by Michael Joseph Ltd.
52 Bedford Square, London WC1 3EF.

Printed and bound in the United States

I was a lonely teenage bronckin' buck
With a pink carnation and a pick-up truck.
– American Pie, *Don McLean*

e is born in a two-room plank house in Tupelo, Mississippi.
he house is raised off the ground on legs of concrete and
rick, has a porch, three windows and a pointed roof. Small,
arrow, redolent of poverty, it resists the heavy rains and the
ummer's dry heat, but otherwise doesn't amount to much.
he floors are bare. There is no running water. Outside is a
hit-house, a pump, some trees and untended grass. A few
iles north-east, in the Princeville Cemetery, his twin brother
buried not forty-eight hours after he is born. Life is raw in
upelo, Mississippi.

t is January, 1935. Highway 78 runs from Memphis to Ala-
ama, passing close to the Presley home in Tupelo. The land
ises and falls, drinks the rain, fights the sun, and is webbed
ith dried creeks and stooped fences. This is Black country.
here are cottonfields and sugar cane plantations; there is
hite trash and black scum. You can hear the two groups
inging with evangelical fervour in those nights when God
eeps them from madness; they both sing the same songs.

bout a year after the birth of Elvis Aron Presley and the
lmost simultaneous death of his brother Jesse Garon, one of
istory's more catastrophic tornados tears through Tupelo.
: spirals blackly to the sky, splitting the dark clouds, ripping
hrough the land with the cold blind malevolence of nature.
t's a nightmare, a dreamer's deep trap, the howling eye of
blivion. It kills a few hundred people, injures more than a
housand, and destroys a great number of homes. It takes
hirty-two seconds. But the Presley shack, in the east side of
upelo, remains untouched.

Now we see them. They are a family of three. The mother has

a face of extraordinary beauty, her hair pulled back tight over
delicate ears, her eyes dark and luminous. The features are
fragile, hinting at deprivation and the sort of religious faith
that can move mountains. She is wearing a cheap, patterned
dress, a belt buckled at the waist; her left hand is looped over
the shoulder of her equally sombre husband. He wears a
faded shirt, a hat tipped back on his head; is lean, hungry and
radiating the innocence of a man who does not hope for too
much.

They are workers and they know it.

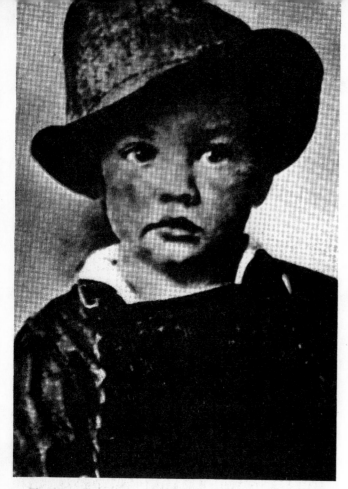

The boy, Elvis Aron, stands between them. He is two or three years old, a real sharecropper's kid. He is wearing dungarees, a grubby two-toned shirt, and has a hat on his head just like Dad. The hat is tipped cutely to the right, slanting down over huge, fine eyes whose pupils seem enormous and give him a penetrating look which is at odds with his round baby face. The nose appears to be flattened, the cheeks are too chubby, and already the now famous curl is distorting his fat lips. He is, in short, an unlovely but irresistible kid – the kind normally doomed to oblivion in a land that eats cheap labour.

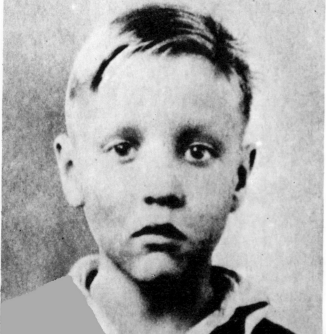

Some time later when the boy is six, there is anoth photograph. It is a head shot. He has developed some of mother's more delicate features, is golden-haired, wide-ey and beautiful. But the famous lip is there, twisted down the left, giving the angel a mischievous look, again irresistib

When at the age of eight he is photographed again, he taller, slimmer and quite docile: every mother's dream chil

In this six years the parents have aged considerably. Th mother is heavier, her hair is loose but cropped short, and th curve to her legs speaks of hard work. The father wears bagg trousers, a worker's leather jacket and a cheap shirt. The boy now called Elvis, is dressed in local style, with a long-sleeve white shirt, open at the neck, and ragged trousers tugge chest-high by braces: he is Huckleberry Finn.

The great myths of America lie behind him. Born of a famil that is scourged by its own poverty, maybe he already dream some heady dreams. In this land that he roams, through th cottonfields and swamplands, the air is heavy with the romanc of its own history. The Union and Confederate armies hav clashed on these slopes, the town has been razed in the fur of civil strife, and the Indians have left names that will ro on the tongue with all the magic of ancient hieroglyphics this land is a dreamer's masque.

The boy will sense this if he doesn't quite realise it. He wi learn to love God, to respect even his worst elders, and t stand by his country right or wrong. He wanders through th bellied fields and the sloping swamplands, puts his ear t the wind and listens closely. The air is filled with singing tha came out of slave ships, now pours from black lips, fills whit churches. It is the singing of the Blacks who have given to th

hite man a culture he will never acknowledge: it is American
ospel. His parents and his country and the First Assembly of
od church are the meaning and marked horizons of his life:
ere is no other way.

His mother has lived in Lee County all of her life, has five
ters, three brothers, a hard time. Her folks had farmed some,
t were otherwise anonymous; just another large underfed
mily, struggling along. When she met Vernon Presley, a
an as poor as she, they had a quick courtship and got
arried; a romantic endeavour. Her husband was a quiet
an, grabbing work where he could, doing his best to get on
this county where work wasn't plentiful at the best of
nes. From sun-up to sunset he hoed cotton and corn, humped
les, delivered milk, sorted lumber – tried just about every-
ing. So he did the rounds, working here, working there,
hile his wife climbed from bed in the cold dawn to make
eakfast then work in the garment factory – twelve long
urs a day. Now the child sees them, is enfolded in their love,
ut knows nothing of how they survive. His mother embraces
m, comforts him, making up for her lost child, soothing this
ne's clinging fears. He will always be loved.

They have breakfast, the dawn breaks, the day begins; it is
unday, it is time for church. His mother takes him by the
and, and with a wave to his father walks him down to the
nall church on Adams Street, where they stand and worship.

It is the Day of our Lord in America in 1943.

Here, and in the fields, and in Beale Street in Memphis, he
arns everything he will ever need to know. Black and white
e apart, but their cultures have merged, and it is nowhere
ore obvious than in music. No one will acknowledge it – it
a tacit understanding – but black religion fills white churches
ways that aren't questioned, and this white boy feels
lack in his bones. The preacher chants fervently, the
ongregation shrieks ''Praise God!'' and gazing out at the
ottonfields, he hears the noise from the other churches, the
ving gospel of the blacks, and takes their rhythm into his
loodstream: when he sings, it's with tainted breath.

The singing comes as naturally as breathing: it is part of his
eritage. He lives in the very seat of American folk music where
hite man and black man swop minor traits. White music is
illbilly, black music is the blues, and some day the two will
ave to meet. His singing, therefore, is not unusual; it is
omething he grows with. It is the enthusiasm with which
e steps forward to do it and the angelic repose of his face as
e utters the words which are remarkable. But he learns early
nd well. He sings gospel in the churches, folk songs on the
orches, and he sometimes sways his body in childish emula-
on of the Blacks he has watched in the fields.

Out of his untutored eyes he observes his parents' withering
overty. They both rise with the dawn and they work hard
ll day and they don't have too much time for pleasure. His
ather keeps changing jobs, they have to keep changing
ouses, endlessly, it seems. He sees his mother's face, feels the
ension in her flesh, and he swears one day he'll mend things.

He is at that time of life when the golden haze of child-
ood must give way to the first buffetings of reality. It is
ossible that he now sees behind their shielding smiles to the
opelessness lying beyond, to the land's clinging poverty.
e sings to his mother when the storms drive them from
ome; he stands up to sing at school and in church, clear,
remulous, uncertain, with an arresting sincerity that brings
ears to the eyes. The songs are bathetic in the country and
vestern vein, tied to blue moons and broken hearts and

trains howling lonesome on those tracks that lead back into
history – the songs of deprived folk. Or they are hymns, the
spirituals of his church, and they are spun with a high Southern
drawl. They are songs at the crossroads.

He's a spoilt child, but he carries it well. Later it will show
in contradiction – in his narcissism and in his private humility
– but for now it protects him. No one who remembers him
will complain of his manners. Sweet and unfailingly polite,
quiet and respectful, the hint of rebellion has never touched
him. Poor but decent, average at school, he gathers flowers
with the other kids, fools around, rarely gets into mischief: an
anonymous boy.

Some things, however, are prophetic. At the tender age of
ten Elvis Presley is entered for the annual singing contest of
the Mississippi-Alabama Fair. He stands up on a chair, sings
Red Foley's ''Old Shep'' and walks off with the five-dollar
second prize. He's sung it at school, and to his parents and
friends, and he will sing it many times in the future – a
favourite song, a real tear-jerker. Some day he will sing it to
the masses.

Now he has a guitar in his hands, bought by his parents.
He learns to play it by listening to the radio, to the hillbilly
stations – to Jimmy Rodgers and Roy Acuff and Ernest Tubb
and many others – all of them steeped in country music. He
listens to the blues, to the proliferating black men, to Big Bill
Broonzy, Otis Span, B. B. King, John Lee Hooker, to Jimmy
Reed and Chester Burnett and Booker White – all steeped in

11

"gutter" music. And finally, most always, he sings in church with his folks, and adds spirituals to his broadening repertoire: he picks them up, he plays tricks with them.

The family moves close to Shakerag, Tupelo's black ghetto, and Elvis finds himself at a new school. He is thirteen years

old and is photographed looking threatening in a cowboy suit in front of a painted western landscape. He is, in this photograph, remarkably similar to what he will later become: his eyes are dark-shadowed, his face is lean and narcissistic and a fancy cravat dangles from his neck; he wears a broad belt that is studded and glittering over a pair of real fancy two-toned pants. He is still thirteen years old when the family moves yet again, migrating like the blacks and the other poor whites from the harsh fields to the bright lights of Memphis – the home of the blues.

In Memphis things are bigger, more frightening, more exciting: the alien streets run for miles. There's a new kind of life here, and a new breed of people; there are cinemas and cars and televisions and juke joints, and the kids are slick and strangely restless. The whole world is changing, and while he doesn't comprehend it, he responds to its secret siren call: he yearns for material things.

It is Tennessee's largest city, and though they live near the commercial centre, they are as poor as they ever were before. They have a one-room apartment and share a bath with three families; the walls are ragged with holes and filthy. He goes to a huge school where the strangeness terrifies him, but eventually he adjusts, makes some friends, dates some girls, and starts to change fast without knowing it.

Memphis envelops him.

While both his parents work, his father moving from job to

job, Elvis finds his way about the streets and local custom. He is growing, getting acne, putting grease on his hair, an though he is still quiet and polite, he is finding the confiden he needs. All the kids now have crew cuts but he wears h hair long, and his sideburns cause more than one fight – H is not slow to swing. Yes, for all his charm, for all his shyne and gentility, he has a violent temper and a certain arrogan that seem totally at odds with his character: he'll cut loose he's pushed.

They move again. This time they are imprisoned in three-storey brick building that looms over the leaning shack of the poorest blacks. Here there are drug stores, beer parlou and factories – and just half a mile away, burning bright in the night, is Beale Street, the home of the blues. There he wander past the pimps and the whores, around the winos and the junkies, walking under the bright lights, treading with car thrilled by the danger, by the strangeness of it all. Blue eye wide and innocent, drinking it in he listens to the music the honky-tonks, the beer parlours, the crumbling room The songs are different from his own, they are crude an exciting; they are shocking words growled by these raw battered blacks to the rhythm of guitars and harmonica they are fresh, more vital. And now the music of his childhoo the country songs and the spirituals, are being fused in h mind with what he hears in this street and will make him th future white negro.

Now sixteen years old he buys his clothes in Beale Street— Black clothes, bright and flashy — he shows a peculiar preference for garish pink and black in the age of the grey flannel suit. Take this, and his long hair and his ever-growing sideburns, place it down in its context, in the Eisenhower years, and you have something outrageous on the loose.

Naturally, he continues to sing, to carry his guitar around He plays occasionally for his friends, in the school's variety show, at picnics and at the local boys' club—never professional He isn't showy with it, is more often reluctant — it's jus something he does – but once he starts he really gets into it.

The length of his hair now appears to be tied to his desire to become a truck driver like his father. But he's like most other kids: trailing the sweater girls, doubling up to go to movies, taking rides at the fair, throwing balls at milk bottles, longing for a car to go cruising in – a pretty average All American Boy.

The adolescents hang out around the drug stores and juke joints, bored by the past, embalmed by the present, and casting their hazy eyes towards the romantic future. This God-given country is going through its dullest phase, and they can't stand their parents for suffering it. It's excitement they want, and it's excitement they will get, but at the moment they just don't know where to turn. The atmosphere is heavy, desolation clouds the brain; they are affluent and don't know how to spend it – *it's all such a drag*. The girls in their sweaters have bobbed hair and lipstick; the guys – slacks and jumpers, domes neatly crew-cut – play sport. On the radio they listen to Rosemary Clooney and Doris Day, to Vic Damone and Eddie Fisher, and that crap's enough to make you want to weep. There is, it is true, a slight rebellion in the air, most noticeably against parents in grey suits, against all that's static. Yet some things are beginning to happen: Marlon Brando is a brute who sends shivers down the spine, there are people called Beatniks in the most alluring cities and, most important, four-beats-to-the-bar are now drawing crowds back to the dance halls. Yes, changes are coming, but no one quite knows what they are – they only know that they are waiting for the Phoenix to rise from the ashes of post-war mediocrity, for some cool and dangerous and sexy redeemer, some Lazarus.

He is here amongst them and he goes quite unnoticed. He is normal. A growing lad. But that's not to say he's ignored.

In 1953 Bill Haley and his Comets have a hit with an item called "Crazy Man Crazy", which words henceforth enter the language. The changes have started.

Towards the end of his school years Elvis starts working part-time to help out his struggling parents. He works as an usher at Loew's State Theatre, but has to quit when he punches a fellow usher. He works the evening shift at the Marl Metal Products Company which is rough, and makes him fall asleep at school. For this reason he quits again.

His parents are still badly off. They are harassed by the Housing Authority, and they never know when they'll have to move again. The debts are piling up, the kid mows lawns for pocket money, yet no matter how poor they might be, they always look after him. They even go so far as to buy him a Lincoln coupé, which ostensibly is for all of the family, but he uses it. Life sways on a tightrope, but considering the circumstances, he has a very good time – goes to parties, does the bop, hangs on juke boxes, gets his oats – but he

never runs short on the gratitude: he returns all the love he gets.

He leaves school in the June of 1953, gets a factory job, then moves to the Crown Electricity Company. Finally he is a truck driver and he loves it: he is earning his keep. People notice that he likes to comb his hair and that he doesn't give a damn who sees him do it. In fact, so little does he think of the opinions of others that he has his hair trimmed in the beautician's instead of the barber shop.

All life is an accident; so might fame be. Certainly, in his case, he comes by it casually enough.

One of the places the kid drives past in his battered Ford pick-up is the Memphis Recording Service in Union Street. It's a modest offshoot of the Sun Recording Company who specialise in private recordings. The kid has never been in there, but he knows all about it, and he wants to cut a platter for his mother – four dollars, two sides.

It is the summer of 1953. A hot, busy Saturday. Every hustler in Memphis carries a guitar, and thinks he's gonna make it real big when he trembles his tonsils. The office is

Left: Graduation picture taken for Humes High School year book, June, 1953, when Elvis was 18. Above: Elvis in Memphis at 19. Bottom left: Talking to Memphis fans at the age of 20, just before the explosion.

crowded. There must be some tension in the air.

The kid sits in a chair, slicks back his greased hair, and waits his turn. The office manager at this time is one Marion Keisker who has recently been Miss Radio of Memphis. She asks him what he can sing, to which he replies: "Anything." Unperturbed, she then asks him who he sounds like: "I don't sound like nobody", he says. He is shy and polite but he really doesn't know what else to say: it is the innocence of genius.

The kid, now dwelling in the safety of this innocence, goes in to cut the disc for his Ma. He sings one of his favourites – the Ink Spots' "My Happiness" – then he tries "That's When Your Heartaches Begin", a real country tear-jerker.

He doesn't like the sound of his own voice.

This studio is sitting at the crossroads where black music meets white. The owner, Sam Phillips, who loves black music and sells it, is on the lookout for a white man who can sing it: this development must come. If the kid is a genius who will never comprehend it, then Sam Phillips is his reasoning second half. Already Sam has cut records that will go down as classics – though neither he nor his staff are yet to know it. It is even likely that the kid in his studio has been influenced by some of the material: Joe Hill Louis' "We All Gotta Go Sometime", Rufus Thomas' "Bear Cat", perhaps even "Walkin' In The Rain" by the Prisonaires, who sound just like his much beloved Ink Spots. Anyway he is here. And strangely, and contrary to the normal house rules, Miss Keisker decides to put the boy on tape.

"Over and over I heard Sam saying: 'If I could find a white man who had the Negro sound and the Negro feel, I could make a million dollars.' This is what I heard in Elvis, this . . . what I guess they now call 'soul', this Negro sound. So I taped it. I wanted Sam to know."

Top left: In Dallas, Texas, 1956. Bottom left and top right: At Union Station, Memphis, 1956, wearing what seems to be the same jacket, but without tie and with a different shirt, about to embark on one of his earlier tours. Above: With a girlfriend, Kate Wheeler, in Dallas, 1956. Note the curled lip and the slick clothes.

The kid finishes and takes his platter home to his mother; his good deed for this day is done. When Sam Phillips hears the tape, he is impressed, but says the boy needs some work. Miss Keisker keeps his address and the phone number of a friend, after which life cruises on in its mellow way. A few months later, on the first Friday of January, 1954, the kid returns to cut another private record. He sings "Casual Love" and "I'll Never Stand in Your Way", then he shuffles out of the studio. He starts learning to be a spark, secretly yearns

Top of page: Two rare photos of Elvis, looking younger than his 21 years at his home at 1034 Audubon Drive, Memphis, in 1956 Above: The Grand Ole Opry. Opposite page: Top left, Elvis with friend George Klein; top right, with dee-jay Dewey Phillips.

to be a singer, and family struggles continue.

About eight months after he has first visited the Memphis Recording Service, they call him up and invite him back to the studio; they have something to try him with.

Sam Phillips has come across a song called "Without You" and Miss Keisker thinks the kid might be right for it. He isn't. He is awful. He just can't get it right. They try it once more, then give up in despair, have a coffee break. Sam Phillips asks the kid just what he *can* do, and the kid replies: "I can

do anything." And by way of demonstration he does western gospel, Dean Martin, Billy Eckstine – you name it, he tries it he does it. And Sam Phillips falls for it.

What Phillips then does is arrange a meeting between th kid and a skinny guitarist known to all as Scotty Moore. The meet at Scotty's house and when the kid walks through th door he is dressed all in pink but for his white shoes. The horse around for a while and are joined by Bill Black, wh isn't at all impressed by this freaky boy. But Bill Black is bass player, and when they get into the Sun studios, there i

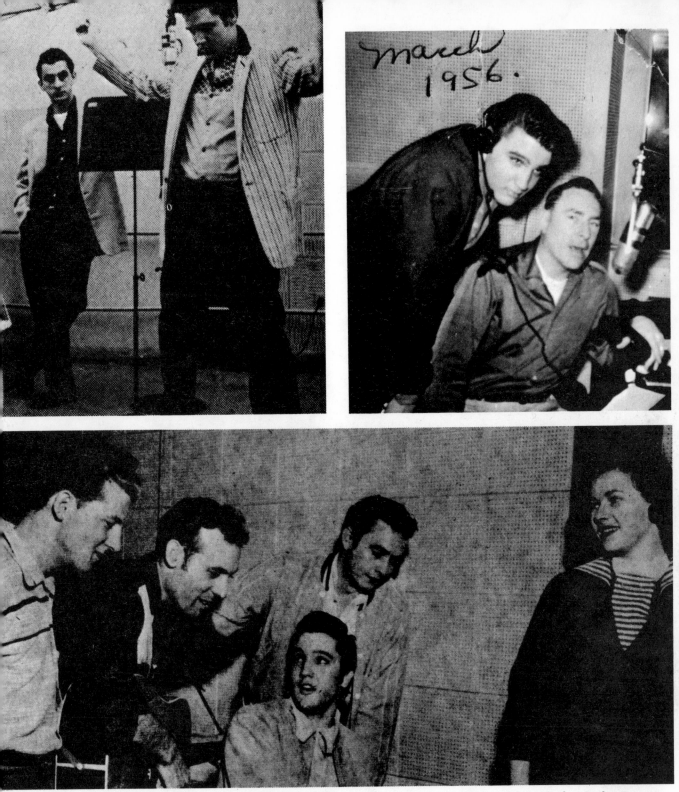

Above: In the Sun Studios, about 1956, with, from left to right, Jerry Lee Lewis, Carl Perkins, Johnny Cash, Marilyn Evans.

just him and Scotty backing Elvis: they will make some extraordinary sounds.

This test session extends into months of hard labour as they work to develop a style. They don't know what they're looking for, and the kid's voice is weird, but for some reason Sam keeps them at it. A couple of times the kid appears with Scotty's band in a local club, but not too many people think it sounds right. They work on. They are not amused. The kid has wild clothes and he's a bit of a looker, but he sure in hell ain't no great singer. Then, after months, out of some intuition, in the hollows of the studio, in that air of desolation, Sam says: "Okay, this is the session." And they turn on the tapes.

The first thing they try is "I Love You Because", a real country weeper so doleful it is more like a dirge. They do four takes of the song and the kid's voice is freaky, pure country but with something else again. He sings high and sings low, sometimes misses a note, and the trembling on occasion seems

17

deliberate. Also, on the first take, he tries a spoken bridge, during which he drawls his words with all the slimy innuendo of a hoodlum inching into the alley. "Honey," he drawls, breaking down any sentiment, "every time I'm walkin' by your side . . ." And the contrast is stunning. But it doesn't make a great song. It is pure country and western, an undefiled corn-cob weeper, and it has all the shameless sentimentality of that particular genre. Still, they keep trying. On the second take they cut the spoken bridge and instead add a whistled introduction. The kid sings it much deeper, guitar and bass are more assured, and it is certainly the best of the batch. They try it twice more, but one take is not completed and the fourth version will never be released.

He has cut his first disc.

After this, they turn off the tapes and try some of "those country-orientated things". Apparently none of them come to much – most certainly they aren't taped – and they settle for having a break. Sam is back in the control room, the boys are slugging Coke, and the kid takes his guitar in his hands and tries one of his favourites. The song is Arthur Crudup's "That's All Right Mama", a jumping blues number, and when the kid cuts into it, singing high and mean, his guitarist and bassist follow suit. The hair of Sam Phillips stands up on his neck: it's electric. He turns on the tapes, makes them run through it again, and that's it. Finally, and almost by accident, he has found what he wants.

The vocal on "That's All Right Mama" is high, urgent, desolate and decidedly sensual. It's pure gutter blues with a pounding bass rhythm, but Scotty Moore's guitar retains a country flavour. It is exactly, to the very last note, what Sam Phillips wants. "On one side we had a country and western

Elvis in the studios, with greased hair and acne, just kicking off on an amazing career. 1956.

ballad with a rhythm and blues feel, and on the other side we had a strictly rhythm and blues song with a slight country feel to it." The latter is "That's All Right Mama"; the former is "Blue Moon of Kentucky". When they cut "That's All Right Mama" they need something to back it, and finally, four days later, they find something. The first take of "Blue Moon" is a brief, medium-tempo, country rocker with a strong and assured vocal treatment. At the end of it, Scotty runs humorously down the chords, that kid takes a nervous breath, and Sam Phillips, with a laugh, says, "Fine, man! Hell, that's *different!* That's a *pop* song!" But they tape another version and this one is much faster, with an extraordinarily driving and eccentric vocal that turns the whole thing inside out. This track it is that will back "That's All Right Mama", and both tracks form a remarkable debut: black music and white music at long last have joined at the crossroads.

It is the Year of our Lord in America in 1954.

"His key is precise, intuitive knowledge of who he is and what he's projecting on stage. His consistency is absolute."
– *Morgan Ames,* High Fidelity

The restless children of America now see standing before
them the product of their most secret dreams. He is over six
foot tall, his hair is greasy and long, he has blue eyes and a
curling, self-mocking lip. He comes on real easy, as if he's
always owned the stage, grins at his boys as if it's all some
kind of joke, then picks up his guitar and lightly strums it,
pretending to play. This boy is no country yokel. Rather he's
Flash Harry, a dreamy-eyed dude, and he knows it and knows
how to carry it. His instincts are sound.

He sees them. He grins at them. It is all they need. They
prostrate themselves.

No one ever knows where he picked up the confidence, the
charisma, the sublime public ease. He can bite his fingernails,
tap his feet on the floor and drum his fingers in acute nervous
spasms – but once in the spotlight he is confident, he knows he
can do it. The young man has learnt quickly, all America is
his, and when he leans toward the mike, when his fingers
caress it, they all sense that he's into some private dream,
willing to share it. He is Lazarus arisen from the ashes of their
boredom: a cool, dangerous and very sexy animal who will
transport them briefly to Heaven.

He is called Elvis Presley.

The rise to local fame is a gradual acceleration which for
most struggling artists would be lightning but for him is a
snail's crawl. He has played on flat trucks and in schools and
in stadiums; he has driven across the South, across Texas,
to the nation; he has lived through those long nights with the
salt of rejection and he has got himself a few pink cadillacs:
he grins crookedly, self-mocking.

He leans forward like an animal, legs apart, body braced,
the guitar hanging loose like a weapon; he purrs like a big cat.

Above left: The slim, smiling cowboy is famed country singer Hank Snow, pictured with Elvis during a Grand Ole Opry tour. The "live" shots on these pages are amongst the earliest ever taken (1955). Bottom right: Elvis relaxes by playing the piano with his parents.

They scream, writhe, wet the seats, tear their hair and claw at their own faces with sweaty hands – he enjoys it. His lips twist in a grin as he reaches out for the mike stand, fingers sliding slowly down it, then curling around and taking hold, rocking it gently. He growls just a little, flicks the hair from his eyes, lets his heavy-lidded gaze burn up the front rows, raises his left hand.

The hysteria is immediate and total.

When he finally starts to sing he knows just how to do it, since the tapes he has put down for the Sun Record Company are the most remarkable ever made by a white man. Like many a great actor, he has worked by his instincts, turning up to record with nothing prepared and then sweating for hours to find material, to find the right approach. Nothing in this particular line comes easy to him: it is all a huge sweat. But the results which are sparse in these first early days make up in quality what they are lacking in quantity: they are gold in the wilderness. He takes pure country songs and then rapes them with the blues; he takes the blues and refines them into pop songs. This, in itself, would be quite an achievement, but it isn't what makes a man myth. No, what he has given them, these bored, restless children, is a raw and untutored sensuality, a first hint of freedom.

He stands in the spotlight and he gives them what they want because it's all that he ever learnt to do. He heard it in the churches, in fields and on the porches; he saw it at revivalist meetings and in the black men of Beale Street. So he sways his body, shakes a leg, rolls his groin, does it first slow and easy, a slithering come-on, then quickens up, turns almost epileptic and makes love to his guitar. This instrument, in fact, will soon be but a prop: a symbol of arrogant contempt, the first real modern phallus.

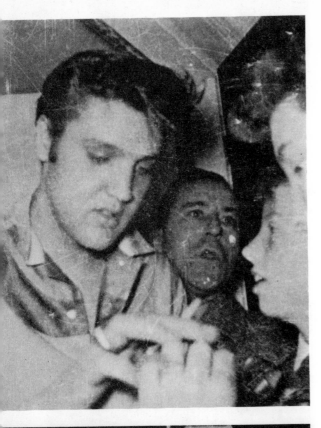

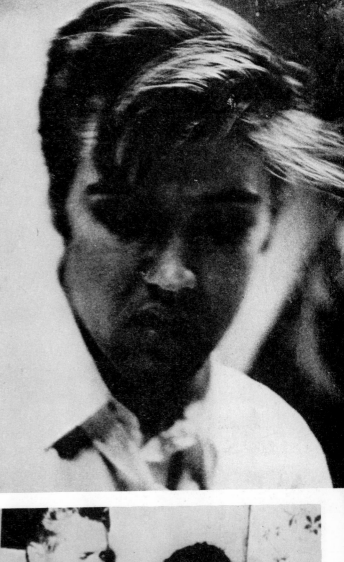

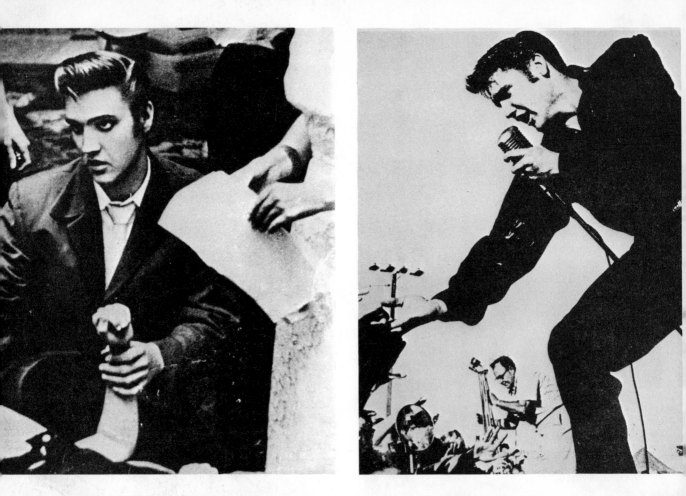

A return to Tupelo on 25 September, 1956, to perform once more in the Mississippi-Alabama Fair where at 10 years old he first sang "Old Shep". Soon after this he would purchase Graceland, 3764 Highway 51, South Memphis (below).

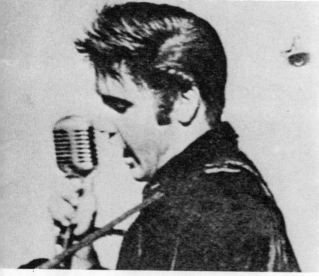

At first he eases into his performance with a sly, [w]icked charm. Walking on without prelude he will lean [to]wards the mike, let loose with the lop-sided grin, burn [th]em up with his eyes. Then, just to tease, he will start with a [b]allad, leaning close to the mike, almost kissing it, breathing [ov]er it, his long eye-lashes modestly lowered, almost effemi-[n]ate. It's a beautiful trick, a sublime delaying tactic: he will [h]old them in the palm of his hand until he's ready to jump. [T]he guitar, very early, becomes no more than an accessory, [a] item to toy with, a symbol, something to stroke. And his [vo]ice, in such ballads, will be close to a groan, a strangled [so]und, strangely orgasmic, drawing them in. He knows what [he] is doing. The tension is rife. And he will dangle his left [ha]nd like a limp, sodden leaf – then twitch, just a little, and [wa]tch the fireworks.

This developing knowledge of the psychology of the [au]dience is something he will never lose. He will watch them [wi]th his eyes, and with his arrogant grin, but his instinct is

what he'll depend on. So, after the ballad, and sensing their tension, he will turn slightly away, mumble out a few words, let the honey of his voice and his deep Southern accent charm them into a soft romantic haze – then he'll cut loose.

In the earliest shows it is "Good Rockin' Tonight" and the throb of Bill Black's bass will set the mood. The kid will shake his left leg, smack one hand on a thigh, jerk his shoulders as if in a spasm, rock back on his heels. The audience goes wild: they have witheld too long; now release is here. He grins, shakes his head, throws the hair back from his eyes, then howls the first word like a hound on the prairie – a long, drawn out, spine-chilling, "Weeeelllll . . ." His rendition of this number is a blatant overlaying of brute lust on pure country corn: it is Brando gone pop. He invites them out back of the barn: there's good rockin' tonight. It is pure come-hither-baby and it works like a charm because the way he phrases "rock" means something else – and you didn't discuss that.

The changes come so fast they're overwhelming, a cyclone of harassment. In 1955 he starts touring with the Grand Ole

27

*hen not being moody out back of Graceland (above), Elvis
*is being scandalous on stage. The performance shown here
d overleaf was in New York, 1956.

pry, a hillbilly show covering the east. He plays in the
ena in Norfolk, Virginia, and he's just one more country
odeller in a cowboy outfit with a guitar in his hands, looking
nesome. There's a long red silk scarf knotted loosely around
s neck, a round-brimmed black hat pushed far back on his
ad, quite exotic, framing pale face and dark hair. Tall, lean

and unusually handsome, he has "a Latin quality . . . beautiful,
smouldering eyes, long dark brown hair and sideburns".
His hips begin to undulate, his head whips up and down, and
he seems altogether to be in some sort of trance, sometimes
smacking the guitar instead of playing it, an evangelical
chanter. Suddenly it isn't the Grand Ole Opry as they've
ever understood it; it's like nothing they have ever seen before.
The adults are revolted, other performers think it's crazy,
but the kids in the audience are pop-eyed and start to go wild.
Yes, he bring the house down, and Hank Snow, who tries to
follow him, is shamefully booed off the stage . . . thereafter,
no one tries it.

By late 1956 he already has his own show and things are
considerably different. He plays the Dallas Cotton Bowl and
the cops are so worried they erect a ten-foot fence around the
stage. The kid, The Pelvis, makes his entry into the field in a
new and gleaming Lincoln white convertible, waving a
friendly hand. The audience, which at this gig numbers a
good 26,000, goes berserk before he opens his mouth – the
formula is set. Now, of course, he has progressed beyond mere
country and western, has discarded the mandatory cowboy
outfit. Flash Harry he is and Flash Harry he'll be, climbing
out of the convertible with his lop-sided grin to reveal, in his
modest manner, "a billiard-table green coloured coat, black
trousers, pleated white shirt, black tie, snow-white boots that
zip up the side, huge cufflinks and a striped cummerbund
around the top of his pants . . ." No horse shit: he's changing.
Then he runs through his hits, does his Dracula bit, and leaves

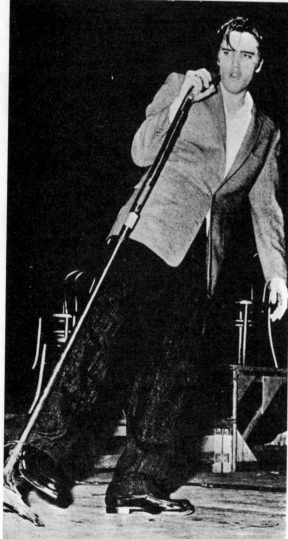

them wasted with a version of "Hound Dog" that would shame a burlesque show.

Naturally, at the gate, one ear cocked to the hysteria, his new manager, Colonel Parker, heavy and benign, is selling Beanie hats, photographs, records and other Elvis souvenirs – since it isn't just a pop show, it's a carnival, and it always will be.

Not too many months later, in the huge Mosque theatre in Richmond, he's still flashy but much better groomed. His body has filled out, he looks sleek and prosperous, and his hair has gone more dark with grease, his sideburns more prominent. In the view of at least one fan, he has "gorgeous, thickly lashed, velvety blue eyes, and peaches and cream complexion" as well as "great poise and distinction". He wears a stage shirt of white silk trimmed in lace, a black suit cut from an extremely rich material, and a pair of black patent leather slippers. Later still, growing ever more flamboyant, he will wear a specially tailored suit of "soft, pliable leather, impregnated with gold . . . the silver lapels and trouser stripes

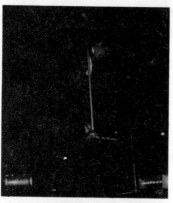

Kansas City, 1956, with Bill Black on bass, Scotty Moore on guitar, J. D. Fontana on drums. Hysteria prevailed.

encrusted with brilliants'', all of which "sparkle and shimmer" in the lights of the stage. They shimmer most particularly when he does his special thing, which is to take hold of the mike, pull it down at an angle, then gyrate his pelvis in an extraordinarily violent bump and grind while his right fist swathes through the hot air: a blatant, sadistic rape.

These are the first solo performances and they're something to see, but within a couple of years he has extended them. By 1957 he has taken his own measure, and he knows that by scaring the sheep he will capture the lambs. So, he is outrage-ous, he is totally wild, he is something from the backwoods of the uncultured American South just come out of the trees for some plunder: this feat is stupendous. He is still indefinable – his background so pious – yet he works with an instinct that can only be genius to contradict every *more* of his breeding: he's a nice boy gone ape.

This persona is an inspired piece of *kitsch*, a remarkable invention. He has the looks of a hoodlum, yet he talks like a gentleman; on-stage he's a maniac, yet off-stage he's a saint; he sums up for his fans the revolt against adults, yet he loves his own folks with a shameless love – the controversy is exquisite.

"I never thought my performing style was wicked. *Wicked?* I don't even smoke or drink!"

Nor does he. He says yes-sir and no-ma'am, sings hymns, collects teddy bears, eats hot dogs, hamburgers and popcorn, never touches the demon brew. A monster on stage, his real life style is a hymn to youthful decency, a catalogue of the mundane and trivial, so "normal" it's ludicrous. He's a devotee of the most plastic verities of American life; he dates only nice girls, only takes them to the movies, never enters a night club or bar, doesn't gamble or smoke. He loves his parents, worships God and God's country, is grateful for everything he's been given – a most loyal son. Yet once in the spotlights, with his sharp eyes highlighted, he sneers and beseeches, seduces and surrenders, spits defiance at everything good children should revere, is no less than the sinner incarnate, the hooligan king. He is the most contradictory image to be placed on the American landscape – and he's marvellous copy.

"I don't know what happens to me when I sing. Maybe it's the music, the song, the crowd or something deep inside me, but to the rock 'n' roll beat I have to move my hands, feet, knees, legs, my head – everything. There were attacks on my singing style in the papers – but I felt that I could sure live them down."

He doesn't live them down – doesn't even bother trying –

33

Top: With his mother and father in 1957. Above: Playing cops 'n' robbers back of Graceland. Opposite: 1957.

instead he plays up to the avalanche of condemnation by becoming even more outrageous than before: black shirts and white ties, phosphorescent pink socks, gold lamé suits; his eyes are pencilled in and his fair hair dyed black to add demoniac qualities to his rough romantic good looks. In his stage act, these attributes are given prominence, high-lighted in the spotlights which pierce through the star blackness when he stands on his toes, makes his hands like two claws, pops his eyes, his curled lip cruel, and snarls just like a vampire – pure evil, a rare treat.

He does "Heartbreak Hotel" when the main lights are turned down, when the spotlights cut into his blue eyes, his lean wicked features. He bends his left leg, supports himself on the right, and then throws out his arms in appeal, like a man crucified. *"Well since mah baby left me/I've found a new place t' dwell/It's down at the end of Lonely Street at/Heartbreak Hotel."* His voice is desolate, raging, standing out on its own, punctuated by a guitar so savage it's like a chop on the neck. Then he swivels his hips, the mike caught between his thighs, head back and eyes closed, a sublimely tortured pose, and groans, almost grunts, monosyllabic and wracked, *"And I'm a so lonely, baby/I'm a so lonely/And I'm a so lonely/Ah could die."* It is blatant theatrics, an acting out of the lyrics, a visualised extension of his voice, of the bleak, surrealist words. When he gets to the bellhop, to the desk clerk dressed in black, he runs his left foot up the back of his right leg, slides one hand on a thigh, leans well back, his mouth open and howling: a wild beast in pain. It is more than they can bear – they are out of their seats – they are rushing for the stage and as the cops push them back he already has gone on to something else, crouching over, hands flailing. The guitarist Scotty Moore takes a mean, lashing break, and the kid is right in there, almost kissing the floor, his body shaking to the rhythm, in a dream, in a fever, then whipping around fast as it finishes, pointing straight at the fans. *"So if yoh baby leaves ya/And ya got a tale to tell/Jest take a walk down Lonely*

34

Street to/Heartbreak Hotel . . .'' Now slurring his words, a deliberate masquerade, he curls himself around the mike, starts the stroking and guttural groaning, that sly suggestion of pillow talk . . . ''*And am a so lonely, baby/Am a lonely/ And am a so lonely/Ah could die . . .*'' Moaning and purring, breathing heavily, sometimes sighing, just rolling on the boards, very casual, calculating, repeating ''*Ah could die, ah could die*'' as if in orgasm.

After this there is nothing he can't do; his freedom is total. In the very early days Bill Black fooled with his bass to add novelty to a straight country act – but all that is now past. Up there is one man, a young demon, a beauty, who will straddle the mike, shake it loose between his thighs, stroke its flank as he lies on the floor, give it head, give it spasms. The cops are in the pits, but for once in their lives they're more wary of the man on the stage than they are of the audience: a wild man, a maniac, a highly paid lout. And dear Jesus, he's corrupting their kids – and the kids love him for it.

The whole thing is a pure hallucination, a spotlit, chaotic dream. From his own vantage point he sees a white haze of bright light, the pure eye of the sun, huddled masses, a shimmering blackness. But they, in the theatre, in the cramped sweaty seats, are looking up at a glittering idol, a golden young god who is the very essence and meaning of glamour – excitement concentrated. This response is part sexual, part romantic, and always self-willed. But he, this young Elvis, will dredge

from their souls every last ounce of fleeting frustration, each singular hope. And this sense of unreality, this well-rehearsed fantasy, is given credence by the crowds, by the darkness, by the blinding lights, and by the monstrous noise that clamps down on the brain and cuts out all extraneous matter: it's a trip through the subconscious.

"People want to know always why I can't stand still when I'm singing. Some people tap their feet, some people snap their fingers, some people just sway back and forth. I just sort of do them all together, I guess . . . I watch my audience and listen to them and er . . . er . . . and I know that we're all getting something out of our system and none of us knows what it is. The important thing is we're getting rid of it and nobody's getting hurt."

His words spiral over the airwaves and into print; a whole world opens out for TV panelists: this subject will feed them.

Yes, this nice boy in his innocence is corrupting our children, encouraging hooliganism, making whores of our young girls, turning nice young men into wild brutes who spit in your face. It's a sin, it's a shame, it's indecent, and it's quite Un-American.

But he's a valuable release for all the tensions that beset the adolescent: he'll distract them from worse crimes. He is there, after all, with James Dean and Marlon Brando. He is violent, surly, rebellious and sexual, but beneath it all he is sensitive, all-aching, a lonely child . . .

He is, in short, a common identity.

He picks himself up from the stage floor, all dishevelled, sweat pouring, and taking up his guitar, he wipes his brow and turns solemnly towards his audience, just laid low by "Mystery

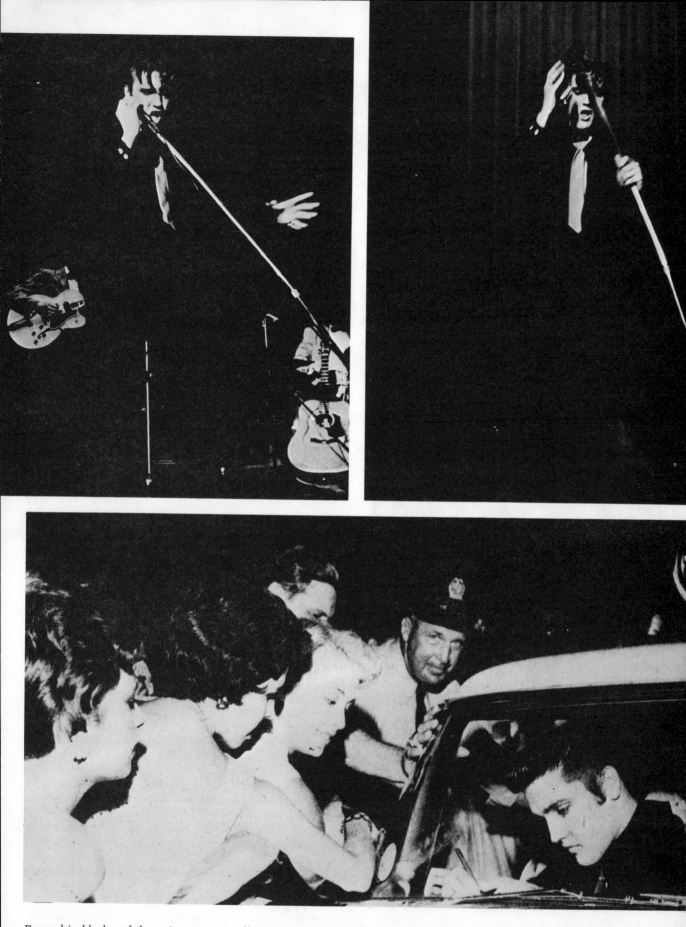

Dressed in black and demoniac on stage, off stage he is sweet when signing autographs. Opposite page: A rare shot of Elvis with Colonel Parker and one brand new car – a gift from the legendary manager. Overleaf: The fireball rocks on.

rain'' or ''Long Tall Sally'', now one huge, black, writhing ass in the dark pit of the theatre. Many young girls in that eat age of yearning are now seeing all their dreams fulfilled, eir secret guilts understood. And the young men — me look just like him, and others sneer and want to get up ere, want to smash him to pieces. Yes, he is something uch more than a crooner: he looks as mean and as rough as ur local redneck and they don't like him threatening them is way — so they hate him, they ape him. And he, who ways watches his audience and listens, gives everyone just little of what they need.

He now takes hold of the mike, offers one solemn stare, wers his long-lashed dark eyes and bows his head. This moment is sombre, all stillness, almost religious. While they are dazed by the violence of his previous number, he sings, near to a whisper, a ballad or gospel song. It is total audacity, pure instinctive histrionics, and the contrast is so brutal that the audience seems staggered, sinks slowly back, reclining, collapsing, hypnotised by his reverence, his intense, tortured face, his slow, snakelike swaying, his lonesomeness, his brimming sincerity. It is all too much (he's so violent, so gentle) and they surrender to pure sensual pleasure, enclosed in their dreams.

The regional flavour of his talent is most evident when he brings on the gospel. He sings it like he's standing at the altar of the church, now heavy with vibrato, now almost falsetto, bending notes, flattening notes, pouring out black, evangelical passion. This is the music of this country and no boy who can sing it can possibly be as bad as he seems: every mother could love him.

Some mothers do, but some mothers don't, because what he represents is a threat to their daughters, to their sheltered lives. And not only their daughters, to their wandering sons, who come in nights in gaudy clothes, hair long and greasy, to stare at them with moody eyes. Promiscuity is rife: the very bone and moral fibre of the age is being smashed by this hoodlum. What's happening to the country – you might indeed ask – when such indecency is allowed on the stage? We just don't understand it.

The schism between parents and children is now almost complete. The old world has died, a new world is in the making, and the casualties are falling on both sides. Now young folk are affluent, they are restless and jaded, and they need their

own leaders to guide them – they want their own world. Politics turn them off, hearth and home are just jokes, and ambition has done nothing for their parents but leave them sucked dry. So, disowning this, they will live for the moment, for the hot glittering instant that has no tomorrow, for excitement, existentialist thrills, success now or never. Yes, they want slick clothes and fast cars and a common identity, and they see it in Brando with his violence and sexuality – and in Elvis with his pink cadillacs, his flash, his freedom.

Everyone gets a little of what they need; he is always most generous. And later he comes in heavy with his new kind of songs, those Big City crushers. He is with RCA and those boys in Noo Yawk, guys who know how to foster an image and write around what they have. The songs are commercialised rhythm and blues, witty and vicious, primitive and exciting, geared to that sense of rebellion that has blown like a hurricane across America; aggressive songs, sexy songs. They will no longer write of blue moons and autumn leaves, of dancing in the dark and holding hands. The Hillbilly Cat, the King of Western Bop, is now Elvis the Pelvis and he'll prove it with bone-hard material. He will sing about sweat, about the fevers of love, about blue suede shoes and gleaming black cadillacs, about mean dirty thrills and raw women: he will sing of the hidden life. "*I want you, I need you*", he groans. "*Make me thrill with delight.*" Then he challenges with panache and a real sense of power: "*Don't you step on mah blue suede shoes*", and he does it with his head back, the left leg like a piston, the guitar slanting upward like a phallus exploring, one hand on a thigh, pelvis rocking, hair flaying his face. Then he drops to his knees, takes the mike along with him, runs his hand right along it and quivers while the shrieks fill his ears. And somewhere behind him, in the black of the stage, his musicians and vocal group will lay down a sound that is almost blocked

by the bedlam. The place is hysterical.

He is banned more than once and they love him because
s dangerous, because he's wild and untamed, and because,
ind this, lies the clean Southern boy who loves his mother,
country and his God. And though they'll never admit it,
the saint behind the beast that allows them this ephemeral
ulgence: he is after all loveable.

The first shadows of mythology now encircle him, enshrine
n in Holy clouds. His life style is the style for a whole
eration, and it's stretching out over the world. In the
gles of Thailand there are Elvis Presley sweaters; in Japan
is a monstrous industry. His voice is unmistakeable, his
e fills sundry dreams, and his first name is part of the
guage, a new word for the cool. He walks on the waters
a fame so complete that it doesn't leave room for human
ts: he is God-like, inviolable.

Somewhere within this the Tupelo child has disappeared,
the Memphis boy has been laid in his grave, the bright deity
created. He is so famous as to be quite removed, a pure abstract
vision.

Remorselessly determined, he always gives a performance
that is never less than total. He never accepts *No* for an
answer: he will not let them rest. Witnesses to these performances will later testify that he never lost sight of the audience,
would never release them. No, he played them by the minute,
by each silence and shriek, and he never let up until he had
them in his palm, until they lay there before him in utter
surrender, were close to the edge of delirium, near out of
control. Only then, and not before, would he attempt to
level them out – with his self-mocking humour, his sense of
the ridiculous, his basic and healthy grasp of the joke,
of his own selfish pleasure. And this hint of remove, this

43

latent lack of conviction, would stand him in good stead in the future, on the day of his resurrection.

"Well, we're gonna do a little ol' bit here . . . er . . . little ol' thing we just recorded in *Noo* York . . .er . . . you know, don't git hysterical down there, kid, ah mean *New* York . . . er . . . a place, you know, with *sidewalks* . . . yeah, well, this little ol' bit here, it's a very tender ballad . . . er . . . real *sweet* song 'bout a gal I know . . . er . . . nice kid . . . just like you, honey, just like you . . . and I says to her . . . I says . . . I mean, breathin' *real* close . . . I says . . ."

And he braces his legs, leans over real low, curls his fingers around the mike and gently rocks it, just teasing, eyes mocking. He grins, the lip curls, it is pure humorous sadism, and they shriek, they howl, they come out of their seats; they are clawing at their own faces, and holding on to each other, tears streaming down their cheeks, some wet between the legs, knowing what he's going to do, hardly daring to believe it, because he's shattered the world with it, stripped away their minds, and it's a number put over like nothing has ever been done before: a real old gutter blues turned into pure wild aggression, a Kowalski song, a thunderous raver, white primitive brilliance. So he starts crouching low,

Left: Elvis sharing a cigar with Colonel Parker. On stage he was someone else again: a demon unleashed.

He performs a bump 'n' grind and makes defiant gestures. Nevertheless, he will soon be a tamed man. It is 1958.

breathing into the mike, running fingers up and down it, almost hugging it, swallowing it, and then purrs, and then growls, and then laughs and starts again – and then suddenly drops down to one knee with fist outstretched and howls this abuse in their faces, this back-handed slap.

Once hated by the Southerners for singing like a black man, he now sounds like a slave in the bear pit: his shrieks are pure rage. "Hound Dog" is the ultimate song of contempt, and he never fails to close the show with it, whipping his audience. They lie back in their seats as his voice flays their minds, as his clawing hands seem to strip them bare, his groin a pure challenge. Then he does a bump and grind, slides one hand down a thigh, tugs his ears, pops his eyes and looks monstrous – they squeal and collapse.

He will sometimes work this song to its ultimate limits, doing as many as sixteen choruses, each building on the last, each leading the audience to new levels of hysteria. He is

now safely shielded behind blue ranks of cops, behind clu[b] and some pistols and heavy men – a president's bodyguar[d] And he does truly need it, forever after will, because wh[at] fills these theatres, these stadiums and auditoriums, [is] something not easily controlled: a frenzied, amorpho[us] beast. And he knows it, and feels it, and responds to its ca[ll,] raging at it with his voice, with his sly sense of mocker[y,] with his matchless ability to pull them from their sea[ts,] take their latent sexuality and whip it to a frenzy that w[ill] only be released in pain and tears.

It can't be done with publicity – it is much more than tha[t,] it is a mystery of the ages, it's real, it *exists*. No one kno[ws] where it comes from, what hidden strength wills it, but [in] some it can not be denied, and in him never is. So he falls [to] his knees, thrusts his groin in their faces, crawls over t[he] stage like a snake on its belly, convulses, jerks uprig[ht,] twists back to his feet, leans into the mike, works in spasm[s,] releasing it all. Yes, he sings sixteen choruses and he thrash[es] himself mercilessly, tries to drag from himself, perhaps ev[en] simulates, the common passions of his juvenile audien[ce,] shares with them this mystery. And when he's finished, [he] doesn't bow, never comes back for an encore, is just rush[ed] away shivering, sometimes crumbling from exhaustion, a[nd] disappears before they know what has hit them.

They then smash up the theatres.

He had wanted to be big and he is big – there will never [be] bigger. He has come at a time when the whole world see[ms] stale, when the young are suppressed and want freedo[m,] and this he has given them. Having, in a real sense, j[ust] ripped off the black man, he will now just as unconsciou[sly]

46

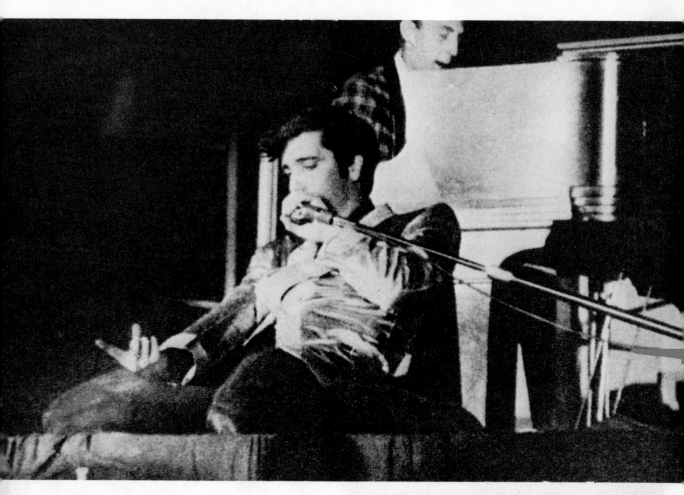

ay back his debt by opening the doors to black music, by
ncouraging the marriage. After this the world will never be
he same: there is a general awakening. White kids will ape
lack kids – their walk, their jive talk – and black music and
terature will flood over the land to change cultural and class
oundary lines, to make visible the invisible man. Yes, he
oes this, and he does it alone – and of everyone involved he
ill be the last person to understand it . . . after all, he is just
ntertaining.

He sings like a black man, but Dean Martin is his idol and
's Martin's world he now will pursue. He will learn to be a
rooner, to be smooth and romantic, to leaven this brew
ith some dry wit and urbanity, to take Hollywood and
onquer the silver screen – to be everything he's dreamed of.
ow ironic, then, to have changed the whole world because
e wanted to be what the new world despises: a common
ntertainer, a "star", pure factory fodder.

So his voice will change and his act become subdued; so he
ill live in a mansion, in a house with a swimming pool. And
ke others he admires, he will surround himself with body-
uards and with yes-men who will never speak out, who will
ways congratulate. And in doing this, he blindly puts
mself, without resistance, even willingly, into the hands
 the promoters, the fat-bellied salesmen. And they will
adow his eyes and put paint on his lips, cake his face and
nooth out his rough features: they will make him look
astic. And once they've done this, they will package him
d sell him to the larger masses huddled around the globe.
d he will accept it saying yes-sir and no-ma'am – a most
edient Southern boy.

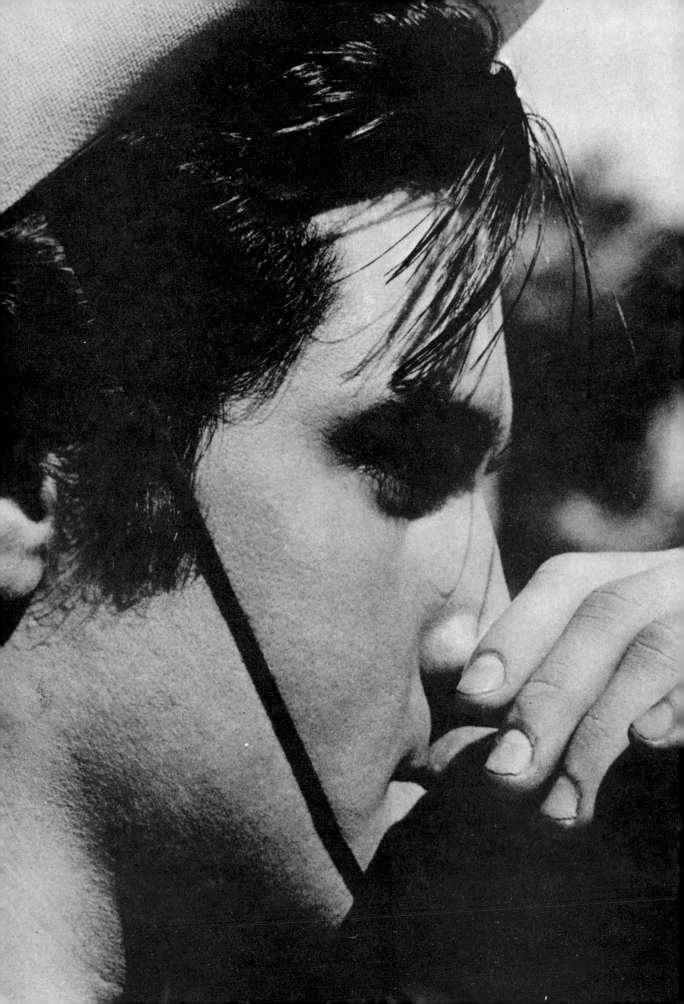

"That's how you're selling me, isn't it? A monkey in a zoo. Isn't that what you want?"
– Deke Rivers (Elvis Presley) in Loving You

is Presley is processed. Bought off Sun Records by the
ge RCA company, the welcome mat laid down before him,
is now a big star. At the first recording sessions at RCA
hville, the studio is bigger, there's more money to burn,
he's surrounded by a tougher, more cunning breed.
ile he sits at the piano, while he fiddles with the drums, he
bserved by Colonel Parker, by his assistant Tom Diskin,
Steve Sholes, by some cronies, by the representative of
and Range Songs, by Freddie Bienstock, the manager of
own music company – all watching pure gold being pro-
ed.

Now the writers are under contract, the dubs come in huge
s; the whole thing is one huge operation, where nothing
ft to chance. He tries take after take, he works long days

and often through the night until everyone's shattered. The
results are stupendous, all monsters, all destined for fame:
"Heartbreak Hotel", "Hound Dog", "Blue Suede Shoes",
"Don't be Cruel" – these and many others are created in these
days and most of them will go down as classics – commercial
but unique.

The voice is now extraordinary, the most versatile in pop,
and there isn't a trick that he can't use, no tactics evade him.
Now he has a vocal group, four men, the Jordanaires, and
they weave some sweet harmonies behind him, softening the
sound. He uses lots of echo, slaps his hands on his guitar,
thumps his knees, bangs the studio walls, makes some strange
"slapping" rhythms. He is anguished and sexy and con-
temptuous by turns; he is humorous and aggressive and

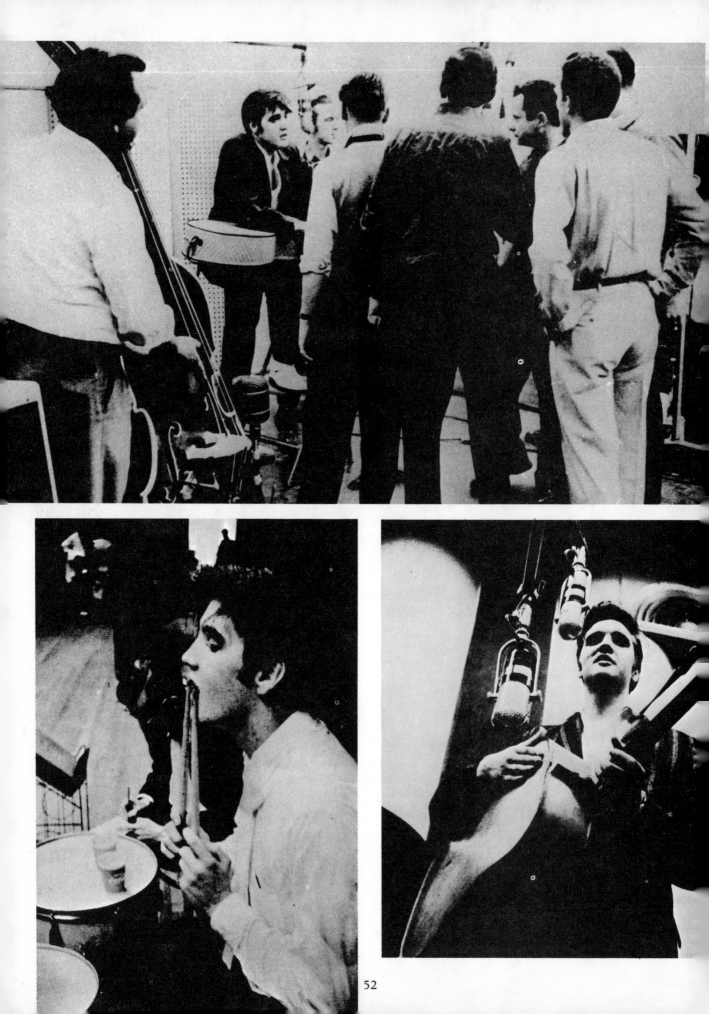

...cording sessions at RCA Nashville, 1956. Top left opposite ...ge: Elvis, watched by Bill Black, talks to the Jordanaires. ...p left of this page: Scotty Moore, seated behind a vigorous ...vis, looks exhausted. Top right: Elvis and the Jordanaires ...n through a rehearsal. Overleaf: First publicity stills from ...56.

malign – never embarrassed. He shows sweat on every track that he makes, lets it ooze from the grooves, has it dripping from his tonsils, bathes the words in it. His productions, indeed, have the raw and guileless intimacy of the greatest lovers and fools known to man: they are quite irresistible.

The first publicity photographs are an uneasy mixture, since his new owners aren't sure what he is and are not yet confident in handling him. The "action" shots are ludicrous: he is posed with arms outstretched, leaning over the guitar, both legs bent – a stiff, grotesque doll. He wears a red windbreaker, white open-necked shirt, black trousers and white gold-buckled sneakers. His eyebrows are painted in, his face is smoothed out, and the background is washed-out yellow:

a representative lunacy. They are better on the head shots, tackling every persona. During one particular session, using very sharp highlights, they dress him up in a flowing green shirt, make his hair stiff with laquer, and take shots that could cover each image, and will in time do so. In one he looks clean-cut, almost Byronic, his eyes moody and piercing in his young, boyish face, the sneer totally removed to show tender lips: a romantic girl's dream. By contrast, in another, the lips are thick and brutal, pure evil – they know how to spit. In this same photograph, the eyes are small and heavy-lidded, expressionless under very thick brows which have obviously been hand-touched; the calculated result makes him look ten years older, one ugly and most unpleasant character, the kind to avoid. Then, at what appears to have been the very same session, his white face stands out in blackness, the profile highlighted, looking out to the side while his ringed hands are clasped on a box that might well be an altar. He is also, to display the young boy in himself, seen in normal light, frolicking with a puppy: a shot for the mothers.

The amount of press photographs released during this time is quite staggering; a veritable deluge, it covers the world, showing Elvis as a saint, as a sinner, as a clean boy, as a beast that should not be let loose, as a dreamy romantic. The photographs are designed to appeal to every kind of fan, and to compliment the frequently bewildering collage of singing styles that young Elvis is offering to a pop-eyed world. He will never be bigger than he is during this period, and the photographs like the records whose style is almost imperceptibly changing are the first calculated refutation of his primitive image. The "mean" shots are quickly dropped.

By 1956 there are Elvis shirts, slacks, sweaters, bracelets, belts, ties, hats, T-shirts, dogs, dolls, greeting cards, bubble gum cards, pins, pens, pencils, buttons, pillows, combs,

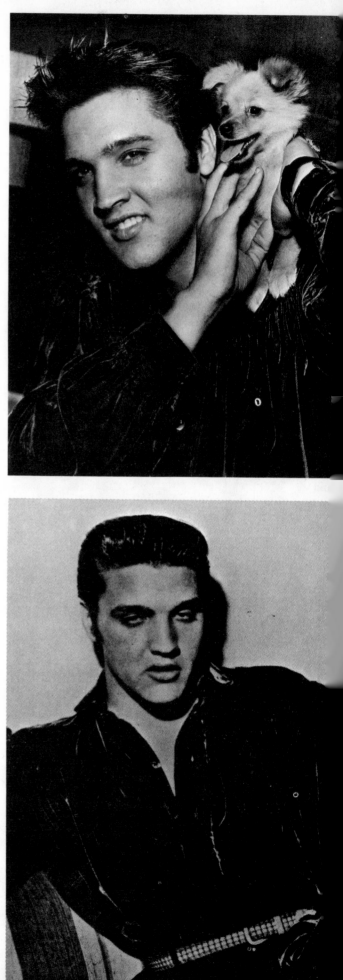

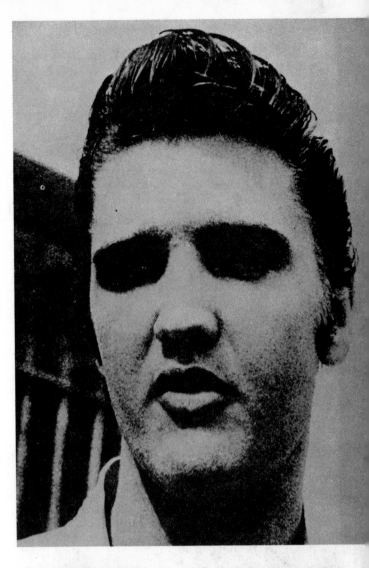

More publicity stills, 1956. Left: Four different faces from the same session. Right: a final "mean" shot.

hairbrushes, busts, bookends, guitars, colognes, lipsticks (Hound Dog Orange, Heartbreak Hotel Pink, Tutti Frutti Red), shoes, shirts, socks, underpants, belts, chains, handkerchiefs, wallets, fan clubs, gangs, sects, sundry other organizations and special photographs that light up in the dark – plus, of course, all the records. (But no tie-ups, of course, with booze or cigarettes.)

Elvis has a gold-leaf suit that cost $4,000 and gold slippers that cost a meagre $100. He has a whole stream of cadillacs – yellow, pink, blue and purple. He has "dozens of teddy bears, a live Australian wallaby, a pair of burros, two monkeys named Jayhue and Jimboe, a three-wheeled Messerschmidt, thirty sports coats and forty sports shirts ('His clothes have to be seen in compatible colour to be believed'), a swimming pool, and a $100,000 mansion that glows blue-and-gold in the dark." The kid knows how to spend it.

It is obviously the best time of his life; he is out to enjoy himself. Colonel Parker is advertising him with elephants and midgets (The Elvis Presley *Midget* Fan Club) and he himself is doing his bit. To calm the hysteria at one particular performance, he quips, "Thank you. You bring a lump to my bill fold." Then, in reply to critics who think he is obscene, he makes a remark that will fill young fans with glee and will become part of pop literature: "They all think I'm a sex maniac. They're all frustrated old types, anyway. I'm just natural." Some time later, accused of signing his autograph on young ladys' breasts, he neatly skips out with: "I've written on arms, legs, ankles – any place decent where people can take soap and wash it off. I don't want no daddy with a shotgun after me." He also bites the hand of a female interviewer, explaining blandly: "I was only being friendly like a little puppy dog." And when asked by a woman journalist how he feels about girls who throw themselves at him, he gives her his heavy-lidded burn and says: "I usually take them." Finally, when he is asked why he hasn't gotten married, he comes up with the pure corn-cob reply: "Why buy a cow when you can get milk under the fence?"

No doubt about it: he's got it, he can use it, and he plays with it. He also gets into fights (but always in defence), has a few lawsuits thrown at him by girls claiming to have his child, and has a good time, driving motor bikes and fast cars, dating starlets and painting the town red: a young man in his heyday.

The fans are now spread world-wide and are voracious in pursuit of him. Some pray to his picture before going to bed, carve his name into their forearms with jack-knives, or riot in the streets of what once were staid cities; others get expelled from school for refusing to cut their hair (make no mistake, the crew-cut is *dead*), run away from home to keep vigil at Graceland, crawl through his windows, climb over his cars, steal the trees from his garden, walk away with his statues – and at least ten-thousand of them write him letters each week, in which they express their undying and most suicidal love.

He is now considered to be "morally insane", is described as "an inspiration for low IQ hoodlums" who "ought to be entertaining in the State Reformatory", the reason doubtless being that he is practising "his voodoo of frustration and defiance" and is therefore a "whirling dervish of sex" Consequently, some of his records are publicly incinerated, more live performances are banned, and when he gets on television they wipe sweat from their brows and try straightening him out for the masses – and results are ludicrous.

On the *Milton Berle Show* Elvis wears a tuxedo with lapels that resemble shark fins. He seems decidedly uncomfortable, keeps fingering his bow tie, and at one stage actually mumbles, as if it wasn't rehearsed, "It's not that often that I get to wear the . . . er . . . suit and tails." There are Roman columns behind him, the guitar seems out of place, but his singing gets the message across – there's no holding this boy. So he groans

Above: He sings "Hound Dog" to a hound dog on the Steve Allen Show. Facing page top: Andy Griffith, Imogene Coca, Steve Allen and Elvis (Tumbleweed) Presley. Bottom: Elvis with Milton Berle and Elvis with Tommy and Jimmy Dorsey, 1956.

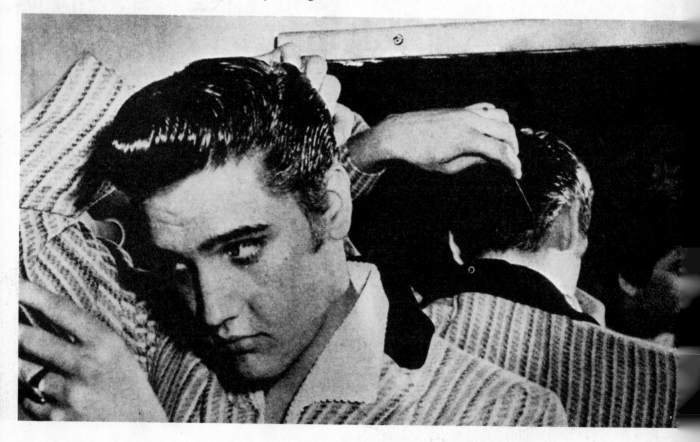

out "I want you! I need you! I love you!" and the girls in the audience start shrieking. This is just the beginning.

The *Steve Allen Show* is worse, pure insanity. With Steve Allen, Andy Griffith and a lady called Imogene Coca, he endures a thoroughly silly and humourless Western sketch based around the selling of a "Tonto Chocolate Bar". It is presumably a satire on the Louisiana Hayride, but it sinks fast under its yipee-aye-ohs. Elvis, known as Tumbleweed, is

submerged in the background and only comes forward on occasion to sing some abysmal lines. He wears a white sombrero and a black cowboy outfit, is handsome and otherwise lost. Then he changes into a tuxedo, they wheel on a droopy dog, and Elvis chants his song right in its face, before kissing its nose. He doesn't get to move much, but he sneaks in the odd shiver, and that just about wraps it up for the day. The show is a huge success.

On the *Ed Sullivan Show*, where he's told to stay subdued, he manages to be better: he insinuates. Against a dark, light-flecked background, his hair shining with laquer, he runs through "Don't be Cruel", starts to sway just a little – and is promptly cut off at the waist. He then introduces "Love Me Tender" – the title song of his first movie – and he sings it by plunging his fists in his pockets and rocking back slightly on his heels, his lip curling, just teasing. He is lazy, greasy, and he's Rudolph Valentino – sliding a hand down one thigh, shrugging his shoulders just for kicks, and very slyly mocking the sentiment of the song, sometimes rolling his eyeballs. The

girls go bananas, their shrieks shake the cameras, and Mr Sullivan is losing pounds as he stands in the wings. Later, Elvis Presley saunters back before the cameras to publicise his newest LP. His hands hang loose and limp, he sways dreamily from side to side, he cups one hand over an ear in imitation of Johnny Ray, and on the last line of "Love Me" – a long, drawn-out "OOOHH!" – he suddenly grabs hold of his head, shakes it vigorously and howls "*Love me!*" as if he's been knifed by a madman. It brings the house down.

But these television shows are a harbinger of things to come. As his records change, softening his approach, spreading over the whole spectrum of popular music in an attempt to corner all of the market, so he achieves the desired effect. As he comes on with the ballads, with the teardrops and perfume, he is, with his very sound instincts, preparing himself for what he will need when he gets to Hollywood – which, to be sure, is where he's heading. If he never leaves America (and as a performer he never does), the silver screen will carry him to foreign lands, make him a household word. He will be like Dean Martin, Bing Crosby, Frank Sinatra: he will aim for an Oscar and retire, a respectable man. Rock 'n' roll is a fad, has no hope in Hell of lasting, and if you want to survive you get out while the going is good. In this, as in many other myths, Hollywood is the answer.

His debut is one of the most entertaining camp performances of all time. Originally called *The Reno Brothers,* the movie is

Below: Elvis signs up with producer Hal Wallis to a killing seven-year contract. He'll seldom look so happy for some time after. Opposite page: Love Me Tender *(1957).*

etitled *Love Me Tender* (1957) to cash in on the kid's latest hit. There aren't supposed to be songs, but when they realise what they're dealing with, they promptly slip four of them in.) Very much a "B" grade look at the American Civil War, it features young Elvis Presley as an innocent ploughboy who falls in love with, and then marries, his brother's girlfriend. The brother, who was thought to have been killed by the damned Yanks, returns to try and start life again – which makes for embarrassment. The rest of the film is a confused, grainy sortie into shootin', lootin' and general mayhem, during which the greasy kid performs four country songs and manages to die, after much heroic lingering, with his own ghost singing lazily about him – a fantastic finale. As for Presley's performance, it is passionately sincere, if wildly off-key. Fans will later complain about the "almost childlike persistence

of the other stars in trying to 'better' Elvis's lines" – but the other stars show more sense: they simply sleep-walk around him.

The film does, however, prove that Elvis has real presence, a most natural gift for projection, an animal vigour. The songs are disappointing to those expecting hard rock, but are the only kind possible in a period piece. Later they will stand up as undefiled hillbilly boppers, sung crisply and with unerring instinct; but at the time they are forgotten as throwaways, last minute additions. Still, the kid quivers and shakes like a jelly, legs bending and rolling in spasms, the guitar pointing skyward. It's the very first time that non-Americans have seen him, and what they see doesn't disappoint them: he is dreamy, sublime, the greatest thing since James Dean. And who wouldn't weep at such a death scene?

The film *Love Me Tender* enamours no critics, makes
fortune at the box office, and causes more riots in the streets
After being informed that his "dramatic contribution is not
great deal more impressive than that of one of the slavering
nags", young Elvis, undeterred, tries another. *Loving You*
(1957) is more ambitious (technicolour, no less) and its main
theme is simply the rise to success of a young man much like
Elvis himself. As a film it's much better than it is ever given
credit for – a woefully sentimentalised, but otherwise quite
accurate, examination of the rise of a pop star in the American
south-west.

Elvis plays Deke Rivers, a small-town boy with a natural
ability for putting over his own kind of music, specifically
rock 'n' roll. He is picked up by a beautifully, calculating
press agent, who sees in him the chance to revive the flagging

ve Me Tender (1957). A 20th Century-Fox release,
*duced by David Weisbart, directed by Robert D. Webb,
*d co-starring Richard Egan, Debra Paget, William
*mpbell, Neville Brand and Mildred Dunnock. The film ran
*eighty-nine minutes which was approximately eighty
*nutes too long (Elvis sang the other nine minutes). A
*fused, grainy sortie into shootin', lootin' and general
*yhem, it gave Elvis four country songs ("Love Me Tender",
*et Me", "Poor Boy" and "We're Gonna Move") and
*owed him finally to die, after much heroic lingering. A
*tical disaster, it made a mint at the box office and turned
*is into the new golden boy of Hollywood. Above: Elvis
*gs to his family on the porch, including Debra Paget (as
*wife) and Mildred Dunnock (as his mother). Opposite:
*onel Parker, Elvis, William Campbell and El's cousin,
*e Smith, on the set.

Left: Another still from Love Me Tender. Below left: A r...
shot of Elvis recording the film's soundtrack, with
J. D. Fontana on drums. The guitar pose was taken during
filming, but not actually filmed. Meanwhile, other work
(and play) continued. Bottom: Elvis running through a son...
with the Jordanaires. Opposite: various "candid" shots of
boy on the loose. The one at bottom right is a classic exam...
of young lovers in the fifties, complete with Eisenhower
clothing and transport.

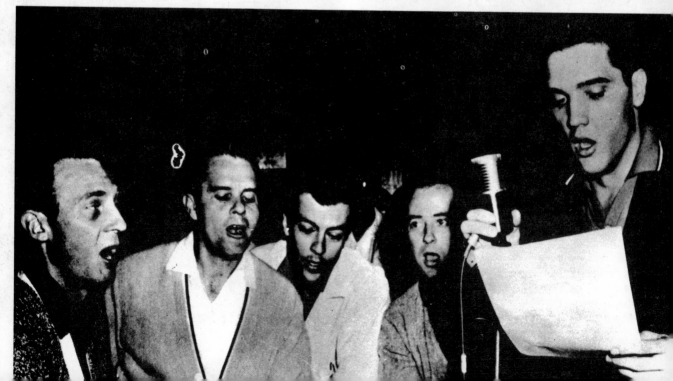

Loving You *(1957). A Paramount Picture, produced by Hal Wallis, directed by Hal Kanter, and co-starring Lizabeth Scott, Wendell Cory and Dolores Hart. Critically underrated at the time of its release, it is now considered by some to be one of the best of the genre. A reasonably accurate examination of the rise of a young pop star in the American south-west, it unconsciously mirrors Presley's own changing career – from blue-denimmed rough-neck (above) to phosphorescent dream-image (opposite page). The film used lots of shadow and romantic back-lighting to emphasise the "mythic" qualities of its star; it also smoothed out his face, painted his lips and eyes, and offered him up as an aphrodisiac to the needy. Actually seen playing with Elvis in the movie are Bill Black (bass) and Scotty Moore (guitar). Shortly after this these old friends would go their separate ways.*

fortunes of her ex-husband's simple country band. She takes the kid on tour with them, but pretty soon he's much bigger than the band he's supposed to be aiding. This leads to jealousy and resentment on the part of her ex-husband, who views the kid as a threat not only to his own career but to the love that he still has for his woman. On top of which (a most cunning device) the kid is sensitive, lonely, bewildered by his success, and unaware of how he is being used: instant audience sympathy.

The film uses this simple theme as a basic prop around which to hang some good production numbers; it presents the songs well and it's the only one in his career that seems to have a firm grip on what he is. It also manages, for the first and the last time, to present Elvis as he is on the stage . . . well, not quite, but close enough. And finally, most certainly, it

...arks the beginning of the tidying up of Mr Presley: the ...nooth-faced, unreal man.

It takes Presley's own history – his humble background, ...s rise to fame – and neatly ties it to the current craze for ...rtured teen heroes. He is therefore shown singing and ...ghting and quietly brooding, talking often in a whisper, face ...ramatically shadowed, a real blue-denimmed child of the ...ties, struggling through. It also emphasises, since it is ...rrently fashionable, that he really doesn't give a damn for ...s success: he just wants some lovin'.

Its technique is lascivious.

He is first seen in a very natural light: wearing denims, ...oking grubby and unsure of himself. The first song is ...rformed while he's still wearing these clothes, standing on

the back of an open flat-top truck, legs spread and a guitar in his hands – the quintessential Elvis pose. The song is the first version of "Got a Lot of Livin' to Do", and he starts it looking nervous, glancing cagily around him, holding on to his guitar as if for comfort, not really involved. Then, as he starts to get into his bit, he rocks back on his heels, lets his left hand hang limp, and simultaneously shakes his left leg – a modest, witholding version. He finishes by quivering, swinging his right arm and then breaking a string on his guitar: a foretaste of the future.

As the film progresses, as Deke becomes more popular, we see him performing on the truck and in marquees and getting just a little wilder each time. He does "Hot Dog" and "Party", and though he's still in blue jeans, he is more the Elvis we know, swinging arms, shaking legs. One of his favourite tricks is to rock back on his heels, let the spasms jolt up through his body as if through his feet: he's not really moving, he's just quivering all over; he's like something plugged in to a power point, being jolted to death. And indeed, since the

always places him before an audience, the shrieking
the screen is often indistinguishable from the shrieking
hose in the cinemas. Much craftier you can't get.
The film now outlines the way in which pop stars are
cessed. Deke Rivers grows more famous, sings ballads
softer rock, dresses flashily and enters real theatres where
decor is abstract. "Teddy Bear" is a rock song sung almost
whisper – and the singer is the kind you don't find in the
ets. His hair is stark black and shiny, his eyes are inked in,
wears tight red trousers with white seams down the sides,
his shirt is phosphorescent, a light-reflecting silk, all
ite but for the collar, shoulders and cuffs, which are red
h white flowers and fancy patterns. The stage behind him
dreamy, a veritable rainbow of colours, and the shadows
crimson and mauve on his smooth, suntanned face. He
esn't play the guitar, he just holds it at an angle; and he
resents a creature so wonderful as to be beyond the
lms of mere mortality: a highly glamorised, perfect male.
Prior to this he has tackled "Lonesome Cowboy", and
ugh he hasn't yet reached the very heights of golden
ter, the presentation is just as dream-like. He wears a
ckered shirt and necktie, never plays his guitar, and is
n in a spotlight that cuts through the darkness to highlight
deep, long-lashed eyes, his hair shining like cut glass.
en he spreads wide his legs, turns slightly to the side,
ws a clenched fist and swings one strong arm: he is no
n to mix with.
This film does, in fact, use lots of shadow to emphasise

Elvis in action in Loving You, *singing "Got A Lot O' Livin'
To Do". He will never be as wild as this again.*

Opposite: A dramatically shadowed Elvis in Loving You.
Above: Highly stylised publicity stills from the film.

e mythic qualities of its star. It also smooths out his face, aints his lips and his eyes, and offers him up as a meal for the ungry dreamer. (When the kid has a fight it is not his own ult: he is set upon; when he loves it is definitely without enitals: his kiss is a climax.) If the film is not great art it is ill an accurate representation of the emotional climate of its

times, one of the very best of the "teen" movies. And Presley's performance, though no confident earth-shaker, is perfectly matched to its material and remains quite undated. In fact were he not a pop singer, maybe he would receive more serious attention than he is going to get. The pity here is that his personality is such that it can't be ignored by the

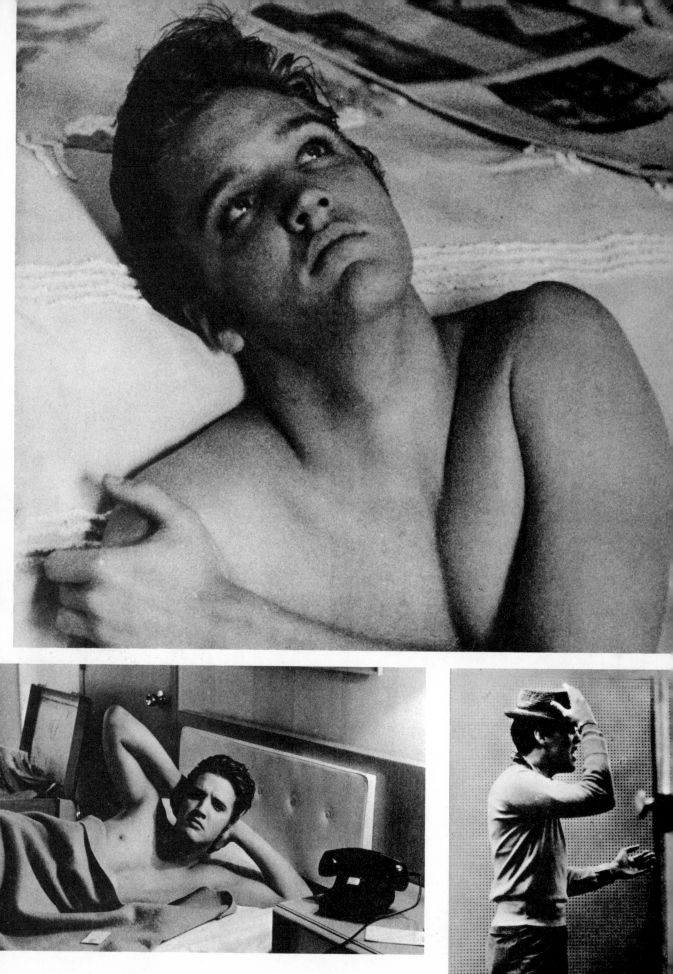

s: and after all it is just a rock movie.

ut for rock 'n' roll movies, it is very good indeed, showing
ur prime performer as we most prefer him: gyrating his
n, swinging his arms, pumping out his hips, shaking all
, and dragging his bent left leg along a stage ramp like a
ple reaching out for the sacred cup: pure untrammelled
wmanship.

aturally, the film is a smash, causing riots and huge
ies. It is condemned from the pulpit, often viewed by the
ce, and even banned in some backwater counties where
think it's a devil's tool. Meanwhile the soundtrack is
ed out and snapped up, while some singles taken off the
chunder straight up the charts. The movie has proven
Elvis can hold the screen, but in doing so it changes his
ction, sweetens his image. He is now in the arena of the
t family audience and certain items have to be considered
ch as children and grandmas. It won't happen abruptly –
changes will be subtle – but the changes must definitely
e and are already prepared.

house Rock (1958) has become the epitome of "punk'
ies – a nice, greasy film about arrogance and deceit, about
ition and greed, about a slick sonofabitch who claws his
to the top and leaves his footprints on the faces of his old
ds . . . but it ain't what it seems. It shines the spotlight
ife's most human vermin, it is cynical and brittle and very
ny. But within all the toughness, the comic-book realism,
e beats the soft heart of a sentimental hack.

he film is made at the height of Elvis's fame, when he is still
ved as a revolting teenage fad, the first of the tough,
k rock singers. The producers, therefore, aren't about to
the ship: they want to sell him to the fans, to all the kids

Jailhouse Rock (1958). An M-G-M Picture, produced by
Pandro S. Berman, directed by Richard Thorpe, and co-
starring Mickey Shaughnessy, Judy Tyler, Jennifer Holden
and Dean Jones. Disdained by the critics and condemned fro
the pulpit, this highly entertaining look at a hoodlum pop
star has since become something of a cult movie. Above: Ou
hero is stripped to the waist and brutally flogged. Left: He i
corrupted by worldly Mickey Shaughnessy. Opposite page:
Three classic examples of this new, and thrillingly nasty,
Elvis. Top left: He tackles Judy Tyler, growling "That ain't
tactics, honey, that's jest the beast in me." Top right: he
sneeringly offers popcorn to a dumb blonde (Jennifer Holden)
Bottom: He is filmed through the legs of a stripper with his
gaze very cunningly aligned. Overleaf is the flamboyant
"Jailhouse Rock" dance routine.

who like this snake, but they also want to broaden the scop
to add tears to the tantrums. So they have him real mean,
real fireball and sexy, and they lay out the shock effec
nicely before pouring the cream. Thus, he is miraculous
brought back to basic decency – to the real, softer *him* ar
in doing so they manage to weight the scale at both ends
and destroy an almost perfect piece of *kitsch*.

Once more the simple theme is the rise from rags to riche
but this time the gimmick, the irresistible novelty, is that th
kid is an unrepentant ex-con. At first he's a nice boy – just
little bit wild – but then, when he gallantly defends a lady
honour, he accidentally kills her tormentor and gets sent u
the river.

The injustice of this makes him cynical. And once inside the Big House, he learns the ways of the wicked world, has his lovely locks shorn (the biggest gimmick in the movie) and gets blamed for a riot he didn't start. He is then stripped to the waist and quite thrillingly flogged (the second biggest gimmick in the movie) and goes back to his cell gritting perfect teeth.

He has now been corrupted by the corruption of the world and he'll go out for all he can get: his soft heart has been hardened. Remarkably, he learns to play the guitar; even more remarkably, he manages to make an appearance on a show that is televised from the prison. And to stretch credibility even farther, his cell mate (Mickey Shaughnessy) gets his signature on a contract prior to his discharge from the brig.

"Watch out for the teeth, sonny", he's advised when he departs. "It's a jungle."

So the kid sneers and leaves, his eyes cold as ballbearings, and meets up with a lovely press agent who starts turning him into a star while she fights off his uncouth advances. "I like the way you swing a guitar", she says lasciviously – and then turns all puritanical when the brute lifts his huge paws. "Don't try your cheap tactics on me!" she primly tells him. To which he replies, with his lip curling superbly: "That ain't tactics, honey. That's jest the beast in me."

He gets famous as a singer, buys himself some fancy gear, and starts knocking off the birds right and left because his agent rejected him. He then goes to Hollywood, has parties by the pool, buys some dogs and treats them better than the humans, most of whom he just tramples on. He spits on his friends, almost cuts his true love's heart out, and says to Mickey Shaughnessy, who now walks all the dogs: "You're just gettin' bitter, old buddy." For which there is good cause.

Towards the end of the film, he's attacked by his dog-walker because he's been so mean to his true love, whom the

for Elvis's performance, which is even more entertaining tha
Mickey Shaughnessy's. He is arrogant and sexy, violent an
sarcastic, and he delivers his lines with a soft icy edge th
enlivens them more than they're worth. It is true of this fil
that until the very last reel he doesn't even bother trying
woo his audience; he stifles his natural charm. But the film
rigged to make each nasty trick seem the product of som
deep inner hurt: he is merely defensive.

What really comes out in the film – and it's a harbinger
the future – is the degree to which Presley has been stylise
The most celebrated production number is the "Jailhou
Rock" sequence, which is big, bold, brassy and as slick as th
come. But Elvis's free-wheeling style, which *Loving Yo*
managed to catch, is here tightly controlled and drastical
subordinated to an immaculately choreographed routi
which entertains without exciting. Elvis moves like a snak
is professionally beyond criticism, but one feels that an
male chorus dancer could have done the thing for him. What
missing is the element of violence, of visual surprise; what
left is a competent but standardised Hollywood gang show.

There are two other rock songs in the film, but neither
presented well. He sings "Baby I Don't Care" by the side of th
swimming pool and his gestures, which are supposed to b
sophisticated, are merely grotesque. The second rock song
his classic version of "Treat Me Nice" – is presented as a stud
recording, which necessarily limits him. He occasionally sna
his fingers, sways his hips, shakes a leg, but for the most pa
he is subdued, a mere Hollywood swinger. The last song in t
film, which should have been a real raver, is a ballad which
offers with glistening eyes. And it is this calculated ru

Above: Jailhouse Rock's arrogant Elvis explodes into action.
Opposite: The Big "E" with his Harley Davidson on the
M-G-M lot between takes on the Jailhouse Rock film.

dog-walker also loves. He loses his voice (sighs of dread in the
cinema) and it looks like he'll never get it back – thus he
instantly repents. As is true in real life, repentance always
works the miracle, and this film doesn't argue with that.
Elvis takes off his bandages, looks at his true love, almost
weeps and then opens his golden throat – the violins come
rushing in.

Hardly a synopsis to suggest a softening process, but the
soft soap is definitely there. The film will become most famous

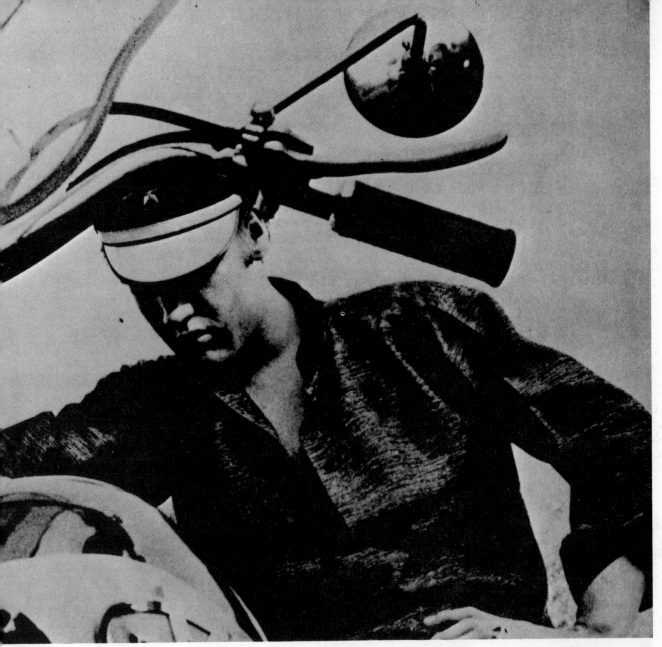

vn – from hard rock to soft ballads – which will guide the
g sequence of his next movie: he will leave them in tears.
He is now a long way from Memphis, even farther from
pelo, is ensconced in the whirlwind and glitter of Holywood,
ting records in Culver City, at the M-G-M studios, and
ing out with his "ol' boys" in the biggest hotels, hiring
vies, drinking Cokes, and sneaking out in the morning
rs surrounded by bodyguards, with his "mafia" and yes-
n, to try to have a little fun without the fans swarming
vn on his mortal flesh. Sometimes he visits Graceland,
blue-and-gold glowing mansion, and he still makes live
earances between film commitments. But now the army
s him and he wants to do it right, so he makes one last movie
ch will be his best – though it will show also with a
ressing skill that the rocking Elvis Presley is about to be
ied in favour of a more general approach: he will finally be
oth.

hin its narrow limitations, *King Creole* (1958) is a film almost
ectly realised and executed. Shot in black and white on

location in New Orleans, it is directed by Michael Curtiz with a great eye for detail and shows his ability to get the best from his actors. The supporting cast is any young actor's dream: the superb Walter Matthau, Carolyn Jones and Dean Jagger, not to mention the underrated Vic Morrow as the local flick knife. It is further enhanced by having Presley's finest sound-track collection – though the treatment of these songs will be the most disappointing aspect of the production.

The film opens with some beautifully lit shots of desolate, rain-damp, early morning New Orleans' streets black woman trundles her cart along, singing out to adver her wares. Elvis, playing a kid named Danny Fisher, comes on his latticed balcony and sings "Crawfish", an excell pastiche Creole song. He leans on the railing, tucks in his sh

*ing Creole (1958). A Paramount Picture, produced by Hal
Wallis and directed by Michael Curtiz. Labelled by some
critics as the "Blackboard Jungle" of pop, it was Elvis' most
violent film – and certainly his best. The supporting cast
was any young actor's dream, and included the superb Walter
Matthue, Carolyn Jones and Dean Jagger, with Vic Morrow
s the only delinquent to equal Elvis. Elvis obviously learnt
lot from these professionals; his performance was excellent.
Unfortunately a major mistake lay in reuniting him with
Dolores Hart, surely one of the most saccharine girls in the
lm business. His love affair with her was only matched by
he insipid treatment of some otherwise wonderful songs.
hese pages show the "smooth" Elvis performing his numbers.
rom left to right: "Trouble", "New Orleans" and "As Long
s I Have You". Overleaf: Elvis mixes with some bad com-
any – with the exception of the lovely Lilliane Montevecchi.*

d sways his hips ever so gently: a smooth, sinuous per-
rmance.

The kid is basically decent, but he's dissatisfied and
bellious, and considers his father a weakling. He isn't
tting on at school, is not particularly interested in anything,
d cleans up in a local night club to bring in needed money.
is morning, when he goes to the club to clean up, he meets
pair of local hoods and an alcoholic moll (Carolyn Jones).
ey want some music, but it isn't available, so they insist
at the kid sing a song. He does "Steadfast, Loyal and True"
is school's Alma Mater – his hands folded primly in front of
n, his voice nervous but true. When he's finished, one of
e hoods assaults Carolyn before turning on Elvis himself.
vis smashes two bottles on a table and seems to know how to
e them.

"You're a pretty fancy performer, kid", says one of the hoods.

"Now you know what I do for an encore", Elvis replies.
The kid now has to go to school, so he shares a taxi with
iss Jones, and when they get there, she insists that he kiss
r. The other kids see this, start hooting and hollering, and
vis loses his temper and takes a poke at one. For this minor
fence, he's told that he won't be graduating, which is news
at could cripple his father. Then, on the way home, through
e dark-shadowed alleys, he's waylaid by Vic Morrow and
s gang. Vic pulls out his flick knife, but is grabbed by the
roat and slammed violently into the nearest wall. So
pressed is the hooligan by this brilliant display that he
omptly invites Elvis to join his gang. Elvis refuses.

"Good boy," murmurs Vic, closing up his glittering knife.
ights real dirty."
When Elvis arrives home he breaks the bad news to his
her (the excellent Dean Jagger) and this causes yet another
w between them. Elvis, disgusted, stomps out of the
use and decides to join Vic's gang after all. The idea, would
u believe, is that Elvis sing in a store to distract the staff
d let the boys knock off some goodies. This they do, in
ery amusing scene, while Elvis strums his guitar and croons
over Doll", a modest but catchy ballad. Then Elvis makes
ate with a cute salesgirl witness, and he gets the hell out of
store.
That night, in the Blue Shade, Elvis speaks to the boozing
y, who is accompanied by the dreaded Maxie Fields
alter Matthue), the crooked owner of this colourful den.
lter orders him to sing, so the kid gets right up there,

looks real mean and evil, and let's rip with one of his all-time
classic numbers: "*If you're lookin' for trouble/You've come to
the right place/If you're lookin' for trouble/Just look right in ma
face . . .*" The song is an intriguing mixture of blues, jazz and
rock, and it's raw vocal treatment is superb. The visual
presentation is smooth rather than aggressive – a finger-
snapping, hand-waving performance far removed from real
rock. And it encourages the owner of a rival club to offer
Elvis a job as a singer. This he does *not* refuse.

For his try-out performance at the King Creole club he
does a hand-clapping "Dixieland Rock". It's a pure rock song
with a Dixieland backing, and though the vocal is superb,
the visual presentation is once more pinioned on the altar of
a "sophisticated" approach, more suitable to Hollywood
than to rock fans. Apart from shaking his head and snappily
clapping his hands, he doesn't really do all that much. But
he is, of course, a huge success.

The kid is now involved with Dolores Hart, who is virginal,
and with Carolyn Jones, who is not. ("That's a pretty piece of
material", he says of Carolyn's dress. "You ought to have a
dress made out of it some day.") In between these minor romps
he sings a ballad, "Young Dreams", and a superb gutter blues,
"New Orleans". In both of these numbers the lighting is
excellent, but the presentation is woefully stifled. He sings
the ballad in a chair, snapping fingers, kicking legs, and
otherwise looking quite trapped. Then, on the blues number,
he's smooth and sinuous, but only his hands really move.
It is, however, the best number in the movie, and the recorded

version is really quite remarkable: a stuttering, half-talking, and frequently howled piece of pure gold.

We are now only half-way through the film and the last rock song is sung. It's called "King Creole" and Presley's vocal is excellent, but he sings it without moving much. The legs are epileptic, the left hand hangs limp, but basically it's a static performance, nicely lit and well-regulated. And for the second half of the film there'll be no rock at all – we are now being prepared for the future.

Elvis is drawing all the crowds away from the wicked Walter Matthue's club, which doesn't please Walter at all. He thus employs Vic Morrow to involve the kid in a crime, which he can then hold over his head like a noose. Elvis's father has taken a job in a local pharmacy where he is constantly humiliated by the manager. Knowing that Elvis is much disturbed by this, Vic suggests that they beat up the manager, and Elvis agrees. Unfortunately they beat up his father instead – which leaves Elvis open to Walter's blackmail. Elvis is given no alternative but to sign up with Walter and move away from the King Creole club. During his farewell performance he sings "Don't Ask Me Why", and then gives a sad speech and disappears. He now works for Walter.

The rest of the film is a very fast-paced, if somewhat melodramatic, sequence of events. The kid's father goes to Walter to plead for the release of his boy and is informed that his son led his own attackers. This breaks him up, and Elvis, quite shocked, brutally beats Walter around his own flat. Walter then orders Vic to carve the kid up, which Vic manages to do before Elvis kills him. The wounded Elvis, his left arm pouring blood, staggers back to his father's front door, where he is promptly rejected. He staggers away, eventually faints

84

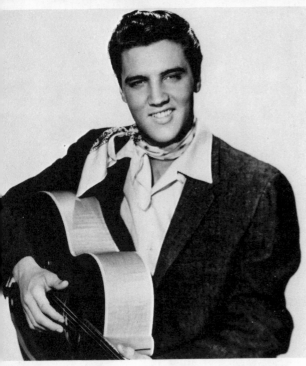

...g Creole marked the end of the "rebel" Elvis. Opposite: ...th Dolores Hart and, above her, Carolyn Jones. Above: A ... "mature" Elvis in a publicity still from the film.

...m loss of blood, and is rescued by the repentant Carolyn. ...e drives him to her hideaway, a shack by the sea, and to-...her they share an idyllic few days. Then Walter comes ...ng with a pistol in his hand, shoots at Elvis and hits ...rolyn instead. It is now Elvis's turn, but a dumb kid he ...ce befriended drags Walter into the sea where, quite ...raculously, he shoots himself. Carolyn gives a sweet dying ...ech.

The last touching scene has Elvis back in the King Creole,

heavily shadowed, with a guitar in his hands. He is reconciled with his father, who is watching the performance, and he also has his true love in the audience, namely Dolores Hart. He lifts up his eyes, which are sparkling with tears, and he sings to his father, to his true love, to his audience, the very pertinent "As Long As I Have You". A most tearful finale.

An overdose of sentiment and some lurid melodramatics overpower *King Creole* in the end – but otherwise it does stand up. It precedes *West Side Story* as a "realistic" musical and is less embarrassing. Elvis gives a performance of finely graded animal naturalism – a consummate acting-singer acting well – and he does, beyond doubt, transcend the antiquated morality of the film's romantic main theme. And the film, besides being the best of his career, is a disturbing glimpse into the future, a drastic change of direction. It is obvious from viewing it that the rock is being dispensed with to build him up as a romantic ballad singer; thus all the rock songs are crammed into the excellent first half and the second half presents a new Elvis: the Family Favourite. For this reason, as distinct from the excellence of the whole production, it is the most crucial film of his career.

The changes in Elvis begin on television and are finally made manifest in Hollywood. He's been sweetened and groomed and convinced that he's an actor, and now he will leave rock behind. He will go into the army and do his two years and prove that he's as good as the rest of them. This period in his life (which costs the tax man a packet) is used as a platform for new things. So patriotic is the country, so obsessed with his image, that they see in his service, in his willingness to do it, a man whom any parents could respect.

His hair is cut short, he suddenly looks like your own son, and it is obvious that beneath all the glitter he is just like the rest of us. Then his mother dies, he weeps brokenly and publicly, and after this there is no one against him: he is pure as the driven snow. And so all this is used, with a fine sense of timing, to set him up as a good decent boy, as a man all the family can see.

Elvis Presley becomes a Matinée Idol.

I can't see my reflection in the water
I can't speak the sounds that show no pain
I can't hear the echo of my footsteps
I can't remember the sound of my own name
– Tomorrow is a Long Time, *Bob Dylan*

vis comes out of the army in 1960 and goes straight into
...ddle-road show biz. The first thing he does is tape a show
...th Frank Sinatra at the Fontainebleau Hotel in Miami. He is
...ep in the mortuary of the purple-haired ladies and we're
...ver to know if he likes it. His long locks have been shorn, he
...made to wear a tuxedo, and he's told not to move while he
...ngs: he is truly obedient. He sings his current hit – "Stuck
... You" and "Fame and Fortune" – but considering the tuxedo
...d the command not to move they really aren't given that
...ch elbow room. He then sings Sinatra's "Witchcraft",
...ey both duet on "Love Me Tender", and the whole thing is
...ally quite dreary - besides being ominous.
   The first post-army LP is called *Elvis is Back* (1960) and it
...mes in a nice fold-out booklet. The booklet is decorated with
...ctures of Elvis in the army, but luckily the contents rise
...ove these. Obviously carefully angled to cover most of his
...les, the album utilises the songs of Jerry Leiber and Mike
...ller, Stan Kesler and Otis Blackwell, blues writers Jesse
...one and Lowell Fulson, and it's beautifully produced. It also
...cludes, by way of nods to the mainstream, fresh versions of
...ggy Lee's "Fever" and Johnny Ray's "Such a Night".
... challenge Peggy Lee is a challenge indeed, but the Presley
...ersion is smooth and very sexy, just as good as the original.
... for the Johnny Ray number, which Ray handled dead-pan,
...vis bucks up the pace, salts the sex with some humour, and
...rns it into something immaculate. He also sings a few ballads,
...me foot-tapping rock and three genuinely exciting blues
...anters. The voice is now deeper, much smoother and more
...sured, but it still manages to work wonders with insinuation

and wit on such items as "Stuck on You" and "Such a Night".
It is a promising return.

His first post-army single is received by many people as a definite statement of intent. He sings "I'm stuck on you" to a lovely rocking beat and it thunders up the charts as expected. But the following single is a remarkable turnaround – an updated version of the operatic "O Sole Mio" – and since this one, a non-rocker, is played on numerous mainstream stations

G. I. Blues *(1960). Above and opposite page: With Juliet Prowse. Right: with Harris Strickland Jnr. and cousin Paul Morgan in the Fontainebleau Hotel, Miami, before the Sinatra TV Special.*

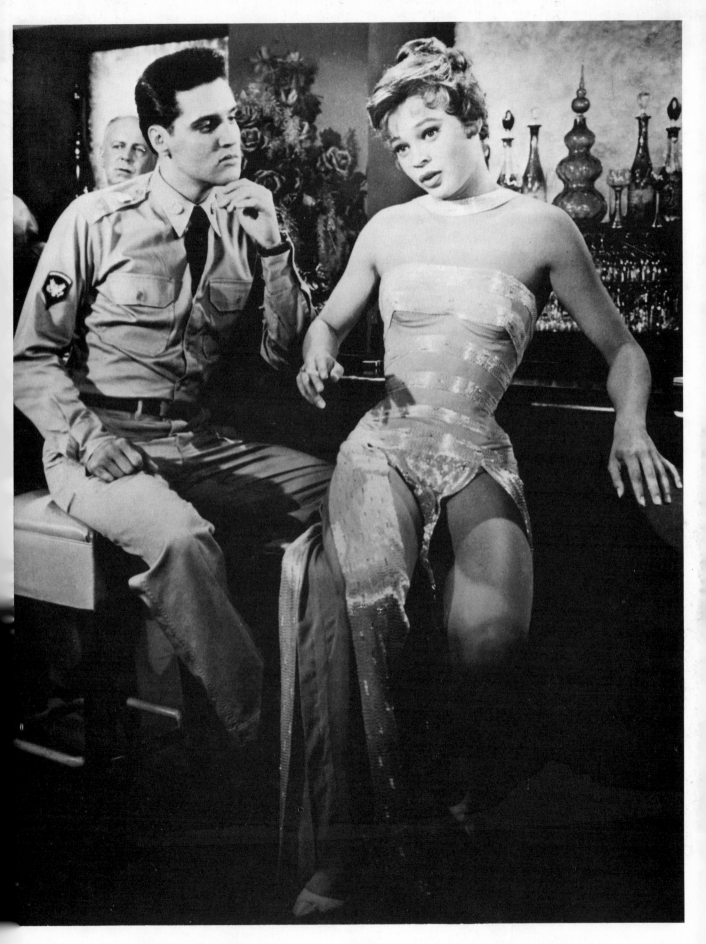

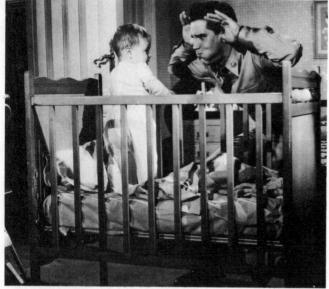

it. Elvis sings in beer gardens, in cable cars and trains, sings to children and puppets and the army, *looks after babies*. He also wears a soldier's uniform, drives a tank and tours the Rhineland and falls in love with a sexy German dancer. This girl is Julie Prowse and she walks away with the movie by performing an erotically charged dance that makes Elvis look tame. As for Elvis's rock numbers, they are few and far between and none of them is anything special. "Shoppin' Around" is a smooth and infectuous toe-tapper, but Elvis doesn't move much beyond some shoulder shrugging. "Frankfurt Special" is better, a sharp, snappy chanter, but it's performed while he's sitting in a train, surrounded by buddies. As for the title tune, it's as far removed from the blues as the earth is from Alpha Centauri; it is, in point of fact, one of the first really bad songs that have obviously come off the conveyor belt. Elvis's mode of presentation is to sing in deep voice while his buddies, a

it becomes one of the biggest grossers ever. His next single, therefore, is "Are You Lonesome Tonight", an old Al Jolson weepy that was also once recorded by the Ink Spots. Elvis and the Jordanaires simply imitate the Ink Spots, but add the novelty of a soulful spoken bridge: sales-wise, it's a monster. And if there are still any doubts as to what direction Elvis is headed, his first post-army movie will resolve them.

G. I. Blues (1960) is first and foremost an exploitation movie that cashes in on Elvis's two years of service. It marks the true debut of the "family" movies and it isn't embarrassed to show

I. Blues *was Elvis's first post-army movie and these scenes* *ore or less speak for themselves. The sideburns cropped off,* *e face well-fed and clean, he sings to puppets and children* *d ladies, then finally bolsters the morale of the army. The* *usicians are actually actors, the plot is pure Doris Day, and* *e whole dismal affair makes a fortune. Elvis, perhaps* *nsing the trap he was falling into, then attempted to make* *o serious movies. The first one was* Flaming Star *(1961), a* *n Siegal western in which Elvis portraying a bitter half-* *eed Indian (right) gave his finest screen performance. The* *lowing pages demonstrate how well he suited the role — but* *only sang two songs (one over the credits) and thus the* *m didn't do as well as the previous ones. Still, it remains* *e of his best.*

usicians, chant "Hup-two-three-four" as if they're practising eir drill in a slime pit. His leg movements, God help us, are a mulated army march and his guitar is not synchronised to the undtrack. The last song, "Didja Ever", utilises the Stars and ripes, and it has to be heard to be believed. The movie makes fortune and its most popular moment is when Elvis sings Wooden Heart" to the puppets. This becomes a hit single.

This film is the model around which the later films will be ased: some comedy, some love interest, some children, some ice scenery and a handful of "situation" songs. Later, in esperation, they'll add motor cars and boats, motor bikes and eroplanes, some animals and a lot of plastic girls, most of them irginal. As for Elvis himself, he'll be gradually castrated into everlasting pubescent boy. And as movie follows movie, ch one worse than the last, he will actually start resembling a unuch: a plump, jittery figure. Meanwhile, his fans will wear its and buy houses, clip their hair and move back into steady bs while a whole new generation of young people will get p on revolution. Yes, the youth culture that he started will ourish and grow while Elvis starts to rub noses with droopy

93

dogs, hold hands with virgin girls. At the moment, however
he hasn't quite sunk that far, and is about to take a last daring
gamble.

It is possible that at this point he actually sees what is
happening and attempts to break out of the trap. He has always
been serious in his desire to be an actor — was in fact more
excited by the good reviews of *King Creole* than by anything
else in his career — and he might therefore have viewed *G. I.
Blues* as mere commerce, as a means of reinstating his drawing

ver. Packed with songs, full of colour, with just a little bit
verything, it will reach a wider audience than he ever had
ore and will consequently give him some leverage. It is
certain, but it is possible. If he makes this one sure thing,
n the gates will be opened and he can tackle anything
desires: even try serious acting. So he makes his family
vie called *G. I. Blues,* and it's a monster and he gets what he
ts. He tries a couple of serious ones.
n both *Flaming Star* and *Wild in the Country* his potential is

grasped. The former is based on a screenplay by Clair Huffaker
and Nunnally Johnson, directed by the excellent Don Siegel,
and includes in its cast Dolores Del Rio, Richard Jaeckel and
John McIntyre: a notable crew. The latter is, if anything, even
more extravagant in its credentials, being based on a superb
novel by J. R. Salamanca, written up for the screen by Clifford
Odets, produced by Jerry Wald, directed by Philip Dunne,
featuring Tuesday Weld, Hope Lange, Millie Perkins and John
Ireland, and with music by Kenyon Hopkins. It can be said of

Flaming Star *(above) was followed by* Wild in the Country *(1961). A sombre movie with many serious flaws, it was enlivened by the presence of Elvis and sexy blond Tuesday Weld.*

both movies, though neither is perfect, that they seriou present Elvis with a challenge and help him to meet it.

In *Flaming Star* (1960) Elvis is the half-breed son of a f blooded Indian and a white man. Brought up in the wh community, he is agonizingly conscious of the problems t his mixed blood presents; when the Indians go to war agai the whites, he is forced to choose between conflicting loyalti In setting up this situation, the film zeros in neatly on Presle own personal attributes: he is moody, violent and posses of an animal grace; he is volatile yet strangely dignified. A Elvis's performance, if not up to Brando standards (the p was in fact originally conceived for Brando) still manages convey, with a fine sense of balance, the pained dilemma the man who doesn't belong anywhere – society's outsider

In *Wild in the Country* (1961) he's again an outsider, but t time the conception, from the production roots up, is son what less than convincing. In all fairness to Elvis, the probl isn't in his performance, but in a surprisingly banal screenpl by Clifford Odets. Cast very much in the "Peyton Plac mould, it has Elvis as a young man with a personal history violence and a latent talent (if not genius) for writi Included in this steamy saga of small-town gallivantings i love-stricken psychiatrist, a drunken uncle, a sex-cra cousin, a sadistic father, a virginal lover, one near murder, c near suicide and numerous other entertaining sub-plots quite a peppery stew. It does, however, present Elvis with t role that suits him well: once more he is moody and rebellic and romantic, a beautiful young dreamer whose pent-violence is but a sign of his frustrated creativity. It's a hoa old theme, but it's expertly produced, and though Elvis surrounded by a team of professionals, it is he and he alo who carries the film.

The critics praise him again, but though the films make
~ney they are, compared to his more musical efforts, relative
~ds.

Now the mystery resides in who makes his decisions: is
~is himself so cut up by the failure that he simply can't face
~ loss of audience? Or is it (and on this his fans will definitely
~ the blame) his management that now sings the new tune?
~The most interesting myth is that his manager is all power-
~having a hold over Elvis that no one comprehends, but a
~d that somehow can't be broken. Certainly, in later years,
~is will appear so passive as to be positively devoid of all
~ition – a mere functioning machine. If he does what Parker
~s, even if Parker was to wreck his career, well, so be it, he
~ not stoop to argue, he will row the boat. It is, in its intricate
~ intriguing possibilities, one of the more enduring riddles
~pop – no one yet knows the answer. But whatever the
~sons, Elvis is now about to embark upon a voyage into
~stic failure, into the darkest backwaters of the most
~lime mediocrity. Yes, if Elvis stops singing the cash
~ister stops ringing; so from now on he will sing and be most
~npathetic – and there ain't another thing to discuss.

Hollywood spreads its tarnished wings.

Already he has considerably cut back on his non-film recordings. He releases *His Hand in Mine* (1960), an LP of religious songs, and most of it is really outstanding. But as far as singles go, he offers only "Wooden Heart", and "Surrender", another rehashed Italian song, albeit sung superbly. The next single will be the title tune of *Wild in the Country*, a mod little ballad heading nowhere. It is backed by a great version "I Feel So Bad", a rocking Chuck Willis blues number. this side is buried, not approved of by his new fans, a might well be a fresh nail in his coffin. He will shortly rele a rocker, the excellent "Little Sister", backed by the m

Opposite page and first left: Elvis as a serious actor takes his final bow in Wild in the Country. *Below left: A rare shot of Elvis in white dinner jacket during a personal appearance at a benefit show in the Ellis Auditorium in Memphis, 25 February, 1961. On 26 March, 1961, he flew to Hawaii for another public appearance in Pearl Harbor's huge Bloch Arena. He did a very long show, moved around quite a bit, and finished with sweat on his brow. As the photos below demonstrate, he pulled in some old friends to accompany him. Behind him in the Memphis shot is J. D. Fontana on drums. In the Hawaiian shots the saxaphonist is Boots Randolph and the guitarist is the legendary Scotty Moore. The Hawaiian show was his farewell performance. He remained there to make* Blue Hawaii *(overleaf), then went home for a string of awful movies, not to be seen "live" again for another 8 years.*

pular "His Latest Flame". Neither record will do as well as e smooth, rhythmic ballads, and doubtless this will reinforce cisions.

In February, 1961, he makes a personal appearance at two nefit shows in the Ellis Auditorium in Memphis. It is the st time he has done so since his discharge from the army, but isn't the good sign that it seems. He wears a white dinner ket, black trousers and tie, and this time he doesn't get nself moist: he is cool and sophisticated.

A couple of weeks later he flies to Hawaii for another blic appearance, this time in Pearl Harbor's Bloch Arena. can't start for five minutes because of the hysteria, but en he gets going he is very smooth indeed. He wears a d lamé jacket, an open-neck shirt, and has a garland of wers around his neck. He sings "Heartbreak Hotel", "Such Night", "Don't be Cruel", "Treat me Nice", "All Shook

Up'', "It's Now or Never", "That's All Right", "Are You Lonesome Tonight", "Hound Dog" and quite a few others. He sings loud and clear, the back-up band is excellent, but it's all very much tongue in cheek: he is mocking himself. And who knows at this time – who would want to believe it – that it's to be his last public appearance for a long, bleak, eight years?

Who knows, indeed? From this point onward the course of his career will defy all effective analysis. Certainly, for someone so inherently outrageous, he will show a stunning lack of resistance, a mystifying compliance.

Some will say that his love for his mother was so strong that her death drained the interest right out of him: he did, after all, only do it for her, to rescue her from the poverty of her life, give her some nice things. There is also the common knowledge that when fame overtook him, his mother couldn't handle it, felt dislocated from her background and frequently displayed real signs of stress, including diet pills and alcohol. If this be true, then it is very possible that he holds himself

Above: Blue Hawaii *(1961) marked the beginning of the second-rate films. Opposite: Surprisingly,* Follow That Dream *(1962) was one of the funniest of the year. Colonel Parker, being held up at gun-point, was not in this film.*

ponsible for her death; and, with her passing, suffers not
y her loss but the ever-gnawing pain of his secret guilt.
s a reasonable, if not too pleasant theory.

Others, less romantic, will say that his management is
iquated to the point of senility. As we know his manage-
nt is, for the most part, a bizarre one-man band dominated by
flamboyant Colonel Parker. An ex-circus barker, a legend-
wheeler-dealer, he was great in the days when pure
n was a commodity, but is now out of touch with reality.
still thinks that show business is the domain of the family
ience, and that sweetness and light, with some ludicrous
micks, will continue to bring the money in. And it is this
ngali, both cunning and benign, this extraordinary show-
n-salesman of the decaying American South who is selling

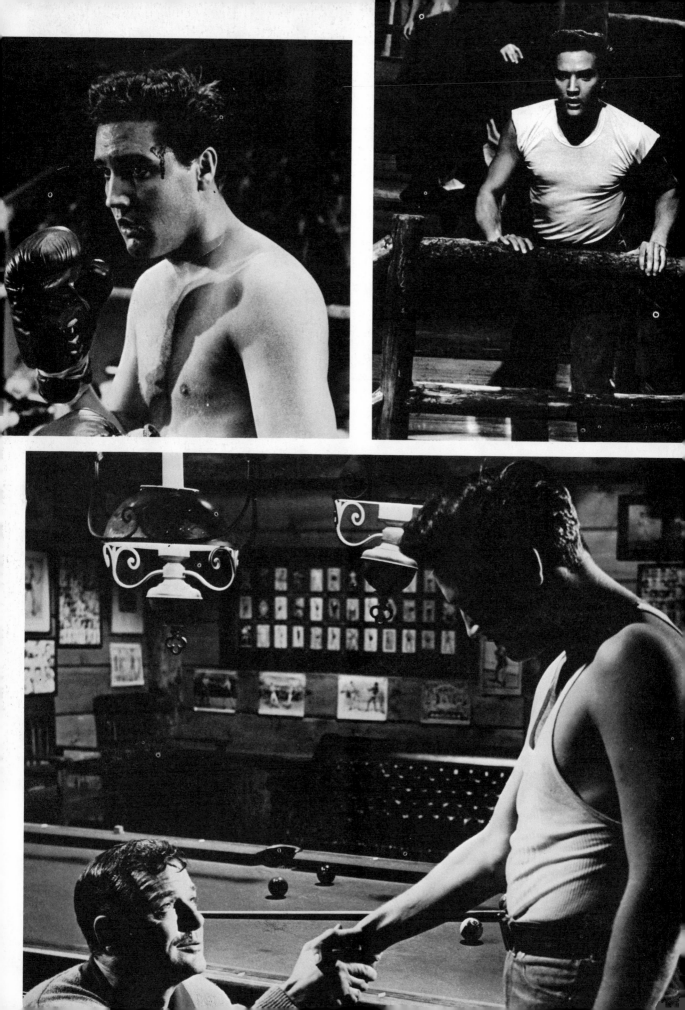

Opposite page: The seeds of confusion obviously began to sprout in Kid Galahad *(1962). Another attempt at blending a "serious" story with some songs, it failed miserably from the first reel to the last. Nor did it fare too well at the box office. By way of atonement, Elvis's next film was again set in his profitable blue Hawaii. It was called* Girls! Girls! Girls! *(1962) and it was every bit as silly as its title. Still, it made a fortune at the box office and thus set the format of future films: cute children, gorgeous gals, exotic locales and lots of songs – all filmed in glorious colour for matinée viewing.* Girls! Girls! Girls! *(this page) had a little bit of everything, and it was a monster in the cinemas and on vinyl. Hereafter the films would become interchangeable – as the pictures on the following pages demonstrate.*

Elvis off, like his popcorn and balloons, on the safest lines imaginable.

Certainly it is true that Parker doesn't read film scripts, doesn't care for the contents, and will only discuss cash at the conference table: he is that sort of manager. But this still begs the question of why Elvis himself, at the height of his success, and certainly with enough drawing power to call his own shots, seems to hand it all over without a word. No matter how bad the movies, no matter how low his record sales, he lets it happen with no sign of resistance – he is passive, a living ghost.

For the moment, however, he is still in Hawaii, to soak in the sun and make the first of the real trash. It's called *Blue Hawaii* (1961), and it's utterly abysmal, but it's packed with sweet songs (pastiche Hawaiian ballads) and the scenery is quite gorgeous to city folk. Needless to say, it's a box-office monster – and not only that, but the soundtrack album becomes the biggest-selling item he's ever had. So this all-singing, girl-chasing, virginal Elvis, in his swimming trucks and thongs, with his surf boards and sports cars, has just proven that the clean lad of *Flaming Star* and *Wild in the Country* is not what the good folks out there want. No, they want a nice travelogue,

filled with songs and sexy gals, and they don't want anything that might threaten them. In short, they want escapism.

As if to prove this point, our good clean boy's next movie is a modest little comedy set in Florida. Called *Follow That Dream* (1962), it has Elvis as the bumbling son of a family of entertaining rural nutters. It is really funny, with Elvis near perfect, showing a natural flair for comedy and timing. But it isn't glamorous enough, there are only a few songs, and it doesn't do much at the box office. He follows it up with a pedestrian remake of *Kid Galahad* (1962), and again, though

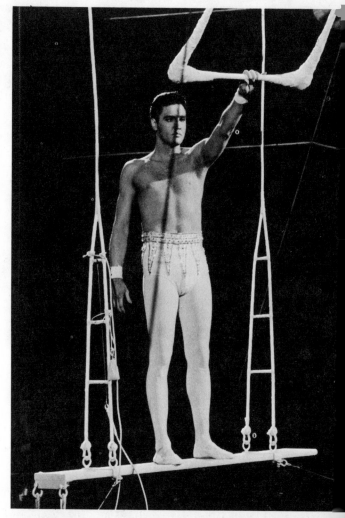

Above and top of opposite page: Kissin' Cousins *(1964).*
Right and bottom of opposite page (with Ursula Andress):
Fun in Acapulco *(1963). Below and bottom right:* It
Happened at the World's Fair *(1963).*

he is good, there are very few songs and the background is
hardly a paradise. It gets a reasonable audience, but it's no
Blue Hawaii – and that's enough news for everyone concerned.
He is rushed straight back to Hawaii, quickly makes *Girls!
Girls! Girls!* (1962) and it's a monster in the cinemas and on
vinyl.

A point has been proved.

For the next seven years, while the real world explodes,
he'll make an average of three films a year, most of them
ludicrous. In few of them will he play a professional singer:
he'll just be a guy who sings for his kicks and some extra
bread. In all of them he'll be engaged in the pursuit of pretty
girls, none of whom will he take to bed. In most there'll be a
fist fight, some children, some animals, and some glittering
machinery: it's the affluent age. And in none will he play
a nasty role – he will always be a bland and straightforward
boy.

The films will degenerate from a reasonable level of com-
petence to the most appalling display of indifference. Written,
produced and directed by hacks, they will stink from the

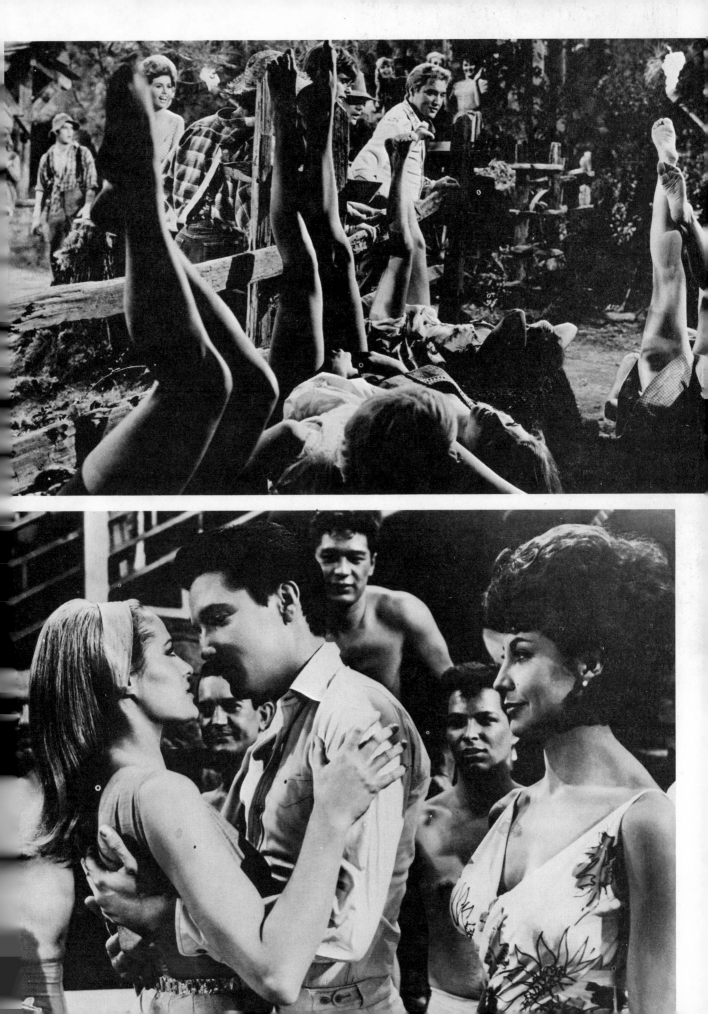

credits to the last mindless reel with the stench of their own appalling taste. Some very talented players will wander through these wastelands, looking desperate or dazed or simply cynical. And the star himself, as if not quite believing it, will finally start parroting his lines like a man in a waking dream – and in the end actually develops a twitch that resembles nothing short of nervous spasms. He will grow fat and lazy, monumentally bored, and as the films pile up like more stones on his grave, he'll recede farther back into the shelter of Graceland, back into his mysterious and shadowed thoughts, back to his memories.

The last remotely decent film is *Viva Las Vegas!* (1964), and it is even more successful than *Blue Hawaii*. They take their

A lightweight affair, but still his best musical in years, was Viva Las Vegas! (1964). The Las Vegas locale enabled them to put in some rock songs – and Ann-Margret, whose image is similar to Elvis's, was a bonus.

time shooting it, the songs are well presented, and Elvis and his co-star, the sexy Ann-Margret, form the most attractive twosome in years. It is even quite possible that the challenging Miss Margret briefly lifts him from the doldrums he's been in; most certainly when they double (as in the very good ''C'mon Everybody'' sequence) the fireworks explode loud and bright. Both performers are sinuous and sensual and assured, and

between them they manage to lift a routine movie far abo what it would otherwise be. But it also has the bonus director George Sidney – and it's the last one that will be blessed. From now on it is Deadsville.

Parker's only concern is that each film should make album that can later be flogged off like toothpaste; for t reason, his only interest in the script is that it leave blanks f

ngs. The songs are mostly ghastly, pure "situation" fodder, ⟨kn⟩ocked together fast in some computerised back room and ⟨of⟩ten manufactured around no more than the title – which ⟨its⟩elf is frequently murderous. What do you do when you're ⟨to⟩ld to write a song called "There's No Room To Rhumba in a ⟨Sp⟩orts Car"? Godammit, you do it. And bearing in mind ⟨th⟩at it's Elvis, and that the boy's got some tonsils, you try some ⟨pa⟩stiche rock, some mock country ballads, some calypso, some ⟨mo⟩dernised oldies and some operatic rewrites – it's all grist to ⟨th⟩e mill.

The titles of these songs are, in themselves, a most illuminat⟨in⟩g summary of their contents: "Ito Eats", "Beach Shack", ⟨S⟩morgasboard", "Wolf Call", "Adam and Evil", "Do The

The best part of Viva Las Vegas! *was the "C'mon Everybody" routine. Above: A respectable Elvis in Graceland.*

osite page, top, he punches someone in Tickle Me *(1965). Bottom, he kicks someone in* Roustabout *(1964). Above, he wrecks
ar in* Girl Happy *(1965). Top left, Jocelyn Lane in* Tickle Me; *top right, Mary Ann Mobley in* Girl Happy.

m'', "Shake That Tambourine", "Go East Young Man",
ga Is as Yoga Does", "Petunia, The Gardener's Daughter",
rt Lauderdale Chamber of Commerce" and, most delicious,
ng in itself, the remarkable "Long Legged Girl With The
rt Dress On" – a real mind-blower. As for the revamped
en oldies, he tries "Santa Lucia", "Old MacDonald's

Farm", "Down by the Riverside", "When the Saints Go
Marching In", "The Eyes of Texas" and "The Yellow Rose of
Texas" amongst numerous others.

When they fall short on these gems they pad out the albums
with a novelty now known as "bonus" songs. Since these so-
called "bonus" songs are pure studio recordings, they are by

111

Elvis in striped coat playing Johnny in Frankie and Johnny *(1966). The Oriental costume is for* Harum Scarum *(1965) and he's surrounded by Mary Ann Mobley (left of picture) and Fran Jeffries. Marianna Hill flashes her legs in* Paradise, Hawaiian Style *(1966); Suzanna Leigh (above) in same flick.*

far the best things he is doing. Perhaps out of a desperation born from singing movie trash, he now concentrates during his rare serious sessions on shaping himself into a crystalline ballad singer – and he succeeds. A phase of his career that is largely ignored, it nevertheless shows that he has not lost his love of singing; that given the right material and some genuine interest he can still manage to convey, with masterly control, a very real sense of human loss and nobility. Starting with his beautiful rendition of "Falling in Love with You", he will continue in this vein with such lovely ballads as "Forget Me Never", "I Need Somebody to Lean On", "Please Don't Stop Loving Me", "I'll Remember You" and his exquisite interpretation of "Love Letters". Unfortunately, so bad is the general quality of the soundtracks that his work during this period, admittedly quite scarce, will be buried on the backs

As the films get worse, so do their titles. Above and opposite: Scenes from Easy Come, Easy Go *(1967) in which Elvis played an underwater demolition man. Top of opposite page is a typical fight from* Double Trouble *(1967).*

of albums that are no longer selling.

In the whole long eight years there will only be three albums of original, non-film material. The first one, *Pot Luck* (1962), is a rather strained attempt to cover most of his more popular singing styles – but his heart isn't in it. "Kiss Me Quick" is a dismal copy of his smash, "It's Now or Never"; "Just For Old Time Sake" is a steal from "Old Shep"; "Easy

Question" is a bid for the Dean Martin Trophy – and so it goes on for twelve tracks. The next album, three years later, called *Elvis For Everyone* (1965), which means that it's a bag of leftovers. It includes throw-outs from *Wild in the Country, Viva Las Vegas, Flaming Star* and *Follow That Dream*. It also includes an excellent bluesy rendition of "Tomorrow Night", originally recorded in 1956; a superb howling blues, "Whe

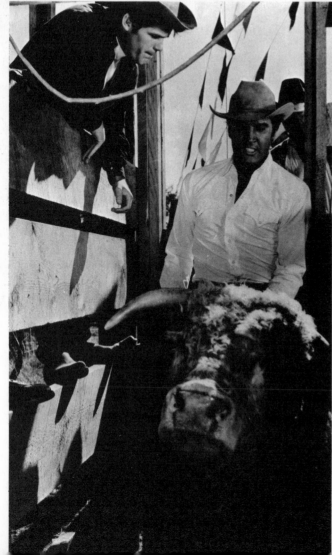

It Rains, It Really Pours'', originally recorded in 195
''Memphis Tennessee,'' originally recorded in 1963; and
good, but obviously antique version of Hank William
''Your Cheating Heart''. The third album of this peric
released a good two years later, is *How Great Thou Art* (196
A religious album, it is reasonable but doesn't match previo
efforts and it seems that even his own favourite music canr
stir much enthusiasm now.

The films roll. He hides in Graceland.

His records rarely see the hit parade; his films are sinkir
Now the movies take a fortnight from beginning to completi
and are starting to go out as supporting features. He hides

his mansion and does nothing; Colonel Parker makes no move. Meanwhile, the world changes, becomes restless and more political, and popular music, to be popular, must reflect this. The Beatles come along to revitalise a dead scene, and Bob Dylan writes songs that eschew false romance and lash out with uncommon defiance. A great admirer of Presley's, he has obviously been influenced by his vocal tricks, his "shock" tactics and his rebellion. But Dylan's songs are more articulate, he is studiously non-conformist, and he will not be enslaved by "show business". He is, indeed, the new prophet of pop culture, and he sings to young people who despise glamour and ambition, Tin Pan Alley and Hollywood, who

demonstrate in the streets and on the campuses for political change. And so the new music follows Dylan, and the Beatles and the Stones, while their hero, Elvis Presley, now well fed and slick, makes strange movies with titles such as *Girl Happy*, *Tickle Me*, *Harum Scarum* and *Paradise, Hawaiian Style*. It's not real. *It's a weird scene, man.*

By this time Elvis must be suffering an enormous lack of self-confidence. He has seen himself tumble from the highest peaks of fame to an anonymity as total as the dungeon: it is close to a nightmare. Hiding out in hotels in Graceland, he is surrounded by his "ol' boys", by the voices of his childhood, and they play silly games and watch out for his moods and

The films don't improve, but the Elvis image does. A side-burned, trimmed down and white-suited Elvis brutally slaps Sheree North in the ridiculously entitled The Trouble With Girls and How to Get Into It *(1969). Below: Another punch-up in* Live A Little, Love A Little *(1968). Opposite: A 'different' Elvis in the ill-fated* Charro *(1969).*

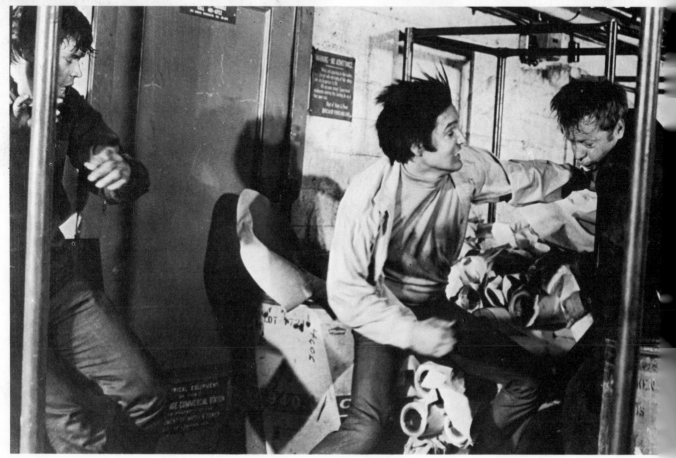

slip notes beneath his door when he locks himself in his room, often not seen for days. Sometimes, sitting in darkness, drumming his fingers as the clock on the wall ticks the hours by, the silence of the years slips around him and enfolds him in thin ice. Sometimes the boys get him out – play some ball, hire a funfair, shoot pistols at flash-bulbs in the pool – but this doesn't last long. He can be polite, or he can burn them with his eyes, ignore their very presence, and most often he retreats. And the fans come and go through the halls down below and start wondering if he ever existed, if he isn't mere fantasy.

What do you do when you have reached the very top before you've even taken a deep breath? Where can you go now? Elvis is rich beyond mere tabulation, yet he doesn't make much use of the money. True, he buys Cadillacs and supports a large crew; true, he lives in grand ostentation. But he never leaves America, has no lust to see the world, perhaps doesn't even know, in his solitude and paralysis, that the

outer world actually exists. Why does he not want to get out, to explore something fresh? – new musicians, new friends, new records, new countries. It never happens, and the mystery of his personality, once so vital and rich, thus spirals into more esoteric shores and leaves him stranded on barren rocks.

Some suspect he's just dumb, others think he's just jaded, yet others will say that his need to perform has been thwarted and is starting to throttle him. And so, as the years pass and he slips into history, he becomes, perversely and in his least productive period, a figure of almost mythical unreality, a folk hero, an idealised memory now frozen in the haze of a romantic past. "Remember *Elvis*?", they now say. "He *was* great." But the very fact of his disappearance, of his strange, oblique retirement, turns him into an American legend: another corrupted dream.

The films continue to come out at regular intervals, each one worse than the last. Elvis sings in settings made of

More scenes from Live A Little, Love A Little *(Elvis fighting and Elvis leering at the cardboard girl);* Charro *(Elvis with cigar and on horseback) and* The Trouble With Girls and How To Get Into It *(with the blonde, with the brunette).*

ardboard and plastic, he plugs a morality that went out en years earlier, he prays at altars and romps in sports cars nd splashes in water and chases girls, grinning like some uge dopey kid when they let him hold hands. When the ongs are set up, he's surrounded by bikinis and guys who an't play their guitars. Though maybe he snaps his fingers, ways his hips just a little, he's embarrassed in a way he never ad to be before. But he always wins his races, always marries s gal, and never opens his mouth without violins — a true, utmoded beach boy.

These films represent the very nadir of his career, but no one ever works out why he does them. He is obviously under contract and that must count for something — but even starlets have been known to have tantrums. What few understand, and what many can't forgive, is that he never steps forward to complain. Stories emerge of his boredom and disgust, but no sign of revolt is forthcoming. He flies in for a fortnight, does his bit and gets out, back to study the gilt walls of Grace-land and remember better days. It is life in a glass bowl; he has lived with the same people for near to thirty years and anything beyond them is alien, a world he can't handle. And now, it is said, he never looks you in the eye, mumbles his words, keeps his gaze on the floor, then drifts away like the ghost in the mansion, just looking for privacy.

Eight years, indeed, is a long time.

In the May of 1967 Elvis Presley is married. The girl is Priscilla Beaulieu, an old Memphis sweetheart. Nine months later, blessed day, they have a child and reality steps in.

Now he suddenly starts moving and no one quite knows the reason: whether becoming a father has given him back his drive, whether his manager has pulled off some extra-ordinary deal, or whether Elvis himself has finally vomited up the crap and is taking things into his own hands. No matter. He is changing.

The first change comes in September when he goes back to Nashville to cut some intelligent records. Included in this session are "Guitar Man", "Big Boss Man", "High Heel Sneakers" and "Just Call Me Lonesome" — all pertinent, all gutsy. The next noticeable change is in *Stay Away Joe* (1968), a zany little movie in which Elvis, once a nice boy, has a riotous time playing a contemporary Navajo Indian who smokes, drinks, jokes, sings, fights and does a lot of woman-ising — a considerable turnaround. Then, in another movie, *Live A Little, Love A Little* (1968), he actually shares a lady's bed and sports sideburns. Both movies sink fast, but the

121

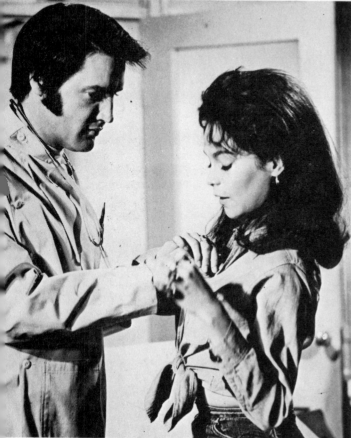

Above and below: Change of Habit *(1969) gave Elvis his las acting role. Handsome, sideburned, he played an expensively dressed doctor slaving religiously in a Hollywood ghetto with a bunch of pretty nuns, one of whom he falls in love with. The film sank like a stone, but when it turned up on televisior it was better than its synopsis would suggest – and Elvis's performance, if not particularly demanding, was fluid, relaxed and full of charm. He has not acted since. Top left opposite page: The new-look Elvis comes back with a bang in his 1968 NBC-TV Special. Top right: The sideburns creep downwards as can be seen in this shot where he talks to Colonel Parker on the set of his last film,* Change of Habit. *Bottom left: Elvis, on horseback, comes out of seclusion to meet fans in the grounds of Graceland. Finally (bottom right), a sideburned, trimmed-down Elvis is about to enter the seventies.*

point has been made, and in *Charro* (1969) the change is ev more evident. A lousy Western film with some very phon sets, it nevertheless has Elvis looking brutish and unshave and its one song is buried behind the credits. Elvis doesn't a well, but then neither does anyone else, and the direction, put it mildly, is basic. In his next film *The Trouble with Gir* (1969), in which he might be described as a ''guest'' star, wears a white suit, a brimmed hat and huge sideburns; a suggests to a lady, with a nice lop-sided grin, that they co tinue their conversation in bed.

He looks just like he used to.

The Presley resurrection, at the end of 1968, is as swift

his first rise to fame. It comes out of the blue with a television special that puts paid to his years of drudgery. Apparently, whilst making it, he was a bundle of nerves, a man facing a live audience after eight years in solitude and suddenly very conscious of the distance – but once on he is dynamic, he has presence, he jumps right out of the screen.

Immediately it seems as if those eight years were mist, as if the Presley we knew had never really been away and had never let himself get out of touch. He looks extraordinarily different from his bland film persona, is remarkably handsome in his very tough way. And his voice which in Hollywood was "that curious baritone" is now raunchy and sensual and threatening: a miraculous revival.

Sometimes dressed in black leather, sometimes wearing a white suit, he moves his body with the lithe grace and finely tuned instincts of a performer in total command of what he is and what he can do. And in the selection of songs, in their mode of presentation, he wipes the floor with his rivals.

The world sits up and blinks, shakes its head in disbelief, then rushes out to snap up the soundtrack album. The closing song, "If I Can Dream", is pushed out as a single and becomes a million-seller in no time. Elvis then goes back to Memphis for the first time in fourteen years and sweats through his most productive session ever. Backed up by real musicians and some genuine songs, he sums up his career and then puts out an album, *From Elvis in Memphis* (1969), that is one of the best he has ever done. A string of hits is to follow.

Suddenly, miraculously, and with mystifying ease, he is back with the world at his feet.

It is instant hysteria.

Date: 3 December, 1968. A sensual, black-clad Elvis in the NBC-TV Special that resurrected him. The King has returned.

5

*"Elvis Presley remains the quintessential American
pop star: gaudy, garish, compromised in his middle
age by commercial considerations, yet gifted with
an enormous talent and a charismatic appeal beyond
mere nostalgia. Presley remains a true American
artist – one of the greatest in American popular
music, a singer of native brilliance and a performer
of magnetic dimensions."*
– Jim Miller, Rolling Stone

his first public appearance after eight years in seclusion,
vis goes to Nevada, to those diamonds in the desert, to
Vegas, the first genuine lunar base. A city of dreams,
ilt from plastic and neon, it casts phosphorescent messages
er the wilderness desolation, is a jewel of cold electric fire
rning bright in the night. An Aladdin's cave of the American
bconscious, both promise and prison to all who would
ter, it is, to be sure, the one place on earth in which a legend
reignite its own image.

Here, with the machines, with the blackjack and baccarat,
th the dealers and the hookers and the criminal and the
ane, in the glitter and timelessness (no clocks, no windows,
day or night), he will resurrect an American myth. The
k will be a parody of what has gone before, a sublimely
f-mocking resumé of his own great achievements; but it
l, in its humour and its superb presentation, give back the
excitement to the watcher: he knows just what he's doing.
The white columns soar upward through the dark humid
encircling a metallic globe, surrounded by flags, domin-
d by the huge boards that hurl out towards the Strip the
ssage that Elvis is back, his face multiplied. And the lights
these boards form a glaring fluorescence, a staggering

orange, an ever-changing yellow and crimson that dazzles the eyes. And the sum of the whole, in all its architectural arrogance, is like a launching tower built on the moon, hypnotising the multitudes.

The myth looks even better than he ever looked before, coming on with trumpets and drums and guitars, to an explosion of flash-bulbs and hysteria. Now the audience is predominantly middle class and middle-aged, no longer rebellious but playing the system, safe in their money, in their own ideas of purity, finally arrived, in the year of 1969, to let nostalgia fill them and lay them waste. And there, on the stage, stands the highlight of their lives returned to flesh and blood, rising up from the tomb. One hell of a man, truly tall, dark and handsome, he sports a black Karate suit, a wicked grin and bushy sideburns; he is pure and untrammelled *machismo* hunched over a guitar.

A wave of nostalgia for the fifties has been sweeping the country. Whether or not this has encouraged Elvis back, it certainly does nothing to harm him. No, rather he plays on it, on his knowledge of his own history, and so turns his first season in the showroom of the International into a classic revival in every sense.

He kicks off with "Blue Suede Shoes", charges through "I Got A Woman", then leans over the mike in that old seductive pose and starts growling from the back of his throat, a sly, honeyed come-on. They may be middle-aged, have cropped hair and bouffants, but they are out of their seats like teenagers and the applause is enough to shake the stage. So he rocks the mike gently, hums and growls, fools a little, than lets rip with a fast "All Shook Up", his legs jolting like pistons. A decade disappears, they are back where they started, and as he spreads wide his legs and rakes the mike across his body, he comes over much stronger than any reality they might yet have known.

He understands this very well – and he knows his own age. So he works along the safe lines of instant nostalgia, but he does so with a style and panache that come close to pure magic. Lithe, raunchy, the sweat pouring down his face, he now moves with the precision of an athlete, the grace of a dancer. His movements, in fact, no longer seen uncontrolled, but

instead are stylised, immaculately choreographed, and splendent with high visual dramatics.

He throws in Chuck Berry, and Leiber and Stoller, Carl Perkins, and he re-works the Sun songs, some old ballads, some new, each building on the last, each beautifully controlled, hips swaying, hands chopping, his teeth and eyes flashing, held in the spotlights, surrealistic in the strobe, sometimes falling to his knees, sometimes frozen in black silence in controlled karate poses that turn him obliquely into something much more than he is: a figure in a ballet, no

Date: 31 July, 1969. Location: International Hotel in Las Vegas. Elvis's come-back performance was a triumph in every sense. These photos recapture the exitement.

poised for a pirouette, now imitating a *pas de deux*, unreal, unearthly, a black dream of pure motion – Nureyev in a jumpsuit, no less.

It is no exaggeration. Of all the rock singers who have aged with the times he is the only one who has kept his sense of grace. Flamboyant and flashy, sexy and self-mocking, he works with the instincts of a genius to give poetry to the basic rock performance. Thus he spirals around, his hand sweeping through the spotlight, and falls down to one knee, his head back, a fist clenched, and is frozen for an instant in a thin blade of silver. And he rises up slowly, curving snakelike, hypnotic, while the violins soar to new heights of cliché, which surrender before him. Then the drums thunder out, a guitar whips the silence, and he is suddenly moving, his groin swinging, head jerking, a diamond-studded fist swathing through the hot air like the whip that will bring the band home, cracking on towards the climax.

There is nothing remotely real about this performer: he h lived with us too long. Now he is a legend who will charge adrenalin merely by the fact that he is *there*. But he's go and he knows it, and will offer it leaving nothing to chan He leans across his guitar, strokes its flanks, croons above grins wickedly and rolls his head slightly: we are back in fifties. Yes, and he even repeats his little speech bef "Hound Dog", a brief, rambling monologue, quite sensele great fun, that mint 'n' julep voice coming out of the speak like the ghost of a lover in the cold sheets, just playing w memories . . .

"When I, ah . . . when I tried to think of a special song tonight . . . huh, huh, huh . . . ah . . . special song that rea says something, if you know . . . ah . . . a *message* song . . ah . . . ah . . . I, ah . . . What'd I do? Oh yeah! I came up w this . . . I looked her square in the eye . . . because that's all had . . . this one big square eye in the middle of her . . . ah

I said, Baby . . . huh, huh, huh . . . she was weird too, you know, she . . . ah . . . huh, huh . . . I got real close up to her, and it was a very tender, touching moment . . . ah . . . and I said:

"You ain't nothin' but a hound dog!"

And they're out of their seats as the years roll away, as the snap of the drums and the savage guitars cut a path through the decade he wasted. It's a much faster version, more contemporary, less exciting, but the delivery weighs nothing against the sentiment. Now, as he moves, as his lean face pours sweat, it's impossible even to think of the bloated buffoon who wasted eight of his years in bum movies. (Did they ever, in truth, really exist? Did he really live in that vacuum, in the dark rooms of Graceland, nameless, like a man without a face?) Whatever ghost he has exorcised, whatever fear he now destroys, he is performing like a slave released from chains, like a man with a hunger. So he lets go the guitar,

Above: Mixing with the fans after the 1969 come-back.
Opposite: Rehearsals for the second bout at Las Vegas.

slaps one hand on a thigh, then starts swinging his fist at the group like a demon unleashed. It's a circular movement, syncopated to his hips, and it takes us right back, through the years of oblivion, to the days when he shocked the whole world, when he seemed like a monster. But now, as he does it, he is grinning, self-mocking, and the movements are seen to be a choreographed gesture towards those roots that are now far behind him: he recreates his own history.

These first Vegas performances are masterfully controlled tributes to that past which has made him what he is. In the sense that he is out to recapture the faithful, he is working to very fine rules. Thus he runs through his hits, begs their tears with his ballads, and climaxes with a very lengthy version of his latest big smash. It is not an accident that this song, "Suspicious Minds", is a mixture of the old and the new, a supercharged rhythmic ballad. For indeed they are ballads that this gentleman prefers, and he offers them up with the sort of emotion that his rock songs can no longer have. "Suspicious Minds" is a bridge song, a fine mingling of both, and before its surging rhythm and some spiralling vocal harmonies, he uses his baritone and his trembling vibrato to pour into it all the emotion he can muster. Then, in the middle of it, he drops to one knee, clenches a fist, and with head bowed takes a gospel-like break, linking up all the influences. He is crouched over, worshipping, transfixed in the spotlight, and his voice warbles and groans, and comes out like an anthem, against nothing but the audience, the band almost silent, and then – "Yeah! Yeah! *Yeah*! YEAH!" – and *bam*! the band is back, the music piles high, and he rises like a black snake from the dark of its lair and starts shaking his torso to the rhythm, socking it to them. The song is a pile-driver, over six minutes long, and he slides across the stage, legs bent back and outstretched, spine curved with the mike held above him – then springs up, his hair flying, never missing a note, leading into the multiple finale . . . . "*Well don't ya know*"/BAM! BAM!/"*We're caught in a trap*" (fist swinging, hips rocking) /BAM! BAM!/"*Ah can't walk out*" (legs stabbing, heels pounding) /"*because I love you so much, Babe-ay-ay-ayay* . . ." Then takes it down to a silence, and then builds it up again, takes it down, builds it up, repeats it once more, then starts kicking across the stage, high kicks, fast and vicious, athletically, beautifully, karate-chopping through the strobe

lights in a blur of pure motion, until he climaxes with a shimmy, a good old-fashioned shake, and then drops to one knee, head bowed and arms outstretched, and is finally, and most gracefully, finished.

A way-out performance.

These shows are masterly, but they also are tied to a past he no longer seems to want. They have given him confidence, put him back where he was but now he will follow his own desires. Thus, six months later, when he returns to the International for the second time, he reduces the golden oldies to jokes, works out some new material. He is now usually all in white, either sequinned or tasseled, the stiff collar turned up over lean, shadowed cheeks, the lopsided grin mischievous, his eyes glittering with mirth, one cool lover, one conqueror, one walking dream. And though there is a confidence that borders on arrogance, his sly, self-mocking humour will assuage it. And his grasp on the choreography of pop is now even more controlled and impressive: he explodes out of stillness.

Las Vegas is cabaret land, a club room, and he knows where he's at. He is smooth, sleek, witty and wicked, a more God-like Dean Martin, a rough-rocking Sinatra, an unreachable legend dressed in light-reflecting white, stepping forth to prostrate his waiting flock, the backdrops a rich imagery. True, there is a rock group (and a good one it is), but the orchestra is massive, there are *two* vocal groups, and even the back-up musicians sing harmony – one huge sound, one spectacle. And he does, to be sure, put on a show, he hypnotises his audience. It's a well-rehearsed routine of almost operatic ballads and some sophisticated, theatrical rock: it is something for everyone.

He opens with a modern version of "See See Rider Blues" and it is fast and vicious and precise. The girls swoop in behind him, pumping out a gospel sound, and the group play a mean, rocking rhythm. But the brass is going mad, working hard to pin it down to the level of a cabaret opener – the conductor's hands wave. Still, it works, it's a hard, raunchy assault; it's a bit of fair rock, whipping up the nostalgia, and it leaves room for play in other fields, prepares the new ground. So he launches into "Release Me", bounds through "Sweet Caroline" and then moves pretty fast into ballads, the real heavy production jobs. He does "Mary in the Morning"

*This page: Winding up rehearsals in the M-G-M studios.
Opposite and overleaf: Las Vegas, August, 1970.*

and "Bridge Over Troubled Water", and the performance is superb. His body quivers in spasms, his head rolls on his shoulders, he clenches his fists and lets the sweat pour down his face, and when he gets to "I've Lost You" he is down on his knees as if death is the only alternative: the tears streak the mascara.

Yes, sir, it is brilliant. It is also sincere. And if he's guilty of many things, he's not guilty of slacking when it comes to giving value for money: he does not disappoint. And if the rockers are fewer, they are also more spectacular, laid out with the panache and sense of dynamics that turn modest numbers into ball-biters, into visual fireworks. Thus in "Polk Salad Annie", which is one of his best, he starts off with a monologue, slides into the song, starts winding up the girls, shuts them down, turns them on, and then whips up the band with that famous swinging fist, with those extraordinary gyrations – all Mick Jagger violence and Nureyev grace at once – and finally finishes as a blur of pure motion in strobe lights, a white-dazzle hallucination, and comes out of it all looking drenched, the grin arrogant, sublime.

The monologue itself is a masterpiece of timing, slurred, honey-toned, sometimes mocking, always sensual, each sly word fitted in to the snap of the drums, the walk Southern and lazy, a Dean Martin pastiche, and then – *whap! whap!* – to the drums, his hand slapping his thigh, before spiralling and slipping smoothly in with the rhythm, singing, "*Down in Louisiana . . . where the alligators grow so mean . . .*" and he is

that alligator, and you are right down there, and then whips it all up and the stage is pure frenzy, and there's nothir in your eyes but this gyrating heathen, this hypnotic blur the craze of the lights, and the sound rapes your ears and t flashing blinds your eyes – and then suddenly, shocke silence, it is over, he is frozen, one white God.

Did he ever go through all those movies with no sweat c his painted brow? Impossible to believe that this theatric wizard ever let himself do what he did, didn't go quite insan Even more impossible – as he pirouettes to catch the mik as he slides across the stage, as he rises like a dream in slo motion and crimson light, as his hand curves through tha thin blade of silver, falling lazily, outstretched – impossible believe, as he does this and more, that he would ever let him self slip again.

And yet the echoes of his former career are now ominousl present. Already, after one season of highly successful roc he is returning to the realms of middle-road show biz. C course he can do it – no one doubts that he can – but then n one understands why he would want to.

There is a sweet old cliché called the Trap of Success, an it is possible that even Elvis can't escape it. A consummat artist, he is cornered by his own image, by the breadth of hi audience, by the size of his fame, by the mystique of his ow presence, by financial considerations, by his age, and by th cold fact that most rockers lose their dignity in the end. Th permutations make mountains, building higher each year, an as he squats on the top, growing loftier by the minute, he i bound by necessity to move away from what he is into area of even broader acceptance.

Yes, over the years he's sung every conceivable kind c song in an attempt to catch all of the market; now, when he i back, when the world is at his feet, he will find that the aud ence he made for himself will demand what he gave ther through their lives – a little rock, a little blues, a little country a little gospel, plus pastiche Hawaiian ballads, some Neopolita and operatic chanters, with a few sophisticated swinge thrown in (most particularly in Vegas). The audience is va and its appetite is huge; thus the voice that can feed it mu suffer. He does it very well – no one else could quite manag

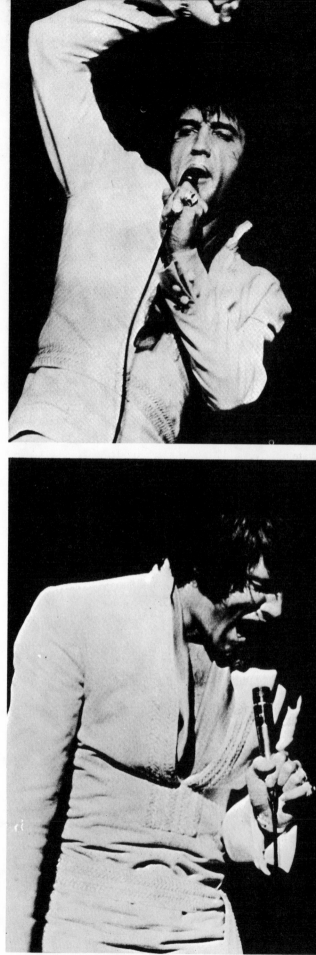

it – but before very long the actual singing will give way to a spectacle that represents more than it is: histrionics will dominate.

Then, of course, there is the narcissism, that intriguing self-absorption, that sublime vice which gave him universal appeal and yet finally locked him up in himself, surrounded by mirrors. He still lives with his "ol' boys", with the voices of his childhood, and even now at the height of his resurgence he's removed from the outer world. So he doesn't return to Memphis, he starts making sloppy records, he travels in the glass cage of his own God-like stature; as he must, he slips back into a parody of his own quite remarkable achievements. And it doesn't take long.

Yet no matter his carelessness, his indifference to criticism, his insistence upon working with his old friends and cousins, he is stunning when he walks on a stage. For this reason there is no comparison between the records he's putting out and the performances he gives in the flesh. Elvis "live" is superb.

Part of the American consciousness, he now tours the country that made him. From 1970 to 1973 he is swinging high. He goes to Phoenix and Detroit, to Albuquerque and Little Rock, to Houston and Miami, to San Francisco, Los Angeles, San Diego and Denver, to Oakland and Portland and

ttle, to Madison Square Garden, New York. He travels by
vate jet, flying in to enormous crowds, looking garish and
mond-studded, his eyes hidden by huge glasses, his bulky
ure surrounded by bodyguards, by gleaming black limous-
s. And he greets all the people and accepts the city's keys,
d is rushed away to hide in hotel suites, to rest before chaos.
ough now he is indifferent to the studios, though he makes
records too quickly; if his sales are already dropping and
movies are dead – no sweat. In the flesh he is monstrous, a
al sell-out – and he seems to be captured by the contact.

His flash clothes are even flashier, his arrogance is stupend-
s, and his theme tune is "Thus Spake Zarathustra" – the
rld-Riddle Theme, the God Theme. No one else could get
ay with it (though others will imitate it), and the sound of
t introduction will send shivers down the spine as the
tlights wander over the stage, as the tympany thunders.
ch a tune conjures up all the mystery of the universe, and to
ny in the void of their own lives, this myth on the stage is
t that. Thus the band tails "Zarathustra" with a fierce,
ving rhythm, an apocalyptic sound, and the legend bounds
a flash of white with a gold cape, studs glittering, tassels
ing, and hits the mike like the Man on the Mount.

He burns through "See See Rider" or "That's All Right
ma", leaning forward on one foot, braced lightly on the
er, the guitar slanted upward, a mere prop that he plays
th, fingers snapping or curled round the mike, which he
netimes nearly swallows. His body is pneumatic, almost
lling through the boards, exploding with tension and con-
ned rhythmic drive as he swivels on one foot, points a
ger to the side, and then falls into a crouch as the guitarist
es a solo, grinning wickedly, punching upward with his
n guitar, not playing, just fooling. It's a moment of self-
ckery, a pure recall to the fifties, and as the applause
lodes over him he returns casually to the mike, shrugging,
se to giggling, then takes hold and rocks it roughly before
wling back into the song, his eyes closed, left leg shaking.

And then, as he finishes, as the trumpets kill it off, the guitar
punches back and forth, in a blur, with blinding speed, and
he is taking his bow before the last note is hit – while the guitar
is sent spinning like a missile through the spotlight to the
hands of a lackey behind him.

It's a gas of an opener, but before thay can recover he's
already well into the second song. The brass is staccato, the
rhythm section punches out, and as lovely Ronnie Tutt takes
a dive bomb on the drums, Elvis stretches out his right hand,
an aeroplane's wing, and then sweeps in a perfect circle,
crouched low and taut, and comes up with legs parted, the
mike to his lips, and is into "Proud Mary" with a vengeance.
Not stupendous on record, it makes stupendous viewing as he
gyrates his hips, karate-chops across the stage, kicks his legs
and then starts swinging that right fist, teeth gritted, sweat
pouring. "Rollin' . . . rollin' . . . rollin' down the river . . ." And
he rolls and punches forwards and stabs the air with his feet,
and then carries it on home to a grand Kung Fu climax.

His greatest gift to pop is his air of the untouchable combined with the illusion of intimacy. The most remote star in
history, he nevertheless manages to reduce a massive audience
to mere Family. Thus he wanders across the stage, through a
flood of golden light, and makes small jokes that could only be
personal. He unzips his jumpsuit, fiddles distractedly with
his belt, wipes the sweat from his face with a scarf and throws
it out to a lady. "Lawd have mercy", he says in that most
Southern of honeyed drawls. "I'm outa mah mind, I'm outa
mah body, I'm jest goin' crazy up here!" And then starts singing "Love Me", wandering lazily back and forth, leaning down
to kiss the girls, accepting gifts, giving scarves – pure primal
show business – and cooing with sly mockery as some lady
grabs his leg, "Oh, honey-chile, I ain't what you think I am."
It is narcissism and self-awareness neatly embraced: the saint
and the sinner, the romantic lover and the stud, the little boy
who came out of the backwoods and the legend he now is.
"Good evening, ladies and gentlemen . . . I mean, afternoon,

ladies and . . . or *night* or whatever . . . Hey, man, what show *are* we doin' today? Just *where* are we, man?" And then goes "*Whoops!*" and shakes his head in mock bewilderment, and murmurs, "I think we better stop right this minute, folks. Howyaall? Nice to see ya." And even as he's saying this, the bass begins to throb, a deep, hypnotic chant, and you can see that left leg moving, first twitching, then shaking, then the fingers start snapping, very casual, quite precise, and then *chop!* go the guitars, and *slap!* goes the hip, and then the girls begin to clap, a sharp, staccato rhythm, and then the small talk is a monologue and then the monologue is a song and then *whap! whap!* and he's off, into "Polk Salad Annie", and he's riding her good, bearing down heavy on her, singing meanly, "*Yah know what I* mean *now* . . ." Of which there can be no doubt.

Elvis is presented as a man with superhuman attributes, yet he always contradicts this very stance. This contradiction in itself is what makes him magnetic, since enigmas are the roots of obsession. He is dressed like a prince, the diamonds glitter, the cape waves; he is tall and athletic, and in the cunning play of lights (all that pale blue and crimson) he seems as unreal as the ghost of a Greek god, the original perfect male. Who cares if he's made up? if the lights are deceiving? if the tune of "Thus Spake Zarathustra" makes you fall for the trick? The fact remains that he *is*, that he floats through countless dreams, and that whatever he was, or wherever he is going, he is now, at this moment, the living symbol of freedom and light. Yes, it is all too much – he has been with us too long – by all the laws of our logic he should find it impossible to descend from this. And yet he does – or he weaves this fine illusion; he stands up before thousands and he draws them all to him, and the sly-

ness is in the silk of his talk, in his wit, in his self-effacem Supernatural are the surroundings – the dazzling lights, drowning colours, the glittering orchestra and the bri group and the sexy girls, the mean man himself in his jewe suit – but he gets down there amongst them, takes their har drops them kisses, is insinuating and sincere and someti violent: he takes no shit from anyone. Yes, one minute g ning, like a schoolboy, like a stud, the next he will turn some loudmouth beside him and the tone of his voice is p venom: "Just cool it, man! *Cool it!*" It is true. He does t And whether genuine or staged, it encourages cold chi makes the flesh creep. Will he actually *do* it. Will he *smash* t guy? And then, before it happens, he has shrugged and turn away, perhaps hitching up the belt, grinning lopsided self-mocking, saying cheerfully, "Oh, boy! There's some *p* out there!" It's either unblushing showmanship or genu emotion, but whatever, it works, makes him fascinating. Y forget "Zarathustra" and the spectacular backdrops, and y think, Christ, the guy's just like *me* – he is human, he *fe* things. It's cool, it's even *natural*, and you can't help believe it when he looks at one of his group, shakes his he and grins ruefully, then murmurs, "Lord, man, I just *dr* this whole thing." The band plays. He starts singing.

He sings the ballads as if he's standing in church, as if h back beside his folk, back in time, back in memories, as if h suddenly lost sight of where he is. He usually sings them w eyes closed, head back, one fist clenched, a foot tapping, h swaying abstractedly. The voice is now deeper, more matu quite immaculate, and it floats upon a tide of true emotic sometimes quivering, not lying. It is, without embarrassme and with a quite guileless intimacy, a voice that conveys r

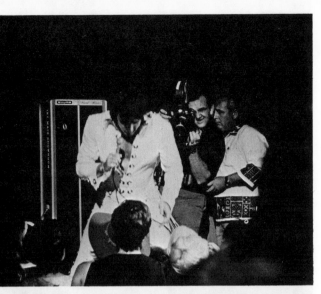

loss and grief. It is also, beyond doubt, quite instinctively and nakedly, a voice of the most romantic sensuality. If he sings of the spirit, he imbues it with the flesh; if he sings of desire he speaks of love. *"Who will I find to lie beside me?"* he sings, and the words, which are simple, which are quite simply desolate, are filled with the tragedy, with the crystalline grief, of a flesh that might never be touched. *"Leaving me lonely,"* he adds, and the last word is a killer, a knife through all hope, a common word transformed to pure poetry by its tone of delivery: an anthem, a hymn.

It is indeed the hymnal quality of his delivery that transforms the most mundane offerings into miniature classics. Just as during his film period his better ballads were ignored, so now, as he tours, as he lays waste to America, he will fight against a barrage of criticism for deserting rock music. And it is true that during 1973 he slows down, starts reducing the temperature, and seemingly oblivious to the cries of the be-

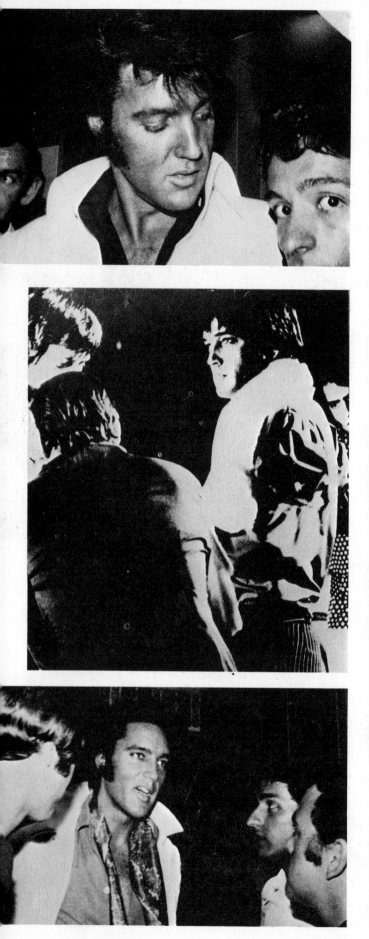

trayed, insists on building up his repertoire of ballads.

Possibly he does this because he knows that he is agin
that he's now reaching forty, that sooner or later he mu
forget the past, leave the young man behind, and build up
new kind of audience. If this be true, then it shows astu
thinking, a firm grasp on what he is and where he must g
And no matter the reason, small difference in the choice, he
doing whatever he is drawn to, and doing it well. Ballads the
may be, but the delivery is beautiful, a very rare combinati
of pure vocal pyrotechnics and superbly delivered histrionic
he comes across like an actor.

142

s Vegas becomes a stint as regular as the movies – but at
*st he starts touring America. The only films during this
*e are two documentaries: Elvis, That's The Way It Is
*71) and Elvis On Tour (1973). Both films show Elvis on
ge and at rehearsals; both are disappointing.

It is said that most good singers are by nature good actors,
*d certainly in Presley's case this is true. Most actors work
*t when they are faced with an audience, when they can feel
*response, and this too applies to him. If his years in the
*vies nearly murdered his talent, if they threatened to crush
*beneath the weight of their anonymity, he now proves
*t he has much fight left in him. Yes, he sings like an actor,
*acts out the words, his face is a mirror to the emotions he
*veys and his hands which are large, diamond-studded and
*delicate weave hypnotic arabesques in the spotlights.
*lis eyes close. His head turns slightly sideways. He seems

to fall asleep above the mike in his hand, gently swaying, just
hanging loose. The stage lights dim. A mist of lavender emanates. The orchestra is silhouetted in a backwash of pale blue,
like those figures we view in our dreams, never moving, just
present. And now seen from the chest up, the white jumpsuit
dazzling his Adonis face highlighted and close to unreal, he
becomes a kind of strange, abstract vision – it's pure cinema,
a fantasy world. And just as you forget where you are, who
you're watching, the music floats in and he is singing.

"*When you're weary/Feeling small/When tears are in your
eyes/I will dry them all . . .*" And he's leaning slightly forward,
braced on one foot, breathing over the mike like a man above
his mistress, his free hand before him, gently weaving in the
air, suddenly quite delicate, an Oriental girl's dance, a story in
mime, the fingers floating in space between the song's painful
words, conveying more than the words themselves could ever
do. "*I'll take your hand*", he sings, clenching his fist, bringing
it to his forehead, a pure Brando gesture as the spotlight thins
down and leaves blackness on all but his face: one face floating, a lover's dream. And his voice at this moment is a thing of
pure nobility, hovering in silence, isolated in stillness, before
rising operatically, coming out in full force against the brass
and the violins and the vocal groups: "*Like a bridge over
troubled water/I will lay me down . . .*" And his spine curves
impossibly, his head falls right back, and as the spotlight widens
and the stagelights blaze forth, he is curved like a bow, like

a spring at its limits, the mike held in both hands, a glittering instrument, pointing straight down at his sweating upturned face. And as he sings the last word, his voice climbs up and up, his head shakes from side to side, his body trembles as if about to explode – and then it does – it explodes: his hands suddenly fly apart, his body twists, the mike goes flying, and as someone jumps to catch it he is going to his knees, like a graceful blur, pure beauty in motion, and ends up leaning backwards, one hand resting on a hip, the other lying on a raised knee, his white-shining spine curved – a statue, one glittering god. Then his head drops. The music stops. Silence. And then sheer pandemonium.

It is acting, most assuredly, and of a very high order; it is in fact the new form of theatre. He will take his audience and he will convey to them emotion in a manner more direct than any other. And like the good actor he is, he will constantly surprise them, will keep slipping and sliding through a variety of moods with the guile of a salamandar in the flame. So before they can breathe, before the tears dry from their eyes, he says, "Oh, boy! A good 'un! Just laid us out!" And he waves to the guitarist, and a wah-wah tears the air, and he shrieks, kicks the air, and then drops down very low, and then gives us his new brand of fireworks: karate to rock music.

It's graceful, athletic, modestly exciting, and it probably marks the end of an era, the final fling of The Pelvis. He will put on a show, and he will make sure it's good, but he's taken his measure and he knows his own age, and no matter what they say he'll leave rock behind. The new Elvis Presley is in the beautiful "I'm Leavin'", in the rhythmic "Let Me Be There", in his exquisitely acted version of "Softly, As I Leave You", in "Why Me Lord" and "Help Me"; in the superb "Loving Arms" and, most of all, in "American Trilogy". This is where he now stands.

As a performer, Elvis Presley has never left America, a it's now very doubtful that he will. Just as his isolation shrined him in his own past, so his indefinable lack of volit has enslaved him to his own country. It has been sugges and is very likely true, that he now views himself as a p ticularly American phenomenon and can scarcely conce of anything beyond. He's religious, patriotic, totally stee in his own music and possibly, in private, just as rural n as he was when a boy back in Tupelo. The myths of Ame

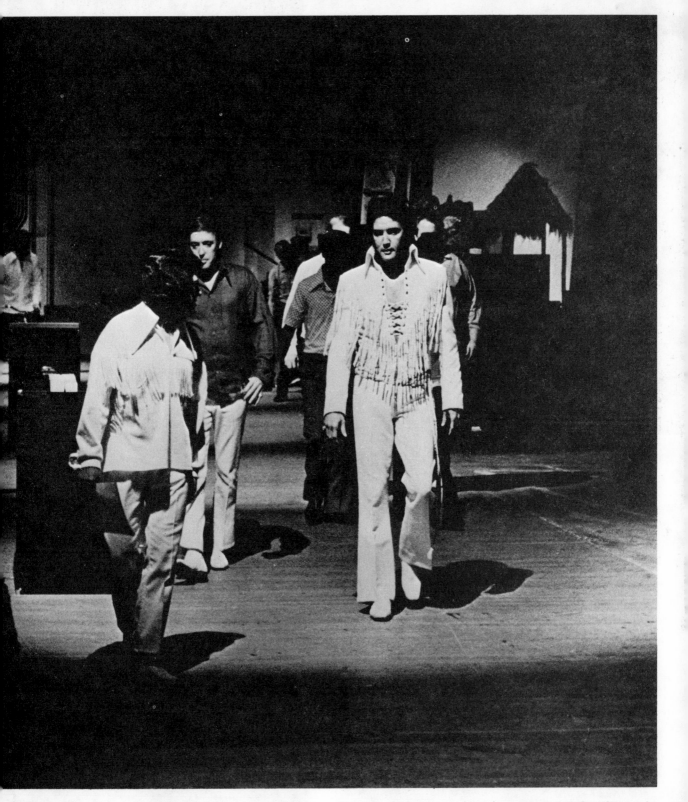

behind him; they nurtured him; they protect him. Now aching middle age, impaled on the pinnacle with half his life live but no new heights to be scaled, he might well be draw-g closer – if closer he can get – to the friends and the memor- and the emotions of his past, to whatever is most familiar d unchanging. If this be true, it could account for his creasing love of gospel music, country songs and American diences. Certainly only Elvis could sing gospel at Las Vegas nd certainly Elvis's treatment of "American Trilogy" (now almost his anthem) is an eloquent testimony to where he stands.

He recently sang it in Memphis.

The stage lights dim – dim almost to total darkness – and Elvis walks to his man, has a quick drink of water, then turns around to be fitted with the gold-lined cape. He then walks back to the mike, a spotlight covers his face, and he takes the mike off the stand and bows his head. He turns slightly side-ways, and in this moment of silence the reverence is enough to move mountains. Then, most gently, as if offering the

tablets, Elvis simply raises his free hand and points.

The treat now begins.

To an acoustic guitar and almost imperceptible back-up vocal, Elvis Presley, dressed in diamonds and emeralds and gold, mournfully (and immaculately) croons: *"Oh I wish I were/In the Land of Cotton/Old folks there/ Are not forgotten . . ."* And now raising his head slightly, his gaze cast afar, one hand high and glittering in the spotlight: *"Look away/ Look away/ Look away/Dixieland . . ."*

A few bars on the guitar and Elvis steps out of the spotlight, and with a choke in his voice murmurs, "Sing it, fellas." Another light falls on the Stamps, a very gospel-sounding group, and Elvis, in the shadows, now stands with head bowed, as they sing, as if in church: *"Oh I wish I was in Dixie/ Away/Away . . . In Dixieland I'd make my stand/To live and die for Dixie . . ."*

Now Elvis steps back into the spotlight, and his head is still bowed, one hand clasped in the other, the mike close to his lips, singing: *"For Dixieland/That's where I was born/ Early, Lord, one frosty morn . . ."* And they're all there with him, travelling back that thirty years, back to the cottonfields, to the poor boy of the South, to where the myths of America are nurtured and heroes are born . . . *"Look away/Look away/ Look away/Dixieland . . ."*

146

And on the last word Ronnie Tutt plays a march on the snare drum, and Elvis starts quivering, lifting high his proud head, the mike tight in both hands, staring up at the heavens, singing, *"Glory, glory, Hallelujah!"* Drawing out and warbling on the word "Hallelujah" until – BAM! BAM! BAM! – the brass (now stage-lit) and the violins (now stage-lit) and *three* vocal groups (now stage-lit) join in: *"Glory, glory, Hallelujah/Glory, glory, Hallelujah/And His truth goes marching on . . ."*

Then the stage lights die out again as the orchestra fades

Elvis adds a gold-lined cape to his increasingly colourful jump suits. Top left: Charlie Hodge encourages Elvis on guitar while the taciturn Jerry Scheff supports on bass. Overleaf: The many moods of The King on stage.

148

away, leaving only one spot-light, burning down like a beacon – on Elvis.

He is sweating and tense, holding tight to the mike . . . His head rolls back on his shoulders, his eyes close; he listens. A lonely guitar plucks out some sad chords . . . And now Elvis leans over, almost eating the mike, visibly trembling with emotion, and magically, most mysteriously, making the most banal words suddenly resonant with the sound of pure faith: *"So hush little baby/Don't you cry/You know your daddy's/bound to die . . ."* And now a lonely flute comes in, and a quiet vocal group, as Elvis, almost talking, his voice hushed and superb, intones: *"But all my trials, Lord/Will soon be over . . ."* And now, yes, they see it, all the distance he has travelled, from a common heritage, into their dreams, sharing their destiny, their history: they reach out towards him. And he, knowing this, turns his back to the audience, bows his head, lifts his head, rocks back on his heels, a tall silhouette, just out of the spotlight, enamoured by the lone trill of the flute, almost tragically stricken . . .

150

151

Then the drums begin to thunder, the full orchestra winds up, the three vocal groups combined sound like a choir in a cathedral, and the strobe lights start flashing; the sound builds and builds, reaches deafening proportions, and the stage lights pour down as Elvis slowly turns around, one hand on the mike, the other holding out the gold cape – yes, pure gold, and it shimmers and flashes, one half of a beautiful sun climbing over the horizon – and then – BAM! BAM! BAM! – Elvis's fist punches three times, the whole stage explodes, and then, sudden crescendo, his right hand above his head, the incredible gold cape waving, a pure clarion call, and they're into the symphonic finale: *"Glory, glory, Hallelujah/Glory, glory, Hallelujah/Glory, glory, Hallelujah/And His truth goes marching on . . ."* And as the last word builds – and builds and builds – the stage lights come on full blast, the whole orchestra

is standing, and there, behind the band, stretching over [the] huge wall, lights flashing all over it like the silver birds [of] truth, is an enormous and most garish Stars and Stripes . [. .] "*And His truth goes marching on . . .*" BAM! BAM! BA[M!] BAAM! BAAAAMMMMMMMM! And Elvis stands with l[egs] parted, his head bowed, his arms outstretched, and the lov[ely] gold cape is a huge sun, burning up the whole audience. [As] they rise to their feet, their tears flow, their hands clap, and [he] falls to one knee, bows his head, crosses arms, and wra[ps] the gold cape around him like a shroud.

The lights dim. He is hidden.

High camp, superb theatre – call it what you will – [it] represents some kind of extraordinary grasp on the psycholo[gy] of a captive audience. He knows what he symbolises, a[nd] what he is and where he stands, and he will take his o[wn] history and wrap it in mythology and serve it up as the tru[th] everlasting, the impossible dream. He has come out of pove[rty] and the child's clinging fears to a world in which reality wo[n't] impinge; he will not let this go. And so he takes what he [has] gleaned, every trick, every instinct, and he uses it to ke[ep] himself on top of the mountain, regardless of what price m[ust] be paid. No longer will he serve as the tough punk rock sing[er,] as the child who disrupted a whole world; rather he will n[ow] take himself as he is and ensure that what he is will be enoug[h.]

He will succeed. He will always succeed. He is now mu[ch] too big for his image to fade; in retirement his legend w[ill] outlive him. A great natural artist, a monumental Americ[an] figure, he now exists beyond mere talent or charisma.

The old Elvis is dead. The new one lives on. Hallelujah[.]

157

Acknowledgements

Anyone tackling an "illustrated biography" of Elvis Presley is bound to run into some headaches. Most of the classic early pictures of Elvis are no longer available from the press agencies, the fans who now hold them are understandably reluctant to part with them, and Presley's management refuses to cooperate "as a matter of policy" in "any literary endeavour." Which makes it a difficult field.

The majority of photographs in this book are the property of the Elvis Presley Appreciation Society which has over the years, with the assistance of its members, built up a considerable collection. I would therefore like to thank all the unknown fans who contributed this goldmine to the Appreciation Society, and the Society for letting me borrow it.

Special thanks must be offered to those individual fans who were willing to trust me with their memorabilia. These include my good friend Pøul Madsen, who sent me an enormous amount of material from Denmark; Penny Sayer, who poured the wine while I went through her remarkable trunk; the lovely Audrey Gussin, who also discussed Elvis at some length over a meal in the Golf Club; and Chris Handy, Melvyn Sergeant, Alan Beresford and Miss S. Whitfield, all of whom sent me material through the Fan Club. Thanks, also, to Lon Goddard of *Disc* for the use of his files; and to Jim Ellis for his general advice and assistance.

Most of the photographs of Elvis at Las Vegas and on tour are from the Metro-Goldwyn-Mayer films *Elvis: That's The Way It Is* and *Elvis on Tour* and are courtesy of that company. Others are courtesy of Rex Features (photographs by Andy Sackheim), Camera Press (photographs by Terry O'Neil), Pictorial Press Ltd., Popperfoto (Paul Popper Ltd), United Press International (UK) Ltd., RCA Records, MGM-EMI Distributors, Paramount Films, Cinema International Corporation, 20th Century-Fox, United Artists, Allied Artists, National General Corporation, National Broadcasting Corporation, and photographers Sean Shavers, Uffe Lomholt Madsen and David Parkinson.

Thanks are due to the undermentioned copyright owners for permission to quote from the following songs: *Heartbreak Hotel* reproduced by permission of Multimood Music Ltd., 230 Purley Way, Croydon, Surrey. *American Trilogy*, words by Mickey Newbury, reproduced by permission of Acuff Rose Music Ltd. *Tomorrow is a Long Time* reproduced by permission of Warner Bros. Music Ltd. *American Pie* reproduced by permission of United Artists Music Limited. *Suspicious Minds*, words and music by Mark James, © Copyright 1968 by Screen Gems-Columbia Music, Inc., all rights reserved, by permission. *Trouble* and *I'm Leavin'* reproduced by mission of Carlin Music Corporation, 17 Savile Row, Lon W1. *Bridge Over Troubled Water*, Copyright 1969, 1970 by Simon. Permission to reproduce lyric granted by Pat Music Ltd., 5 Denmark Street, London WC2.

With few exceptions, the "live" performances describe this book are not of any specific shows, but are compilati of various shows based on fan reports, reviews, newsreel television footage, the two above named documentary fil and the author's own first-hand observations. However, cial mention must be made of Louise O. Spencer of Virgi USA, and Ian Bailye of Leicester for their excellent rep published in *Elvis* and *Elvis Monthly*, of Elvis performin the mid-fifties.

Special note must also be accorded the following bo which gave me additional aid in the writing: *The Great Am can Popular Singers* by Henry Pleasants; *Elvis* by Jerry H kins; *Operation Elvis* by Alan Levy; *The Sound of the Cit* Charlie Gillett; *Revolt Into Style* by George Melly; *Pop F The Beginning (Awopbopaloobop)* by Nik Cohn; *After the* by Ian Whitcomb; *The Age of Rock* by Jonathan Eisen; *The Sun Rock Session File* (Vol. 3) by Martin Hawkins Colin Escott. The most valuable magazine articles were Far Cry From Home" by Pete Fowler and "Black Roots" Clive Anderson, both to be found in the special "Elvis" is of *Let It Rock*, December 1973. I was also indebted to Da Dalton for his excellent report, *Elvis Presley: Wagging His in Las Vegas*, originally published in *Rolling Stone* and rently included in *The Rolling Stone Rock 'n' Roll Rea* edited by Ben Fong-Torres.

A very personal thanks to Tony Atkinson, Todd Slaugh Vikki Slaughter and Manya Starr. Thanks also to all th who made my trip to Las Vegas so enjoyable: David Wa Keith Harris, David Balson (for his protection), Marco der Meij, Mark Wesley and Pierrette, Bill Conroy (say more), Pøul Madsen (again) and of course the unforgetta Kirsten Ede.

Finally, thanks to Steve Ridgeway for designing the be Julie Harris for assisting him, and Tony Power for his mo mental patience during the final two weeks.

Allen Harbinson
June, 1975

HARDY ROSES

HARDY ROSES

An Organic Guide to Growing
Frost- and Disease-Resistant Varieties

Text by Robert Osborne
Photography by Beth Powning

A Garden Way Publishing Book

STOREY

Storey Communications, Inc.
Pownal, Vermont 05261

A Garden Way Publishing Book
First published in the US 1991 by
Garden Way Publishing, Storey Communications,
Schoolhouse Road, Pownal, Vermont 05261

Published in Canada by
Key Porter Books Limited

The name Garden Way Publishing is licensed to
Storey Communications, Inc. by Garden Way, Inc.

91 92 93 94 95 5 4 3 2 1

Typesetting: MACTRIX DTP
Printed and bound in Canada

Page ii: Königin von Dänemark
Page vi: Leverkusen

**Library of Congress
Cataloging-in-Publication Data**

Osborne, Robert A., 1949-
    Hardy Roses : an organic guide to growing
frost- and disease-resistant varieties / Robert A.
Osborne : photographs by Beth Powning;
illustrations by Catherine Venart

    p. cm.
"A Garden Way Publishing book."
Includes bibliographical references and index.
ISBN 0-88266-739-4

1. Roses — Varieties. 2. Rose culture. 3. Roses —
Frost resistance. 4. Roses — Disease and pest
resistance. 5. Organic gardening. I. Title.

SB411.6.083 1991   91-55013
635.9′ 33372 — dc20   CIP

For our families,
our friends,
and for the soil
from which all life springs

Contents

Preface

FOR ME, A GARDEN IS A PLACE OF DISCOVERY. EACH TIME I WALK down the paths of my garden, everything is different. The time of year, the time of day, the sun, the clouds, the rain, the fog and the wind—all combine to influence the plants, which themselves are ever-changing. Muted tones of winter flow into the spectral riots of spring and summer and on into earthen fall. The plants grow wider and higher, break and split, flower and fruit. Spiders wait on dew-hung threads to strike, and birds sweep and call. Shafts of light break through the trees, and the patterns dance across the ground.

Gardens are planted and nurtured by our efforts. Our ideas mold gardens into forms, but a humbling magic transforms them into something greater than the sum of their parts and beyond our initial dreams. We create worlds when we create gardens. The planting and cultivating we do initiate cycles of events. A shrub becomes a haven for a bird. The bird eats the caterpillar on the fruit tree. The bird's droppings nourish microorganisms in the soil, and the fine root hairs of a rose absorb the chemical residues left by the decomposing bodies of those organisms and transform them into colorful flowers. Every event triggers other events.

To be a spectator of this fascinating interaction is my greatest reward as a gardener. I revel in the variety of sensations and expectations that a garden offers. The limitless possibilities can overwhelm me as well, and I have to discipline myself to choose avenues of exploration that most appeal to me. After having had countless "favorite" plants, I have abandoned the notion of special status. Each of them is unique and exciting. The rose is not my "favorite" plant, but one that gives me special pleasures and challenges.

Each garden is restricted by its site and climate. You can stretch these limits at times, but not understanding them will lead to failures. My garden is located where winter temperatures can drop to -40°F (-40°C). The firm grip of midwinter can be broken by a mild storm bred in the ocean only to be re-established with intensity as arctic winds push back the warmth. It is a climate that demands endurance and patience both of the gardener and of the plants.

Introducing roses into such a garden seemed a daunting task when I began. The trepidation I felt initially has blossomed into an exhilaration that has me spellbound, not only by the measure of success we have enjoyed but by the sheer variety of color, shape, texture and fragrance that this extraordinary group of plants offers. By accepting the limitations of our cold winters, I was forced to look beyond the more usual offerings of roses—the hybrid teas, the grandifloras, the floribundas—and toward those roses that are less common.

A forsythia blooms in the spring for only a brief but glorious two weeks, yet we treasure it as one of spring's harbingers. Daylilies each last but 24 hours before they are shriveled and done, yet we cannot imagine summer without them. A close examination of a potentilla flower reveals not extravagance but a refined simplicity. Yet, when we see the bush covered with these simple flowers, the effect is overwhelming. We accept these for themselves and find places for them in our gardens. When "shrub roses" are mentioned, though, many gardeners say, "Oh, you mean wild roses" or, "Don't they have only five petals?" If you have passed over the world of hardy shrub roses for these reasons, or if you do not know anything about them, be ready to be enveloped by their beauty and variety.

Any gardener can use and appreciate these roses. Many gardeners see the rose as a symbol of frustration as well as beauty. They may have spent countless hours trying to protect their roses from the ravages of winter, only to be disappointed by failure. Others may have never tried roses because they have heard how difficult they are to grow. This book is an attempt to provide these gardeners with information. Proper nurturing and, more important, proper choice of variety can mean the difference between aggravation and exhilarating success.

It is my desire to convey a heartfelt love of these roses. At the same time, I want to emphasize the need for objectivity in choosing varieties best suited to each gardener's requirements. All these roses are lovely, but all have at least some weaknesses. It is important to define these weaknesses. Therefore I have strived to give a balanced and accurate description of the roses.

Words cannot replace a good picture when it comes to plant descriptions. Beth Powning's photographs are meant to portray each rose's characteristics as accurately as possible. By their artistry, however, the photos transcend this purpose, allowing the viewer to revel in the grace and beauty of each curved petal and the endless shadings of color that make roses so exciting and rewarding to grow.

Special thanks to Freeman Patterson. We would like to acknowledge the help of Sue Hooper, Suzie Verrier, Brian Dykemann and Mike Lowe.

R.O. and B.P.

**John Davis, an elegant and hardy
rose, is close to everblooming.**

PART I

Hardy Roses: The Flowering of a Dream

Creating Tapestries

GARDENS ARE AS PERSONAL AS THEIR CREATORS AND ARE AS varied in style, composition and detailing as gardeners are in their hopes, aspirations and temperaments. This is as it should be. One of the greatest joys for any plant lover is to walk through others' gardens. Each garden is unique and conveys something of the creator's dreams and interests. I know of a small perennial garden on a windswept hill. It is tended by a wonderfully selfless and charming gentleman who has devoted his later life to the study of hardy perennials. His garden has no fancy statues, no carefully contoured or planned beds; it simply flows across the landscape as the roots of a plant might work their way through the soil. It is an unassuming, gentle and kindly place. It reflects the very best of this good man.

Although this garden is unstructured, it works. A garden that works, no matter the style, does so because its creator understands the nature of the plants in it. Each plant is unique, having a certain size, color and texture. A creeping phlox grows only a few inches tall; its fine moss-like leaves are a living carpet. In the cool, early weeks of spring, its small, five-petaled blossoms weave their alluring patterns of white, pink, red or blue. The red oak tree, beginning as a lowly acorn, grows to dominate a landscape. Its broad, strong branches thrust out from a massive trunk of deeply furrowed, smoky bark. The leaves, large and pointed, lose their glossy green in autumn, turn to smoldering red, bleach to camel brown, and then hang persistently till the snow's weight or winter's storms scatter them onto the ground.

The simplicity of rose petals scattered across creeping thyme makes a pleasing contrast in textures.

Just as you would never think of using an oak where a phlox would be more appropriate, you should use similar care in choosing material for your garden. Whether you are creating a reproduction of Versailles or an English cottage garden, if you do not have an understanding of your plants' vital statistics, the results will be chaotic and you will be disappointed. With some care and forethought, however, it is easy to create gardens that work without any limitations on your style.

When you are choosing roses for your garden, bear in mind that a rose is not a rose, is not a rose. Roses come in every size, shape, color and texture. For example, Scharlachglut is a vigorous, wide bush with velvety, deep red single blooms that are often as wide as a hand, whereas Double Scotch White is a petite bush with fine foliage and white dainty double blooms a bit larger than a thumbnail. It is difficult to imagine two more different roses. They evoke totally different feelings and have different space requirements, yet each is enchanting. As the gardener, your task is to place these roses in the garden so that each can grow to its potential and at the same time not interfere with either the growth of other plants or the visual arrangement you are constructing.

Hardy roses are a delightfully varied group of plants. Many of them, overshadowed by their aristocratic cousins, were known only to a small group of astute gardeners. As they become more available, and as gardeners' horizons expand, this vast array of plants we group together as "shrub roses" will soon take its rightful place among its peers. Designing with hardy roses is an exciting challenge, one limited only by your space, determination and imagination.

The terminology of hardy roses is confusing. Hardy roses are most often referred to as "shrub roses." The term is also used to mean a rose having a full and generally vigorous appearance. Indeed, I have used "shrub roses" in both contexts in this book. Be warned, however, that not all shrubby roses are hardy and not all hardy roses are shrubby in appearance. To add to the confusion, many people refer to old-fashioned roses as shrubs and others refer to any roses other than hybrid teas or floribundas as shrubs. No one has yet unraveled this maze of definitions to everyone's satisfaction, so in order to avoid total exasperation, let common sense be your guide.

Roses have a rather special place in the history of gardens. More often than not they have been treated somewhat like gems in need of a crown. Many older European gardens devoted a separate section to roses. Often geometric, these rose gardens rarely contained much else in the way of plants. They were designed to dazzle the observer with the shape, color and fragrance exclusively of roses.

In the past century rose growers of the world have fixed most of their attentions on the group known collectively as hybrid teas. Generally speaking, these roses are grown to show off their extravagantly beautiful flowers. The plant itself has been somewhat disregarded or even ignored. As a result, many of these beautiful flowers grow on rather spindly, disease-prone bushes.

The recent revival of interest in shrub or "old-fashioned" roses

Jens Munk, a semi-double rose, is a continuous bloomer.

reflects a changing attitude toward the rose's place in modern gardens. This trend has been convenient for the northern gardener, as many of the hardiest roses belong to several species commonly used before the advent of hybrid teas, floribundas and grandifloras. Because these shrubs have become more popular again, their availability has increased dramatically. The increased interest in shrub roses has also spurred many rose breeders to create shrub roses with longer flowering periods and increased hardiness and disease resistance. The rose garden will never be the same.

More gardeners are integrating the rose into mixtures of plant species. The vigorous *rugosa* roses are becoming backgrounds for perennial borders. Low bedding roses are mixed with low shrubs or annuals. The combinations are endless. The shrub roses, with their solidity and various textures, are choice plants, but the promoter of shrub roses still faces a challenge. The name "rose" has come to be synonymous with hybrid tea and to a lesser extent floribunda and grandiflora. If shown a shrub rose, many gardeners will refuse to acknowledge it as a "real" rose. It does not fit their image of what a rose should be. Because the shrub roses are a fantastically varied group of plants, a great deal of education is necessary to show gardeners how many different uses these plants can have. Once gardeners realize that this wide array of plants offers an exciting challenge to their designing talents, these roses will assume an importance unprecedented in their history.

CLIMBING ROSES

In most cases, climbers are really trailing or pillar roses. They produce long, vigorous shoots that can be tied up. With the exception of a few tender species with hooked thorns, which can work their way up the branches of shrubs or trees, all climbers must be tied to a structure or other plant such as a tree.

One of the more popular uses for climbing roses has been to cover structures such as pergolas, gazebos, trellises and arches. In the past the northern grower has had few hardy climbers to work with. Recently introduced varieties now give northern gardeners the chance to create arches dripping with roses that they could only dream about a few years ago.

Several of these roses owe their existence to the work of two hybridizers – Wilhelm Kordes of Germany and Felicitas Svejda of Canada. Kordes spent a great deal of effort developing roses with disease resistance and hardiness. Some of his releases, such as Leverkusen and Dortmund, combine extreme vigor with a fair degree of hardiness. Working with material developed by Kordes, and crossing it with extremely hardy material, Svejda created a series of long-shooted vigorous pillar roses, which are admirably suited for use as climbers. They are hardier than Kordes's roses but combine many of their best features, such as glossy, disease-resistant foliage and long flowering periods. Some of the best varieties are John Cabot, William Baffin and Henry Kelsey. Another variety worth mentioning was developed by Dr. Walter Van Fleet of the United States at the turn of the century. Using the hardy Prairie Rose (*Rosa setigera*) and the trailing Memorial Rose (*Rosa wichuraiana*), he produced American Pillar, which is still a popular and reasonably hardy climber.

Growing climbing roses requires training. If you leave climbers to fend for themselves you will quickly discover them arching in all directions with little regard for your carefully placed trelliswork. The plant must be tied as it grows, and some pruning is usually called for to keep the rose from becoming too wayward. When tying, use a material that will gradually break down, as ties made of wire will eventually strangle the branches. I have made good use of fence staples when training young roses up a pole or trellis, but the staples must be loosened before they become too tight.

When creating a structure to support climbing roses, the choice of material depends on aesthetics, availability, suitability to the garden and your pocketbook. Brick and stone are premier building materials for durable walls and arches that can create powerful effects in the garden. Gardeners with some time on their hands and a little instruction can create beautiful – and affordable – stone and brick structures. It may take some searching to discover accessible stone sources or a cache of old brick, but the pleasure of creating a structure of brick or stone is hard to match. Wood has been the favored material for most garden structures. It is reasonably easy to work with and generally available. The structure can vary from the most elaborate trelliswork to a simple arch made of rough logs. Although most people are not skilled in iron-

When tying climbing roses to structures, be sure to leave adequate room for future growth. Check the ties annually and loosen them if necessary.

work, beautiful garden structures can be built with this material. A good blacksmith or welder can put together arches or pergolas that can assume a lightness and airiness that belie their strength. I have also seen wonderful arches made with common steel pipe and fittings. No matter which material you choose, only your imagination sets the limits when creating structures for the garden.

A last note concerning climbing roses. Most people associate climbing roses with artificial structures, and of course they are admirably suited to adorn these forms. However, if a suitable shrub or tree is available, there is no better showcase for climbers. Before attaching your rose to a tree, be sure there will be adequate sunshine for your rose and that your tree or shrub will not be adversely affected by its new partner.

SHRUB ROSES

The number of varieties of shrub or bush roses is immense. Most hardy roses fall into this category. They range from rampantly vigorous shrubs 10 ft. (3 m) high to rather diminutive bushes only 3 ft. (1 m) high. Some are very open, while others are very dense.

The most common use of shrub roses is as foundation plants. A shrub rose can be found to fit virtually any space along a house wall. Taller varieties can be used where height is not restricted, and lower varieties can be used under windows. They can be effective when massed together or when mixed with evergreens, flowering shrubs or perennials to create infinite combinations of color and texture.

The rose hedge gives you the chance to use the solidity and vibrant color of shrub roses to full effect. *Rosa rugosa* is perhaps the most important species used in hedging, and for good reason. The dense, rounded form of the *rugosas*, combined with their healthy foliage and tremendous hardiness, makes them very serviceable as well as colorful. Other species can also be effective as hedges. *Rosa alba* and *Rosa gallica* hybrids might be useful where a low informal hedge is desired.

The choice of support structures for climbing roses is limited only by your imagination.

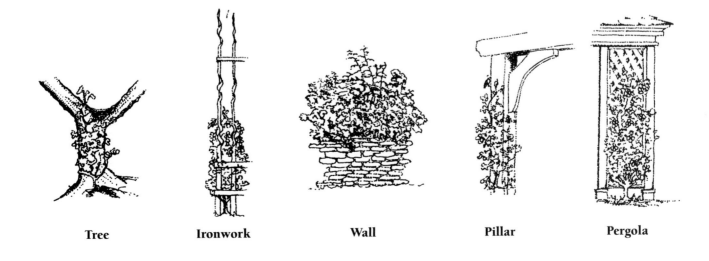

Tree   Ironwork   Wall   Pillar   Pergola

When planted in masses, shrub roses can steal the show from most other plants. The sight of twenty or thirty mature roses in full bloom covering a bed or carpeting a hillside can stir the heart of even a confirmed rhododendron enthusiast. Granted that not every home has the space to house such an extravagance of roses, it is well worth considering when trying to decide how to deal with open spaces. It is important to emphasize maintenance the first few years, but once grown together, a group of shrub roses takes a minimum of care and will repay with an annual display of color that has the power to wash away your burdens and reaffirm to you the gardener the reasons you till the earth.

Shrub roses can, of course, be given their own space in the garden. With a careful arrangement of height, form and color, a spectacular area can be created for roses only. Particularly for the collector of varieties, these "rooms" can provide an area to study, compare and admire. It is worth remembering that if you are planting roses that are not recurrent bloomers, it may be effective to include plants that will be in flower when the roses are not, or perhaps some recurrent varieties of roses, so that that section of the garden is not left colorless for months at a time.

GROUND COVERS

I believe it is fair to say that there are few true ground-cover roses. There are, however, a number of low-growing varieties that can be used to carpet the ground. An example of a ground-hugging variety is the *Rosa rugosa* hybrid Rosa paulii. If grown on its own roots (as opposed to a rootstock), this variety snakes along the ground, never lifting its branches more than a few inches off the soil. It will gradually root into the earth and form a mat, which can be useful to hold steep banks or to form low textural surfaces in much the same manner as creeping junipers. Some trailing varieties can be used as ground covers, though they are not as low and are more cascading.

By using the textures and colors of these lower-growing members of the rose family, you can create exciting visual highlights in your garden. Prostrate varieties can create memorable landscapes when used cascading over a wall or among rocks or specimen plants. Large areas of ground-cover roses, in combination with a high pruned specimen tree or piece of sculpture, can be striking. Low-growing roses placed near water create colorful, patterned edges without making the water seem inaccessible.

A bed of the classic Königin von Dänemark may be used to create a formal look.

2

Wintering

BEAMS OF SUNLIGHT REFLECT OFF THE WARM, PINK PETALS of a rose that is hugging a rocky crag high on a hill in the far north. The steady, cold winds of winter have pressed its red stems against the stones so that they barely rise above them. A month after its fleeting petals are torn away by wind, the first frost coats its leaves. By midwinter the stems are frozen so deeply that a casual touch will shatter them like glass. Yet, under the higher sun of spring, new shoots push from swollen buds, and another year's cycle of growth begins. Farther south, a gardener pokes through her carefully constructed mound of mulch to discover her rose has become a blackened skeleton. All the effort spent in trying to protect the rose from what she imagined was a mild winter has been wasted. How can one rose survive tortuous, frigid winter conditions while the other dies when faced with much warmer winter temperatures? The answer lies in a wondrous process called supercooling.

If you magnified a plant cell, it would resemble a box. The covering of the box is the cell membrane. This rigid structure holds the various fluids and complex structures within its walls, as well as giving the cell its strength. As fall approaches, plants that have the ability to supercool undergo an amazing change. Shorter daylight hours and falling temperatures trigger the cell to reduce the amount of water within it, until all that remains is an extremely thin film of water around the important structures inside the cell. A little-known property of water is its ability to remain elastic well below the freezing point when it is a very thin film. This means that no ice crystals form (ice crystals would rupture and destroy the cell) and the cell can survive extremely low temperatures.

The red rosehips of a Pink Surprise hedge provide sparks of color against a wintry backdrop.

Each variety of hardy plant differs in its resistance to ice formation. The hardiest of these plants can survive in a temperature as low as -40°F (-40°C). This is the cutoff temperature for most hardy deciduous plants, although a few evergreens and deciduous plants can actually take all the water within their cells and put it outside the cell wall, in the spaces between the cells. You can find these plants growing well up into the arctic tundra.

Our super-hardy pink rose hugging its cold, rocky bit of earth belongs to those roses that, through countless generations, have developed the ability to use the supercooling process to its maximum limit. The more tender rose has been subjected to temperatures below what it can tolerate, and the expanding ice crystals have quite literally torn its cells apart. It is the challenge of the northern gardener to discover which roses are the masters of supercooling.

A look at the various rose species can be an important aid in deciding which plants will be worth growing in cold climates. In a given species there is usually a good deal of genetic diversity. Plants differ as we do in characteristics. If a rose species is growing in an area where low temperatures occur, those individuals with a greater ability to use the process of supercooling will be more likely to survive, and therefore to pass that ability on to their offspring. This gradual selection process in time allows species to move northward into colder areas. Many rose species, for example, the popular hybrid tea roses, do not have this selection process for cold hardiness. The hybrid teas, although a complex group, were developed from species such as *Rosa chinensis*, which is a native species of southern China. In its native habitat it rarely encounters temperatures very far below the freezing point. Plants of this species have not had to develop the capacity to endure extremes of cold. When growing roses that are derived from species such as *Rosa chinensis* in gardens with severe winters, the chances for successful overwintering are very poor.

The roses that are successful in northern gardens are derived from species that have been able to adjust to difficult winter conditions through the process of mutation and adaptation. They have become adept at supercooling. Although a large number of species are fairly hardy, only a few have played an important role in the breeding of hardy roses.

The following species of roses form the foundation of most of the hardy varieties in the world. Our best varieties have been selected from these groups. When choosing a rose for your garden, try to find out which species it belongs to. If it comes from one of the following species, it means that it comes from a group with good winter survival skills.

ROSA ALBA

The most expensive perfume in the world pales in comparison to a single bloom from a *Rosa alba*. This ancient species has a special place in rose history and a very precious place in northern gardens. Although little has been done with *Rosa alba* by twentieth-century breeders, the

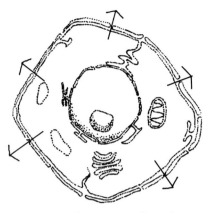

Water being transferred

Supercooled cell

Triggered by the shortening daylight hours and lower temperatures of fall, cells of winter-hardy plants undergo supercooling. Water is transferred outside the cell walls until all that remains is a thin, flexible film of water around the cell's vital components. In this state, the cell can freeze without being ruptured by ice crystals.

older varieties available to us are invaluable. They are generally very healthy, and most are hardy in Zone 4. Some can be grown into Zone 3. Because they do not have a long blooming season they have been relegated to the background of the rose world since the introduction of the perpetual bloomers and the hybrid teas, but I would no more give up my *Rosa albas* than I would my rhododendrons, which bloom for a much briefer time.

ROSA CENTIFOLIA

Peter Beales, in his excellent book *Classic Roses*, tells us that *Rosa centifolia* is not really a species but a complex hybrid comprised of genes from *Rosa gallica*, *Rosa canina*, *Rosa moschata* and others. Be this as it may, the Cabbage rose, as it is known, contains a number of older forms that are both interesting and hardy. Among these are the curious moss roses. These hairy novelties have moss-like glandular bristles that cover the stems and sepals.

ROSA FOETIDA

The double form of this species, Persian Yellow, figures importantly in the breeding of most yellow roses and is the parent of nearly all hardy yellow varieties developed. Considering it is native to southwest Asia, it is an amazingly hardy species, surviving even into Zone 3.

ROSA GALLICA

This species is currently enjoying a resurgence of popularity after having been sadly neglected for nearly a century. Many important varieties were produced in the early and mid-nineteenth century, and these still form the majority of available varieties in the species. However, modern breeders such as David Austin and Peter Beales of England have introduced some stunning new shrub roses with *Rosa gallica* in their blood. Most of the *gallicas* are quite hardy and come in a profusion of colors, including dark tones as in Cardinal de Richelieu, whose flowers are a deep, rich purple. Most have strong perfume, and the flowers are very often double or even quartered.

ROSA RUGOSA

If you had to single out the most important species used in breeding for hardiness, it would have to be *Rosa rugosa*. This native of northern China and Japan has a number of important attributes. Paramount among its virtues is extreme hardiness. Many varieties of *Rosa rugosa* will survive in Zone 2. The flowers of this species are usually large and fragrant, with colors varying from white through the range of pinks to the occasional red. The coarse-textured foliage is unusually healthy.

Blackspot and mildew rarely show up in this species. Lastly, its deep orangey-red hips add a decorative and useful accent to the plant in fall.

My introduction to the world of hardy roses began with the purchase of a Blanc Double de Coubert. Drinking in the sweet, heady fragrance of its first blooms addicted me to roses immediately. This was not a rose that needed to be pampered. It grew defiantly in the garden, scoffing at winter. Ever since discovering this superb ambassador of the *rugosas*, we have concentrated much of our effort on the many excellent hybrids of this species that are now available. If you are living in the very coldest regions, *Rosa rugosa* hybrids are some of the finest and hardiest material.

ROSA SPINOSISSIMA

A species found growing in Europe and Asia, this rose became known as the Scotch Briar rose. It was found in Scotland, and a good deal of selection and breeding work was carried out in the eighteenth and nineteenth centuries in both Scotland and England. From this work arose numerous single and double varieties in whites and pinks. Crossed with Persian Yellow, it gave rise to several yellow forms as well, including Harison's Yellow, the famous "yellow rose of Texas." The small and delicate foliage is unusual. Its thin stems are armed with long, sharp thorns. Generally it flowers once in late spring or early summer, although a few varieties have repeat bloom. One of the better known is Stanwell Perpetual, whose blush pink blooms flower nonstop till frost.

The garden sleeps under its blanket of snow, but its complex pattern of shapes and shadows continues to give pleasure.

3

Nurturing

SUCCESS WITH GROWING ROSES REQUIRES NOT MAGIC BUT knowledge. If you understand the basic needs of your plants and ensure that those needs are satisfied, then the magic that we call growth can take place, and I can think of no more miraculous process than the ability of a plant to suck up water and nutrients, then convert them, with sunlight, into food. In order to make the most of this ability, you need to nurture your roses, to give them all the advantages you can. By providing a healthy soil, adequate water, lots of sun and enough room for growth, you can help your roses reach their potential. Your reward will be the goal of every rose grower – rainbows of sun-washed petals and perfumed evening walks.

SITE

Before you can begin to think about the details of growing roses, you must first decide where you are going to plant them. This can be among your most important decisions. Unless you wish to move, you cannot change your environment. Your position on the globe will determine the general weather conditions and the hours of light available to you. Your particular site will also have a bearing on the garden. Sites differ in soil type, general wind exposure, overall air drainage and, depending upon the size of the site, the alignment toward the sun. Urban environments may affect a site by altering such elements as air quality and light conditions. These are site constraints that you have little control over. Within your site, however, there are often many "microsites." Changing

The soil in which your rose is planted will determine how well your rose grows.

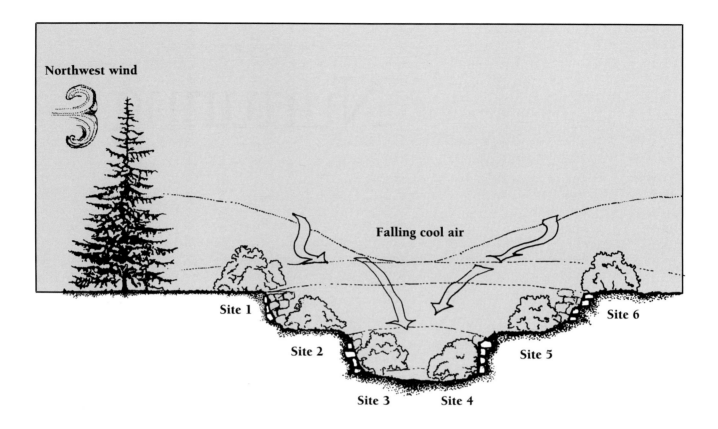

your plant's position within a site, you can often alter the amount and quality of sunlight, the high and low temperatures, the exposure to wind, the water drainage or the soil composition.

When you are deciding where to dig the hole, remember that roses need sunlight. The amount of sunlight will affect plant vigor, flower production and disease susceptibility. The best situation for a rose is full sun from dawn to dusk. Many gardens will not be able to provide this, but try to maximize sun exposure. Roses growing in partial shade will usually be spindly and stingy with their flowers. Roses grown in full shade will slowly die. Sunlight is also an important deterrent to fungal growth. A good dose of sun is far more effective for prevention of mildew or rust than any amount of sprays.

Although we think of ourselves as living in a particular hardiness zone (see the zone map), many sites may contain several microsites that may differ as much as a full zone. The choice of a microsite can greatly affect winter survival. For example, a grove of trees will block the prevailing wind. In winter, a rose planted with this protection would suffer far less from cold, dry winds. These winds can injure a plant by dehydrating it even though the temperature may not be that low. A change in elevation can also be important. On those cold, still nights in spring or fall, frost will form in low pockets where the heavier cold air settles. Higher areas will not be as cold and may escape the frost.

By carefully siting your roses, you can avoid low areas where cold air settles and frosts are more severe. Choose microsites that have protection from high winds, which can lower temperatures and dry plants in both winter and summer. On a typical late spring night, site 1 might be 40°F (5°C), site 2 35°F (1°C) and site 3 below freezing. On a windy winter day, sites 1-4 might be relatively protected while site 5, and especially site 6, may be subjected to severe windchill and desiccation.

Likewise, soil conditions can differ drastically between microsites. Roses are particularly sensitive to wet soils. If their roots sit in water for any length of time, the roots will die from decreased oxygen. In winter, wet soils are colder. Even though the roots have enough oxygen to survive, low temperatures in winter may spell disaster. It is essential that your site be well drained. If you must plant in a wet area, install drain tile to direct water away from the plants. Filling the bottom of a hole with gravel does not solve a drainage problem. If there is no way for the water to escape, the gravel will fill up with water and your rose will suffer as much damage as if there had been no gravel.

The texture and richness of soils will often vary dramatically, even in a fairly small area. If possible, choose an area with a deep, rich topsoil. If there is no such spot, or if your choice of site is guided by other limits, do not despair. Soil is something you can work with to improve.

SOIL

Plants use the soil for anchorage and for sustenance. The soil in which your rose is planted will, in large measure, determine how well your rose grows. A basic understanding of how soil works is essential in managing your garden. Soil is not simply a medium to pour bags of fertilizer on. Rather, soils are complex, dynamic, living systems that react to the changes we create. Gardening initiates changes that affect the soil and therefore our plants.

Nearly every rose book ever written says that roses must have a clay soil to grow to perfection. This emphasis on clay soils is a bit misleading. Clay is consistently recommended mostly because of its ability to hold more water, thus making it less likely that the rose will dry out. Dry rose bushes do not flower or grow well. Another reason clay soils are recommended is because most roses are propagated by budding the desired variety onto a rootstock. Usually the rootstock is either *Rosa multiflora* or *Rosa canina*, species that grow best in heavier soils. However, many of the roses that the northern gardener plants, such as the *rugosa* rose and Scotch rose, actually prefer lighter soils when on their own roots. The important point to remember is that roses must have a consistent supply of water and nutrients to grow to their potential. Virtually any type of soil can successfully grow roses if it is well drained and has enough organic content for good water retention and nutrient supply.

There are very few soils that require no work on the gardener's part to meet these conditions. Most of us live with soils that are not ideal. They may be low in organic material, they may have a heavy clay texture that does not allow the free passage of air and water, or they may be a very light soil that will not hold water and dries out quickly. Your task as gardener is to improve those conditions. Depending upon your soil, this task can be simple or herculean.

SOIL ACIDITY

One of the most important characteristics of soil is also one of the easiest conditions to alter. The soil of any site has a certain level of acidity or alkalinity, called its pH level. The pH of a substance can range from 0 to 14, with 7 being neutral. Most plants grow in the 4 to 9 range. The ideal pH level for roses is 6 to 7. Within this range the rose can make best use of the elements available in the soil. If the soil drops in pH (becoming more acidic) or rises in pH (becoming more alkaline), certain elements become chemically bonded and therefore unavailable to the plants. You can find out your soil's pH by having it tested. If it is too acidic, add lime or gypsum to correct the problem. If it is too alkaline, add sulfur or aluminum sulfate to lower the pH. Your soil test should tell you the correct amount of these additives to bring your pH to the desired level. Most departments of agriculture will perform soil tests, or you can do these tests yourself using reasonably priced kits. Getting a soil test done is simple, yet it continually surprises me how few people take the time to do it. Without an accurate soil test you are only guessing your soil's acidity level and playing roulette with your garden's health.

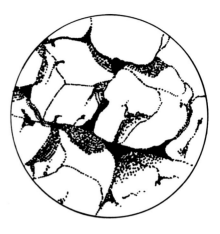

Enlarged view of sand particles

SOIL TEXTURE

"Digging your hands into the earth" is a well-used phrase that deserves closer scrutiny. This phrase evokes images of seeds dropped into hoed trenches, roots settled into their new homes – in essence, the nurturing so central to good gardening. Yet this phrase concerns the texture of soil, and indeed, a soil's texture is of prime importance for good growth.

Soils are divided into two general classifications: clay soils and sandy soils. Clay soils contain a high percentage of minerals such as mica and feldspar. These minerals are made of tiny, flat plates that adhere closely together, making it difficult for water and air to penetrate between them. To break up a clay, it is necessary to mix in large amounts of coarse-textured organic material. These odd-shaped chunks hold the clay particles apart, creating spaces in which water and air can circulate. Because most roots grow near the surface of the soil, it is best to work most of your organic material into this layer. Here the roots will benefit from the increased oxygen supplies and the nutrients that the break down of the organic matter creates.

Sandy soils have the opposite problem. Sand soils are composed of grains of silica, or quartz. These are irregular and have spaces between them that air and water can pass through freely. If there is little organic matter in a sand soil, it dries out quickly.

Water passing slowly through a clay soil dissolves the surfaces of the mineral particles, releasing elements in the process. The particles of a sandy soil, however, do not dissolve easily in water because of their composition. As well, the rapid passage of water through sandy soil tends to quickly drain away what few available nutrients there are. For these reasons, sandy soils tend to be less fertile. However, the addi-

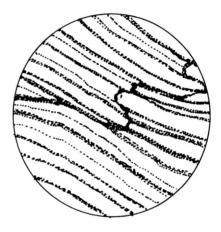

Enlarged view of clay particles

The coarse nature of sand particles allows the free passage of air and water. The flat particles of a clay soil pack tightly together making it difficult for air and water to penetrate.

tion of organic material can rapidly solve this problem. Indeed, some of the best soils in the world are soils composed of sand and fine organic particles. The combination of good drainage and the nutrient- and water-holding capacities of the organic matter create excellent conditions for good growth. As well, loose soils composed of sands and gravels are easier to work with than clay soils.

Most garden soils lie somewhere between the extremes of pure clay and pure sand. In any case, the solution for improving your soil lies in the addition of organic material. Why is organic material so important? Why not simply add the nutrients we need with chemical fertilizers?

Organic material comes from the bodies of plants and animals. When broken down by the soil's microorganisms the elements contained in them are released and combine with water percolating through the soil. This nutrient-laden "soup" feeds your roses. If you examine the roots of a plant, note how the fine roots work their way through the pieces of organic material. They know where the "soup" is being served.

Two well-known sources of organic matter are manure and compost. Another valuable soil conditioner available to most gardeners is peat moss. Its fine fibers have been chemically pickled by centuries of immersion in very acidic water. Although it contains few nutrients, it breaks down slowly and helps hold both water and air effectively in soil for many years. Shredded bark and other forest-industry byproducts are also valuable. Sources such as leaves, grass clippings and prunings are thrown out by countless people, cities and businesses every day. Wise gardeners let it be known that they will accept any clean organic "waste." Properly composted, these wastes will add texture to your soil and will make digging your hands into the earth that much easier.

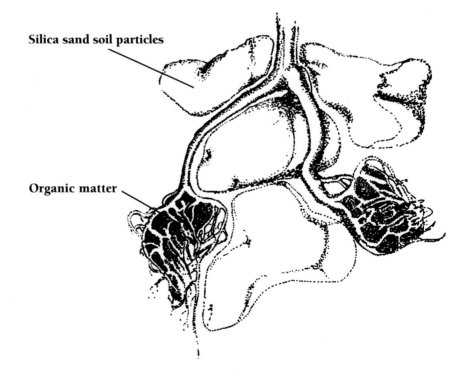

Silica sand soil particles

Organic matter

Fine root hairs surround and penetrate organic matter in the soil, where water is abundant and where the complex process of decay releases nutrients.

MULCHES

I do not garden without mulches. A clean cultivated garden is an unnatural and often hostile environment for a plant. In hot, dry weather it becomes a desert; the surface absorbs and gives off immense quantities of heat and loses moisture rapidly. Rains can cause erosion, and the surface layer can become packed from the impact of raindrops. After a rain, the sun can bake the muddy soil into a hard shell, reducing oxygen levels in the root zone and leading to even worse erosion problems in the next rainfall.

Most plants prefer a "forest floor" type of environment. In a healthy forest, the mulch layer is an equalizer. A mulch on your garden acts in the same way. Its insulating qualities temper the heat of summer and the cold of winter. Mulch absorbs and disperses the impact of falling raindrops, eliminating erosion and preventing soil bacteria and fungi from splashing up onto plants where they can sometimes cause problems. The continual activity by worms, insects and other life encouraged by mulch also creates a network of pathways, which increases the availability of oxygen to the roots. Perhaps most important, an organic mulch provides a flourishing environment for the numerous insects and microscopic plants and animals that are necessary to a healthy soil. Organic matter is continually broken down in such an active community. This breakdown of organic matter releases nutrients into the soil where it can be used by plant roots.

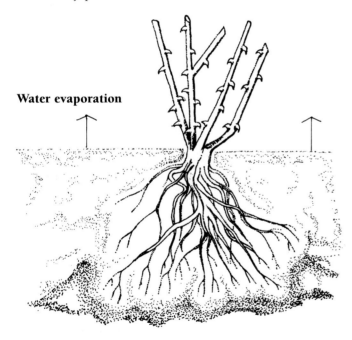

Water evaporation

A clean cultivated soil loses water rapidly in warm weather and roots must penetrate deeply to obtain water.

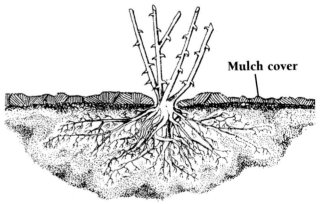

Mulch cover

A mulch cover on the soil reduces evaporation and helps create a wicking effect that keeps water levels evenly distributed throughout the soil. This allows the development of more fine feeding roots near the surface, where soil activity is highest and nutrients most concentrated.

Whenever you add a large amount of organic material to the soil, it is important to realize that the breakdown of that mulch will require nitrogen. Nitrogen fertilizers will provide this, although at the expense of some of the soil's microscopic life. However, if a good quantity of well-made compost is incorporated on the surface just before adding your mulch, it will provide enough nitrogen and will further improve your soil's texture and fertility. If the mulch layer is not worked into the soil, the nitrogen requirements will be smaller. Once this mulch "stabilizes," simply add new mulch on the surface every year or two and the system will not overtax nitrogen supplies. This gradual layering mimics the annual addition of leaves to the forest floor.

Inorganic mulches such as solid plastic sheeting exclude oxygen from the soil and should not be used. Modern landscape fabrics allow passage of water and air and will keep weed growth down, but I have two major objections to them. They are a nightmare if you want to work your soil, and pulling them up after a few years in the ground can be a job to tax the patience of any gardener. Worst of all, they are created from nonrenewable oil products. It is bad enough that we squander these precious resources on things we consider essential, but to cover our gardens with them is not only unnecessary but unforgivable.

PROVIDING NUTRIENTS

A healthy soil seethes with life. The soil's plants and animals go through countless cycles of birth and death. This cycle's waste products, when dissolved in the soil's water, are the nutrients your rose uses for growth. Bacteria and worm and insect manures are the prime sources of a soil's ability to nourish plants.

To create active soils, you often have to "kick-start" your soil with organic materials and sources of nitrogen. The organic material can be thought of as a storehouse filled with the elements that were used to construct the plants that make it up. The nitrogen is the key that starts the process of unlocking that storehouse, for it is at the microscopic level that the breakdown begins. If adequate levels of nitrogen are available, one-celled creatures such as bacteria begin to digest the fibers and other tissues in the organic matter. Soon multicelled creatures consume bacteria. Small insects consume these creatures, and so on. As long as there is a steady addition of organic material, the process will continue. If no more organic matter is added, the nitrogen levels will increase until the existing organic material is consumed; the levels then will fall off quickly. If large amounts of organic matter are added, the process will slow because there will be a temporary shortage of nitrogen for the bacteria. By maintaining a steady input of organic matter and nitrogen-rich materials, you can keep your soil humming with activity, a soil that can provide the nutrients your roses need to grow and flower well.

If you treat your soil as if it is simply a medium into which you introduce needed elements in the form of soluble fertilizers, you will gradually degrade your soil. Without sufficient organic material, the water-soluble elements in the fertilizers pass quickly through the soil. Your plant will absorb a certain amount of them, but most will leach out through the soil, ending up in the water table and eventually in the rivers. This excessive use of fertilizers has caused severe problems in lakes and rivers in many agricultural areas.

Although your plant will have absorbed some of the nitrogen, phosphorus and potassium from the chemical fertilizer, these fertilizers do not contain the numerous micronutrients that are also essential to proper plant growth. Micronutrients are those elements that are needed only in small quantities. They are, however, absolutely necessary. Without the tiny portions of zinc, sulfur, selenium, boron and other such elements, the complex molecules that make up the plant's tissues cannot be constructed. It's like having the steel to build a bridge without the bolts to hold the pieces together. It is the organic material in your soil that contributes most of these micronutrients.

Another consideration when using chemical fertilizers is their acid-ifying nature. As most fertilizers dissolve, they acidify the soil. For naturally acidic soils, it is essential that the pH be adjusted to compensate for this process. Many gardeners complain to me of not getting adequate growth even though they are fertilizing heavily. When I ask whether they have added lime recently, their usual reaction is "I didn't know it was necessary." By adding lime to their soil, they could use a fraction of the fertilizer and have much better growth.

Nitrogen is very important in the formation of the proteins necessary to build stems, leaves and roots. Other elements are important too, but nitrogen is more difficult to keep in the soil. It disperses into the air and is quickly leached away by rains. This instability creates a constant need to replenish nitrogen in the soil and makes it the focus of most fertilizer programs.

If you are committed to raising healthy, vigorous roses, you must be committed to building soil, for the former is dependent upon the latter. Though the soil's activities are complex, the practical solutions to fertilizing your rose beds are simple. Innumerable materials can be used to build better soils, but essentially we are talking about manures and composts.

THE MAGIC OF MANURE

Most people would hardly consider manure a worthwhile topic of conversation. It is safe to say, however, that without using manure as a fertilizer, humans would still be hunter-gatherers. The conversion of human culture to an agricultural base required soils whose fertility could be sustained. The discovery of using manure as fertilizer to increase crop yields and maintain soil texture made the agricultural revolution sustainable.

As food passes through an animal, its composition is altered. Fresh manure contains a high percentage of ammonia. This is partly why manure has such a pungent smell. Ammonia is high in nitrogen and is a readily available source for plants. As soon as the manure is exposed to the air, however, the ammonia begins to evaporate and the nitrogen is lost to the atmosphere. As well, rain percolates through the manure, leaching out the nitrogen. So while fresh manure is a good source of nitrogen, older, exposed manure, although still valuable for its organic content, is not nearly as valuable as fertilizer. A good farmer will work fresh manure quickly into the soil so that the nitrogen will not be lost.

You should be cautious of fresh manure, however. The ammonia it gives off poses a danger to plants. Plants are nitrogen hogs, and will absorb nitrogen as long as it is available. Fresh manure near a plant's roots provides a tremendous quantity of nitrogen. As long as adequate water is available to the plant it will be able to handle the nitrogen. However, if water is limited in any way, the nitrogen will form salts in the plant's tissues, which will burn the plant up. Manure also contains the bane of gardeners everywhere – weeds. Many weed seeds pass through animals without harm. Once put into the soil with the manure, they have not only a place to grow but the nutrition to grow well.

Because many gardeners today live in urban environments, the close connections between farmyard manure and the garden have essentially disappeared. Many gardeners may have only bagged manure available to them. Although often variable in quality and usually pricey, bagged manure is still a valuable soil enricher. It is also usually heat-treated to destroy weed seeds. The bagged manure may lack the nutrient value of a fresh pie from an alfalfa-fed Holstein cow, but it will still work magic.

No matter our source, if we want to use manure to best advantage we need to convert the nitrogen to a more stable form and to eliminate the problem of weed seeds. The answer is to make compost.

THE MIRACLE OF COMPOST

If you know how to make a complete, balanced compost, you do not need any other plant food. Well-made compost should contain all the nutrients needed for healthy growth. It will contain the bacteria, fungi and other microscopic life that work to control diseases in soil, and it will provide valuable organic matter.

The secret of good compost lies in balance. Bacteria in a compost pile feed on the carbon in the organic material and convert it into energy. The bacteria require nitrogen, phosphorus and potassium, among other elements, to accomplish this task. Although phosphorus and potassium are available in the organic material, nitrogen is usually in low supply. We need to add nitrogen to the pile. Fresh manure is the most common source of nitrogen for compost makers, but it is not always available. Many nitrogen-rich materials can be purchased at local animal feed-stores. These include linseed meal, soyameal, cottonseed meal, blood meal, bonemeal and feather meal. If you live near the sea you may be able to obtain fish or shellfish waste. Any of these, or similar high-protein materials, provide the nitrogen necessary to get your compost working.

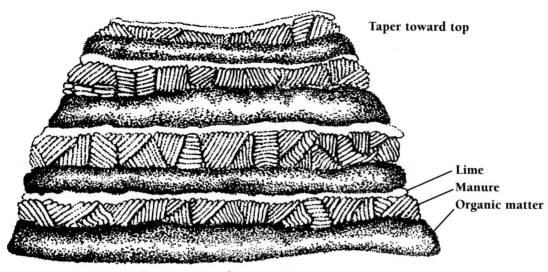

Taper toward top

Lime
Manure
Organic matter

Cross-section of compost heap

A balance must be struck between the carbon/nitrogen ratio in the pile. The proper ratio for optimum compost activity is 30 carbon to 1 nitrogen. To achieve a healthy compost pile with a well-balanced carbon/nitrogen ratio, start as follows.

Spread your organic material into a layer approximately 1 ft. (30 cm) thick. This might include materials like old hay, vegetable peelings, leaves (preferably shredded) or weeds. On top of this, spread a layer of fresh manure approximately 3 in. (8 cm) thick. If you cannot obtain manure, put a thinner layer of whatever organic nitrogen source you can obtain. If you are unable to obtain any organic sources of nitrogen, sprinkle a fertilizer such as urea (42-0-0) very lightly over your organic matter. Sprinkle a few shovelfuls of earth over the whole lot. This earth contains enough soil bacteria to act as a starter for the breakdown process, although many argue that it is not necessary. If you want a sweet (high pH) compost, add a shovelful of lime. Repeat this layering until the pile is about 4 ft. (1.2 m) tall. As you layer your pile, be sure to add enough water to make it thoroughly moist but not soggy.

Once your pile is built, turn it regularly. Turning a compost heap puts oxygen into the pile. This oxygen is vital to keep the bacteria active. Some compost heaps never break down properly due to lack of oxygen. Turning every day or two is ideal, but few of us have that kind of time. If you can turn your pile once a week, or at most once every two weeks, the compost will work well. After one or two turnings, your compost heap should be steaming hot inside. A properly balanced and aerated compost pile will reach temperatures of 160°F (72°C). These high temperatures destroy the weed seeds and any harmful diseases that may be present in the materials. Remember that the size of your pile is not very important. Even a small compost pile will work well if there is a proper carbon/nitrogen balance and if it is damp and turned regularly. If space is limited or tidiness a concern, there are many compost makers available that are easy to use.

Build your compost heap like a giant sandwich, layering nitrogen-rich materials between the bulk of organic materials. Keep the pile moist and turn often to introduce oxygen into the pile.

Once it cools, your compost is ready to use. In the garden it will continue to break down, and as it does so, it will slowly release the nitrogen and other elements your plants need. If your quantities are limited, use it as a side dressing around your plants or incorporate some in your planting holes. If you have larger quantities, use it as a general top dressing on your garden. If you make composting a regular part of your garden program you will see the results in healthy growth and good flowering.

WEEDING

Ask a gardener what they like least about gardening and inevitably the answer is weeding. It is the subject books on gardening tend to avoid. After all, who wants to talk about work when you can talk about the scintillating colors, the exotic fragrances, the joys and beauties that gardening can create? But the truth is, a garden's beauty cannot unfold without weeding. Planting, watering, pruning, feeding and weeding are tasks that must be done so that we can enjoy the results.

I enjoy weeding. After a hectic day I can think of no more relaxing activity than to go into my garden and weed. It allows me to be close to the plants, to touch them, to examine them for any problems, to enjoy them. Gardening for me, as it is for so many, is a spiritual exercise, and far from being repelled by weeding, I find it lends structure and discipline to the experience. At the same time, no one enjoys hacking at overgrown weeds, or working in gardens that resemble abandoned hay fields. The longer the weeding is neglected, the more work it will need to bring the garden back under control. The secret to keeping weeds at a manageable stage is working with properly prepared ground and keeping to a regular schedule of maintenance.

Attitudes toward weeds vary from the relaxed to the compulsive. Whatever your attitude, keep in mind that weeds can teach us valuable lessons about our soil and our management techniques. Weeds are simply plants that are growing where we don't want them, but they are not a homogeneous group. Weeds differ in their habits and needs. By examining which weeds are growing in your garden, you can often discover whether your soil is too acidic or too alkaline, if cultivation is required, if the ground is lacking in certain nutrients and a host of other information. Turn weeding from a nuisance into an opportunity to learn more about your garden.

SOIL PREPARATION

Weeding begins before you plant your first rose. If you are starting with a new piece of ground, the first order of business is to remove as many perennial weeds as possible, being sure to remove the roots to prevent the weed from regrowing. Although it is not exciting work, every hour you spend preparing your site will be repaid many times over in the future. Once the initial preparation is complete, you may want to add compost or manure. (Keep in mind that manure will contain weed seeds.) Once you have planted your roses, seriously consider mulching with a layer of organic material such as shredded bark or other materials that do not contain weed seeds. Many seeds need light to germinate, and the mulch will prevent light from reaching them. A thick layer of mulch will also keep many seeds from reaching the surface if they do germinate. Some will always manage to make it to sunlight, and any perennial roots that remain will send up shoots, but these are easily pulled in a mulched garden, an advantage that will be appreciated by those who have had to cultivate hard, baked ground, in which the weed roots are nearly impossible to remove. A mulch keeps the ground looser and better aerated, making it easy to remove both the top and the root of the weed.

When planning your garden, remember that an isolated plant in a lawn is difficult to maintain. Grass moves in quickly, and keeping your plant free of weeds can be a chore. If you can plant in groupings or beds, you will be able to keep the ground between the plants more easily cultivated. This makes lawn mowing much easier as well. Rather than having to push under a bush from all sides, the mower can simply follow the edge of the bed. This edge should be cut with a spade each spring to prevent grass or other weed roots from moving into the bed. Leave a cut face at the edge; this will tend to "air prune" any roots moving toward the bed. If your garden plan calls for individual plants on the lawn, keep the edge of the cultivated area away from the plants. This will allow you to easily maintain that edge.

WEED MANAGEMENT

Weed new gardens often, particularly during the first few months. At this stage the weeds are not well established and are easy to deal with. If you wait, the roots will quickly spread, and pulling or hoeing becomes increasingly difficult. Begin weeding early as well in established gardens. The spring and early summer are periods of intense growth. By getting to the weeding early you will not have as big a job, and you will be able to relax during the summer when your roses are magnificent and you are warm and lazy.

Most weeding can be done in a mulched garden by simply pulling weeds out by hand. This requires only your hands and gloves, and perhaps the help of a three-pronged hand cultivator. If you prefer to keep your garden clean cultivated, there are several tools to aid you in your work. If you must choose only one tool to have, make it a hoe. This age-old simple device has never been replaced as the number-one gardening aid. Several designs are on the market today, including hoes with triangular blades, push-pull types or ones with open U-shaped blades. The common hoe with a more or less rectangular blade is still the most popular design and, I would argue, the most useful.

Good hoeing is an acquired art. Most people hold a hoe nearly horizontally and hack at the ground. This destroys both the hoe and your arms. A hoe should be held nearly vertically so that the blade cuts away thin slices of ground. Cut these slices from the uncultivated ground, pulling the loosened earth toward you as you work. Walk forward, working in a regular pattern of strokes from right to left or vice versa. If you work as you walk backward, with the blade pushing into the harder earth, you will be working twice as hard with poorer results. Such instructions may sound fussy, but you will be surprised at how much easier and productive hoeing is when done properly.

Weeds can be managed with the aid of chemicals. Called herbicides, these chemicals prevent weed seeds from germinating or destroy existing weeds. The newest generation of herbicides works by interfering with the normal transfer of materials in the plant, killing the plant down to the root tips. Essentially these materials are labor replacers. Labor in agriculture is expensive, and using herbicides lowers expenses.

There is, however, a hidden cost in herbicides. Many of these materials work their way through the soil and into the groundwater, where they then show up in wells, in rivers, and ultimately in the oceans. Areas treated with herbicides often cannot be planted with certain crops for years after the chemicals have been applied. Careless use of herbicides results in the loss of neighboring plants and contamination of soil and water. Children who play on lawns treated with herbicides can develop allergic reactions or illness. It is difficult to measure these hidden costs, but we need to carefully consider the consequences of using herbicides.

Herbicides are another unknown quantity in the chemical onslaught we are inflicting on the Earth. Modern insecticides were introduced after World War II, and their use has accelerated at an alarming rate since then. The harvest of that headlong rush into chemical management is now being reaped. Our water, air and soil are polluted. Plants, animals and humans are being affected in serious ways. Even our food is contaminated.

If we want to clean up our environment, we must make decisions that reflect that commitment. Herbicides are *not* needed in a garden, and I feel they have no place in gardening or agriculture. Any possible benefit we gain by their use is far outweighed by the consequences to ourselves, our children and all life on Earth.

PLANTING

When you purchase a rose bush, you hold in your hand the potential for many years of satisfaction and pleasure. To insure that this potential is secure, you need to properly plant your rose.

The first order of business is to be sure that your rose does not dry out while you prepare the planting hole. As soon as you get your rose, plunge the rootball in water for several hours. This will allow the plant to absorb as much water as it can hold. After the roots have sat in the water for up to 12 hours, take the bush out for planting. If you cannot

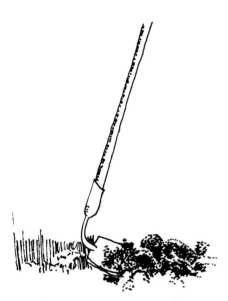

Hoe in a regular sequence of strips, always pulling undisturbed soil toward you as you proceed forward. Keep your hoe nearly vertical so that you slice rather than chop the soil.

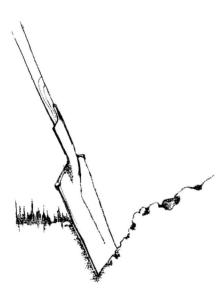

Edge your beds regularly. A steep vertical edge will tend to discourage, at least temporarily, grass and weeds from growing into the bed.

plant it immediately, bury the roots in a trench in your garden or in damp bark or sawdust until you are ready. Remember that even a few minutes in a dry spot, especially in the sun, can mean disaster.

Very often the rose you purchase will be a container-grown plant. If this is the case, be sure that any long, spiraling roots are teased out when you plant such a rose. If the roots have become a dense mass on the outside of the rootball and separating them is difficult, make several shallow cuts with a knife up and down the rootball. This will force the formation of smaller roots, which will grow into the new soil. Rootbound plants, if not unbound, will often not grow into the surrounding soil, and in the worst of cases can strangle themselves to death. Rootbound plants are also easily pushed out of the ground by frostheave in northern areas.

When you prepare the planting hole, first remove any weeds, particularly their roots, from in and around the site. Dig a hole that is wide enough for the entire root system to be spread out, and dig it deep enough so that the roots will be entirely underground. Most roses are budded roses. Such roses have a bud of the variety inserted under the bark of a rootstock. At the union of the rootstock and variety a bulbous crook is formed. This union should be buried at least 4 in. (10 cm) below the soil surface. The soil will protect the union from the more severe winter temperatures and will help prevent suckering from the rootstock. Roses grown from cuttings or layers can be planted at the same depth as they were previously growing, or slightly deeper if you wish.

If you have a reasonably loose loam, it is an advantage to work compost or well-rotted manure into the hole. A handful of bonemeal is also advisable, as this gives the plant a long-term source of phosphorus, which is needed for root development. If you wish to use peat moss, be sure that it is well moistened before you put it in the hole. Be careful not to have the peat moss account for more than one-quarter of the volume of the soil, as this may be too light a mix and may cause the hole to dry out quickly. This is especially important with heavier clay soils. These denser soils will tend to draw water away from the lighter soil within the hole. Your rose will not receive adequate water. If you have a clay soil, it is usually better to replace around your rose roots the same clay you dug out of the hole. Adding some compost and bonemeal is fine. After the rose is planted, place the greater part of your compost and organic materials at the surface, where the feeder roots will form and make best use of these nutrients.

When planting the rose, be sure to work the soil around the root system so that no air pockets remain. These delay the formation of the smaller roots, which are so important in establishing your rose. Once you have worked the soil to the top, tamp firmly with your hands or feet. Leave a slight depression on the surface and fill this with water. Once it soaks in, fill the depression again until you are sure that the entire hole is completely saturated. If you are mulching, spread the mulch on the surface and give one more watering.

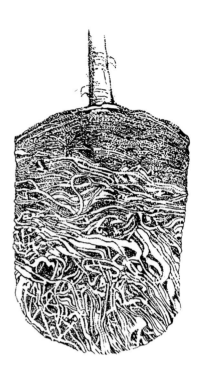

Potted roses can form masses of spiraling roots on the outside of the rootball. These roots must be teased or cut to ensure that the new roots will grow into the surrounding soil.

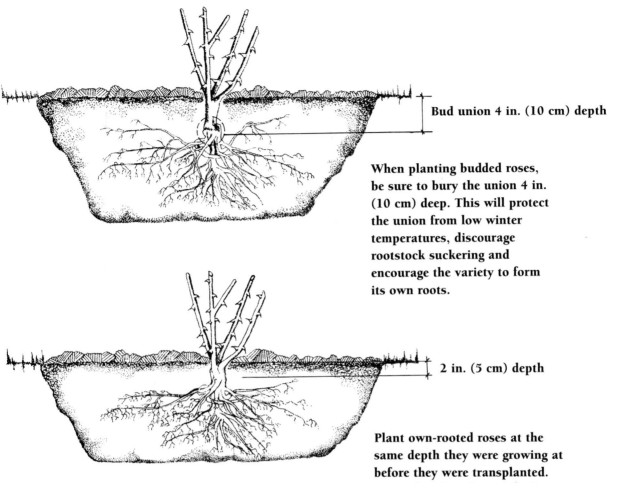

Bud union 4 in. (10 cm) depth

When planting budded roses, be sure to bury the union 4 in. (10 cm) deep. This will protect the union from low winter temperatures, discourage rootstock suckering and encourage the variety to form its own roots.

2 in. (5 cm) depth

Plant own-rooted roses at the same depth they were growing at before they were transplanted. Remember that the width of your planting hole is at least as important as the depth. Most feeding roots are shallow and will spread horizontally.

The most important part of establishing a new rose is watering. Keep a regular schedule of watering, giving the rose the equivalent of at least 1 or 1 1/2 in. (2 or 4 cm) of rain a week. That is a fair amount of water. Be sure to soak the hole well. A few sprays on the surface will not do your rose any good. It takes more water than most people think to thoroughly soak down to the bottom of a planting hole. If you are faithful about watering, your rose will repay you with good growth and more prolific blooming. Even a weak plant will thrive if given enough water. However, a plant can be overwatered, particularly in heavier clay soils. If the roots are kept too wet, they will lack sufficient oxygen. Common sense is your best guide in such situations.

After planting your rose you may wish to prune it back. Be sure to read the section "Pruning the New Rose" for instructions.

PRUNING

Pruning begins before you even buy your roses. It begins in your living room when you are curled up in your easychair deciding what rose to put in which space. The roses you choose all have distinctive growth patterns. If you have a space where you want a low-growing variety, don't put in a vigorous variety with the idea that you can keep it pruned down. Plant a rose that will best suit the space. If you don't, you will constantly be fighting against the natural growth pattern of the plant. You will create far more work than is necessary, and the results will never be as satisfying. Keep in mind that pruning is always a dwarfing process. To better understand what happens when you prune, it helps to visualize how a plant works.

Inside your rose, water and nutrients are absorbed by the roots and flow up the stems to the top of the plant. The top then uses the water and nutrients to make food, which is sent throughout the upper portion of the plant. Any leftovers are sent down to feed the root system. Pruning removes potential leaf surface from your plant. The leaves are the food-production centers of the plant, turning sunlight, water and nutrients into what we call sap. Stems, to an extent, are also involved in the production of food. When you remove parts of the plant with your pruning shears, you are reducing a portion of this "food factory" and thereby limiting the plant's capacity for growth.

Pruning keeps a rose in prime condition by allowing it to form new stems and leaves.

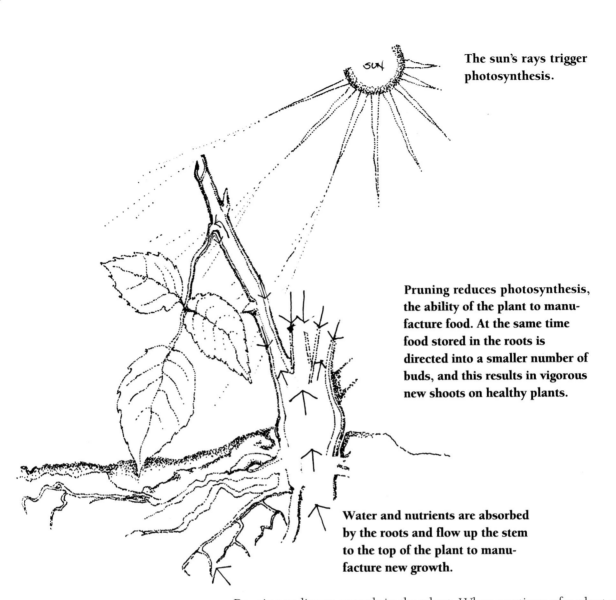

The sun's rays trigger photosynthesis.

Pruning reduces photosynthesis, the ability of the plant to manufacture food. At the same time food stored in the roots is directed into a smaller number of buds, and this results in vigorous new shoots on healthy plants.

Water and nutrients are absorbed by the roots and flow up the stem to the top of the plant to manufacture new growth.

Pruning redirects growth in the plant. When portions of a plant are removed, it uses its remaining buds to form new stems and leaves. The food necessary to grow new parts comes, for the most part, from the root system, where much of the plants' food reserves are stored. If the root system is well established and has a good supply of food, the plant will be able to quickly replace what it has lost and even grow beyond that point. If a plant is weak and is severely pruned, it will take much more time to regain the capacity for growth it had before it was pruned. If the top growth cannot occur quickly enough to replace the food supply in the root system, the roots will starve and eventually the plant will die. It is essential, therefore, that pruning be kept to the minimum necessary to accomplish your purpose. Any more may needlessly weaken your plant.

However, don't be frightened into inaction, worried that you might harm your roses by pruning. Pruning is a useful art, allowing you to keep your roses in prime condition. By and large, the rose is a very forgiving and resilient plant.

Before   **After**

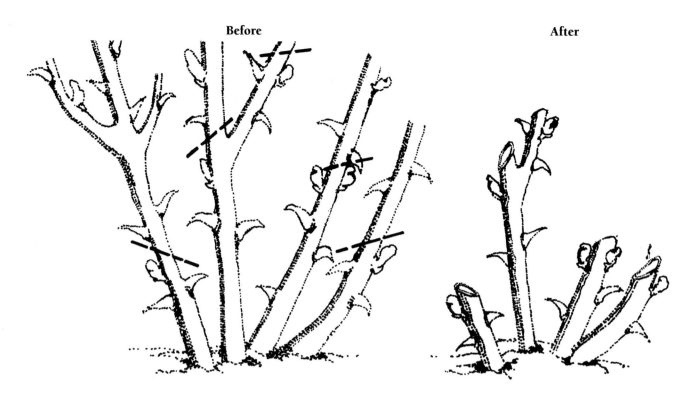

TOOLS OF THE TRADE

To do a good job of pruning, you have to have the right tools. This does not involve a major investment. Although the occasional fifty-year-old *rugosa* rose may warrant a chainsaw, the only tools generally needed are the common hand-held pruning shears or secateurs and, for large old canes, a pair of long-handled lopping shears.

Pruning shears come in several designs and in a wide range of prices. If you are a serious gardener, spend a little extra. A precision-crafted pair of pruning shears that is kept sharp is a joy to use. A poorly made pair will cause nothing but aggravation, will not cut cleanly or easily and will probably have to be replaced much sooner than a well-built pair. The best types even come with replaceable parts. (Quality, of course, should govern your choice of all gardening equipment.)

Another tool you may find useful is a small hand-held pruning saw. With their thin, sharp blades, these are excellent for getting into hard-to-prune areas or for removing branches that are too large for shears. Most of these saws cut on the pull stroke. For delicate work on smaller wood, a thin-bladed sharp knife is often the ideal tool. It is light, easy to maneuver and capable of smooth, clean cuts.

Last but definitely not least are gloves. Going into a rose bush without gloves borders on masochism. You can bet you're going to come out with blood on your hands, or worse, needle-thin thorns imbedded in your skin; if these are not immediately removed, they will remind you of your foolishness for many days. The rose represents both the joy and the pain of love in literature. To a rose grower this analogy needs no explanation.

Pruning back a newly planted rose results in several stocky and vigorous shoots. Pruning to outside buds helps keep the center of the bush open.

PRUNING THE NEW ROSE

A well-grown and well-handled young rose has a healthy root system endowed with numerous small, fine roots and several sturdy stems filled with the food necessary for next season's growth. Such a young rose, if planted in good soil and kept watered, should grow well and require only moderate pruning when planted. Unfortunately, many of the roses that you purchase have been underfed, grown under poor conditions, dug carelessly with a machine set at an improper digging depth or simply allowed to dry out somewhere along the often tortuous route from the nursery to your garden.

The excitement you feel when your new roses arrive often fades when you open the package to find plants with a few dry roots and perhaps some mold growing where the tops were pruned. This scenario should be followed by emergency action. Soak your plants for at least 12 hours but not more than 24 hours. Cut off all dead wood and the top stems to only a few buds. Because the roots are going to be very slow to absorb water, they will not be able to adequately supply it to all the emerging buds and the top will most likely wither, often followed by the death of the entire plant. By concentrating all its energies into a small area close to the root system, the plant can usually supply enough water and food to the remainder for vigorous growth.

With luck your new roses will not be in such a sorry condition. For the average new rose a less rigorous pruning may do. However, as a general rule it is best to prune back a new planted rose fairly severely. By doing so you concentrate the growth in the remaining buds, which will tend to produce several strong shoots rather than many spindly ones.

When pruning your new rose, make your cuts so that the last bud will grow outward. If you leave an inward-facing bud, you will often end up with crossed branches that will need to be pruned again later. Make your cuts so that they slope slightly away from the bud. Cut fairly close to the bud so that you will not end up with a dead stub, which can become infected with canker, but not so close that the bud will be in danger of drying out. An eighth of an inch (3 or 4 mm) is about the right length.

Examine the roots before planting and prune off any dead ones. If the ends of any roots are ragged or torn, prune them off cleanly. Do not prune any more than necessary from the root system. The more roots available to the plant, the more water and nutrients it will be able to absorb and the quicker it will be able to recover from transplanting.

MAINTENANCE PRUNING

Once your new rose has established itself, a program of maintenance can begin. The question of when to prune has always been a source of debate. Successful pruning can be accomplished in either late fall or early spring. If pruning in late fall, wait until the leaves turn color and start to fall. The longer you wait, the more food will be delivered to the root system and the more vigorous your rose will be in the spring.

Pruning too early in the fall can initiate soft late growth that may not withstand hard frost and will winterkill. Most growers still prefer early spring for their pruning, and I think a good case can be made for delaying pruning till spring in the northern garden. Many of the roses we grow in the north will kill back a certain percentage each winter. If you wait till spring to prune, it will be easier to assess the amount of damage that the plant has suffered, and the plant can be pruned accordingly. The dead portions can be removed and the remainder shaped. However, spring can often be a very busy time for gardeners. If you know that time will be at a premium in the spring, by all means prune in the fall. The hardier varieties will probably not suffer. Just leave the more tender types till spring.

When you begin pruning, first take out dead or diseased portions and remove any crossed branches. If your rose has already grown larger than you wish, remove the weaker thin wood and cut back the top to the desired height. When thinning out wood, cut back to the next branch. This will create a more natural appearance and will avoid numerous stubs, which give the plant a butchered look and invite disease. The top branches should be cut so that an equal space is given to each branch. Cut to a bud that will grow into the empty spaces. As the shrub types age, it is advisable to cut out the oldest canes. This will continually rejuvenate the bush, leaving younger, more floriferous wood and helping to keep the plant within reasonable limits.

Many people feel incompetent when it comes to pruning. It is perhaps the most mysterious and least understood of horticultural endeavors. Indeed, the sorry results of unsympathetic pruning can be viewed on any street. Conversely, the result of neglecting pruning can be an overgrown tangle. If you are unsure of how to begin, try stepping back from your subject. Think how your plant should look. Is your rose a vigorous, rounded shrub? Is it a tall, wiry climber? Visualize the perfect plant (of the kind you are dealing with) and superimpose it on your specimen. Pick out and retain the main structural elements. Eliminate the growth that is superfluous to the shape you desire or that extends beyond the limits you want to impose on it. If you can work with the natural growth pattern of your subject, you will be able to achieve a harmonious result. If you are constantly fighting against the plant's growth pattern, the results will look stilted. As with so many things in life, experience is the best teacher. The more pruning you do, the more confident you will become.

PRUNING HEDGES

The first few years are critical when developing hedges. Once you have decided upon the general shape of your hedge, remove the growth that is beyond the imaginary planes of the hedge's sides and top. As the plants continue to grow, your spring pruning will be removing more material each year. It may also be desirable to prune after the first flush of flowering to remove wayward branches. Always be sure to keep the

Keep your hedge widest at the base so that the entire leaf surface receives adequate light.

base of the hedge wider than the top so that adequate light is available to the entire surface of the hedge. If you try to maintain a vertically sided hedge, or try to curve the lower edge to form a ball shape, the bottom section will not receive enough light and will become open with only the branches showing.

As the hedge ages, you should systematically remove the oldest canes in the plants. A few canes removed each year will not create large and noticeable holes, and will encourage new and more productive wood to form. Your hedge will flower better, and you will be creating enough space for light and air to reach the inner parts of the hedge.

Roses lend themselves to an informal style of hedge. Although it is possible to create a more formal geometric style with careful attention to pruning, the continual shearing needed to maintain the sharp edges of such a hedge tends to form a rather dense outer "skin," which does not allow good light and air penetration into the interior of the hedge. By pruning too often you will destroy many of the developing flower buds and your hedge will not be as colorful. If you desire a formal hedge, it is probably advisable to stick with plants that lend themselves better to this use.

If you have a sunny area where an informal hedge would be effective, roses can be a choice hedging material. With gentle shaping and careful renewal, you can maintain a cascading wall of color that will be useful and visually exciting.

PRUNING OLDER ROSES

When speaking of hardy roses, we generally mean shrub types. Many of these are vigorous, permanent elements in the landscape and will endure for decades. As they mature they gradually thicken, often becoming very dense. This can result in plants that are really empty shells. The

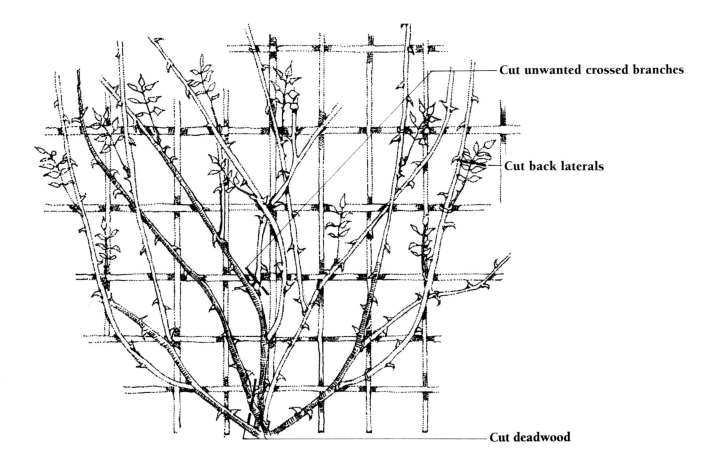

Cut unwanted crossed branches

Cut back laterals

Cut deadwood

center of the bush receives very little light. As a result, no growth occurs on the inside, and only the outside branches put on new growth.

As the pruner, your job is to thin these bushes so that light can penetrate all sections of the plant. Ideally this is an ongoing process, which begins when the plant is young and continues annually. However, you may have to deal with a plant that has been neglected and must be rejuvenated. In the worst of cases it may be advisable to tear out the plant and either replace it or dig out a section of the plant and treat it as a small new plant. If you wish to keep the plant, you should begin by pruning out some of the older canes. This can be a tough job, requiring powerful long-handled shears or a good pruning saw, thick gloves and a great deal of determination. Prune these old canes at ground level. If the plant is very large, prune out some of the canes one year and the remainder the following year. As light penetrates into the plant it will stimulate new growth, which will tend to be more floriferous than the older growth. Gradually cut back the top of the plant as well if you wish to lower the height. Again, this may take a few years. Some old roses can be cut nearly to the ground and will rebound to form a lovely bush, but this treatment can often result in death, particularly for the slower-growing species such as the Scotch roses. Patience is definitely called for with such roses.

Keeping older roses vigorous and productive involves removing dead wood, older canes and thin or crossed branches. The top can be cut back to keep the bush tidy and compact. The severity of pruning should be guided by the health of the bush and the desired result.

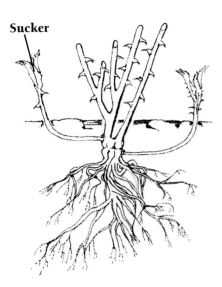

Sucker

Suckers produced by the rootstock should be removed immediately, for they divert growth from the variety and will not produce the desired flowers. Suckers from the variety can be removed or left, depending on how far you want your rose to spread.

SUCKERING PROBLEMS

A rose can be either on its own roots or budded or grafted onto a rootstock. If your rose is on its own roots, then any suckers that occur from below ground will have the same flowers and growth habits. The vigorous shoots that grow from the base of an own-rooted plant will branch and be the source of many new flowers.

If your rose is budded, however, the suckers that grow from below the bud union will be quite different from the top. It is essential that these suckers be removed as soon as they are noticed. They should be pruned off at the point from which they are growing out of the main stem. If a stub is left, it will usually grow several new shoots from the remaining buds. If pruning with shears is difficult, the shoot can be pressed down at the base until it breaks off the main stem. The injury to the stem can result in infection with crown gall or other diseases, but in actuality it rarely harms the plant and is often the most effective way to deal with suckers. Burying the graft union well below the surface will go a long way toward lessening the incidence of suckering.

FURTHER MAINTENANCE

A few pruning techniques can be used with good effect during the growing season. When a cluster of flowers has finished blooming, that section of the stem does not grow any more. New growth starts from the first vegetative bud below the flower cluster. If the old cluster is pruned off, it will stimulate this bud into active growth and within a few weeks, you can have more bloom. This is effective only on repeating roses. Removing the old blooms will also eliminate the possibility of seeds forming. The plant spends a good deal of energy on seed formation, and when these old blooms are pruned off, the plant has more energy to form new growth. Obviously, if you want rose hips you won't want to practice this technique.

Some roses leave their petals in a messy, brown lump when they have finished blooming. The removal of these spent blooms, or "deadheading" as it is called, will help to maintain a fresh look to the plant and, for the reasons mentioned above, will encourage rapid new growth.

Be on the lookout for problems such as rose galls. These swellings are formed by small insects that lay their eggs in the stems. Upon hatching, the larvae feed on the inside of the stem, causing it to swell. If allowed to complete their life cycle they will infect other roses. Cut out any unnatural swellings as soon as they are noticed. Various infections such as cankers should be cut out as soon as you notice them. These often start on dead wood such as pruning stubs or winter-injured branches. They can quickly work their way into live tissue and cause a great deal of damage if not tended.

4

Insects and
Diseases

FROM ABOVE, A CASUAL OBSERVER SEES A GARDEN MURMURING with wind through long-stemmed grasses and fragrant with newly opening roses. But between sand particles, inside last year's decaying stems and on the surfaces of countless leaves and branches, a frenetic drama is taking place with all the cycles of life and death being played out in unbelievably intricate patterns.

It is understandable that many people recoil from insect life. Its forms are so bizarre to us, its patterns so seemingly unrelated to our own. Yet the interested observer who takes the time to gain a better understanding of the insects' life cycles and how they interact in the garden will soon not only develop a fascination for them, but will better appreciate how important the diversity of insect life is to the health of our gardens and ultimately our planet.

There are a number of insects whose lifetime ambition is to suck or chew on rose bushes so that they can obtain all the vitamins, minerals and other necessities needed to produce a new generation to carry on their species. You, the gardener, want to keep your roses healthy so that you can enjoy the sensual splendors they provide. You will need to make some important decisions.

The average manual on roses contains a formidable list of chemical insecticides. Let's take a closer look at what happens to the ecology of a garden when insecticides are used.

Most insecticides kill a wide spectrum of insect species, usually by affecting their nervous or digestive systems. They will kill not only insects inhabiting the leaves and branches of the bush but other

Blackspot appears on leaves in early summer, and can infect an entire shrub.

insects and soil microbes as well when the chemicals wash into the soil. These other creatures may be playing important roles in keeping your garden healthy. As rain and sun wash away and degrade the insecticide residues, insect life returns to the sprayed areas. However, with the numbers of many insects reduced, the new balance is quite different.

Every insect has a predator. Without such predators, we would be scraping aphids off our cars in the morning. When we spray our roses we kill not only the pests we want to be rid of but their predators as well. When the surviving pests, or those arriving from other places, start to reinfest the rose bush, few predators remain to keep them under control. This often results in devastatingly high populations of pests, which, if not sprayed again, will do serious damage to your plants. Predators always reproduce more slowly than their food source, otherwise the predators would rapidly eat up their food source and die. In other words, there must always be a population of food (the pests we want to be rid of) present to maintain predator populations. The key to biological control of pests is to be able to maintain high enough populations of predators to keep pests from doing unacceptable damage to your plants.

When you spray insects with an insecticide, most of them will die, but not all. Every creature on Earth is unique, with its own set of characteristics, its own genetic code. So while most insects in a population will be killed by a particular poison, certain individuals may be tolerant to it. If they survive to reproduce, they pass on their tolerance to the new generation. After many generations, entire populations of insects may become tolerant to certain insecticides. This phenomenon is well documented and has caused much concern in conventional agricultural circles. For several years our nursery sprayed its plants with insecticidal soap. This substance is relatively nontoxic to mammals but is effective against many insect species. We noticed after several years that we seemed to need more and more soap to control our aphid populations. It took a while for the truth to sink in. We were creating a race of aphids that could tolerate soap. We had, in effect, outsmarted ourselves. Genetic diversity had triumphed. It was this fact, together with the realization that an annual spray program locked us into a spray-or-die cycle, that convinced us to re-examine our insect control program.

If you wish to adopt a nonchemical approach to gardening, you must first realize that insects are an important part of the garden. Just because it crawls or flies, an insect is not necessarily an unwanted alien. Nearly all insects in your garden are benign or actually help the gardener by keeping other insect populations in check, by pollinating your flowers, by aerating the soil or by performing any number of countless tasks that keep the garden healthy. There will always be some unwanted insects that will feed on our roses. If we are to make a serious commitment to eliminating harmful chemicals from our gardens and our agricultural community, we must change our zero-tolerance approach toward insects. We must accept a certain amount of damage as nature's due. But if you recruit your allies, this damage can be kept inconsequential.

Spiders are among the most useful insect predators.

The health of your plant is of paramount importance in reducing insect problems. A healthy plant reflects a healthy soil and a proper site. If you have looked after the basic requirements of your rose, you will have far fewer problems. An actively growing plant is less subject to insect injury. There is a growing body of evidence that plants under stress are more attractive to insects. This hypothesis is being substantiated by hard data that suggest that plants under stress emit substances and sounds that can be detected by insects. It makes perfect sense that a well-fed plant is more likely to remain healthy. Good parents feed their children well so that they do not suffer from disease. So it should be with our garden charges.

Gardeners constantly seek out varieties with beautiful flowers, unusual color, good vigor or pleasing form. The gardener who is committed to reducing the use of chemicals will pay strict attention to varieties that exhibit good resistance to insects and diseases. Roses differ dramatically in their tolerance to insects. When choosing varieties, select those roses that will make your job easier. It is encouraging that disease and insect resistance are now becoming important criteria for judging new varieties, a trend that is both welcome and long overdue.

As we sit in our gardens enjoying the pleasures they bring, we often revel in the companionship of birds. Whether calling out their melodious songs or enchanting us with their multicolored plumage, they add a charm to a garden that few will fail to appreciate. But birds are much more than colorful ornaments. They are important insect predators and consume nearly their own weight in food every day. This can have a tremendous impact in a garden. By providing good nesting sites and shrubs or trees for perching, you can enlist one of the most effective means of pest control.

Diversity in a garden is a tremendous asset. Most insects go through several phases during their lifetime. By offering an assortment of plants, you can provide sites for predators to complete their life cycles. As an example, in the fall our grapevines harbour clusters of ladybugs, which often number in the hundreds. Ladybugs prey on aphids. Although we do not know why the ladybugs are there (they do not harm the vines), they use the shelter of the grapes to gather and perhaps mate. There are countless similar examples. A healthy garden is a diverse garden.

Lastly, never underestimate your power as a predator. Often an infestation of insects can be easily controlled by simply going into your roses and picking off the culprits. Some small sucking insects can be washed off your roses with a strong spray of water. Once on the ground they are easy prey to the insects that patrol the soil surface. If you know your roses' enemies, you can be a deadly predator.

COMMON INSECT PESTS OF ROSES

If you choose to use biological methods against insects, a better understanding of insect pests is your best weapon. This section contains information on some of the more common pests of roses in northern areas.

By learning about the life cycles of these insects you may discover ways you can interfere with cycles and prevent large populations from building up in your garden. There is no doubt that we can learn from listening to the advice of experts, but remember that anyone with the ability to observe can find new solutions to old problems.

APHIDS

Aphids are perhaps the most common pest of roses. They are small, soft-bodied, usually lime green creatures that puncture the soft new growing tissues with their mouths and suck the leaf juices. Severe infestations will cause the young leaves to curl and dry up. Aphids are nearly always found on the undersides of the leaves near the ends of the shoots. As they feed, they excrete a sticky residue that is attractive to ants. Certain types of ants feed on this "honeydew" and will even protect an aphid colony from other insects. If there is a great deal of "honeydew," it will often appear blackish on the stem's surface as molds and fungi begin to grow on it.

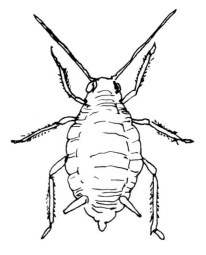

Aphid

Aphids are one of the most prolific insects in existence and also have one of the most amazing life cycles. They overwinter as tiny blackish eggs on the stems, usually near a bud. In the spring small nymphs hatch from the eggs and quickly grow to full size. These first aphids are called stem mothers. They have the fascinating ability to hatch their live young without fertilization from a male. Several generations are produced in this manner. Then a generation is born with wings. These winged aphids, called migrants, fly to other plants, some to the same species of plant, others to a summer host plant, usually an annual of some kind. These continue to produce generations of unfertilized young throughout the summer. As the days grow shorter a generation is produced that contains both winged females and winged males. The females, called fall migrants, fly to the kind of plant on which they started in the spring, then give birth to wingless females, which must be fertilized by the males to produce eggs. The eggs are laid around the buds and crevices of the plant. In the spring these hatch out and the cycle is complete.

Each aphid is theoretically capable of producing millions of aphids by the end of its cycle. The reason we are not swimming in aphids is because so many other insects and birds consume aphids. Early in the spring small solitary spiders can be observed catching and eating aphids. Soon such predators as the small gall midge and the larvae of the syrphid fly begin feeding on them. As spring progresses, the most efficient enemy of the aphid appears. When aphids begin to multiply, adult ladybugs arrive at the aphid colonies and lay their eggs. After about two weeks, tiny, opaque and ravenous larvae hatch and begin feeding. They hold the aphids in their large mandibles and suck their insides out. In only a few days these larvae grow to nearly twenty times their original size and eliminate the colony of aphids. They move from colony to colony until they reach full size. They then form a hardened shell and pupate. In two weeks or so they emerge as the winged ladybugs that most everyone recognizes. They are rounded beetles, usually red or yellow with several dark spots on their wings. Although they eat some aphids at this stage, it is their young that are every aphid's nightmare.

It is imperative that you do nothing when aphids first appear on your roses. Spraying at this stage, even with soap or similar nontoxic substances, is a tragic mistake, for the ladybug's eggs or larvae, as well as other predators, will be killed. You must grit your teeth and bear them for a while. After two weeks or so you should begin to see the small ladybug larvae at work and will notice colonies of aphids reduced to empty white husks. Once the ladybugs establish a presence, the aphids will be kept to minimal levels. If your roses are growing in a light sandy soil, you may find that ants are protecting aphids from predators. This can be alleviated by spreading a thick layer of mulch in the garden. Ants prefer dry, well-drained conditions; under a mulch there is a great deal of moisture, and the ants will not be encouraged to build their colonies.

If you are raising roses in a greenhouse, where ladybugs cannot enter, you have several options. It is possible to buy predators from companies that specialize in biological controls. Another simple but effective control is to hose plants down regularly with a well-directed and strong stream of water. Insecticidal soap can also be effective against aphids, and may be necessary in the greenhouse, where normal insect relationships are disrupted.

Roses vary tremendously in their attractiveness to aphids. One hardy old favorite, F.J. Grootendorst, is notorious as a gourmet treat for aphids. At the nursery we used to spray this variety often to try to keep the aphid population down, with only limited success. Once we let the predators do our work, we found that, after the required waiting period, our Grootendorst becomes a wonderful place to study predators in action. Now our Grootendorsts stay relatively clean all season. In contrast, a new variety, Champlain, must be last on the aphid's list of restaurants, because we never see the pests on this rose.

GALL WASPS

Gall wasps are tiny insects, usually black or orange. They are so small that a hand lens is necessary to see them well, and they are usually noticed only when the gall forms around the larval stage. The galls interfere with the flow of water and nutrients to the sections of stems above them, and occasionally large numbers of galls are noticeable. Where no control is practiced, infestations can build up to levels that can seriously reduce the vigor of your roses.

In the spring, adult wasps lay their eggs in the stem of the rose. These eggs hatch in approximately four days. Once the larvae begin feeding, the plant reacts by producing masses of tissue around the larvae. The larvae overwinter in these protective galls. In spring they pupate. When their host plants are at the proper stage, the adult wasps eat holes through the sides of the galls, emerge, then lay their eggs to begin the new generation.

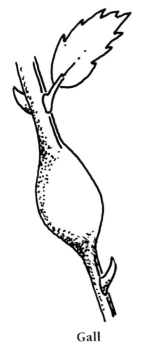

Gall

Gall wasps are seldom a severe problem. To control them, remove the galls as soon as you notice them. If you cut the gall in half with a knife, you will be able to see the larvae inside. Bury or burn the removed galls to ensure there is no threat from another generation. If you keep an eye out, you will notice galls on oak trees, goldenrod and other plants. Each species of gall wasp is specific to a certain species of plant, another testament to the immense diversity of insect life.

LEAFHOPPERS

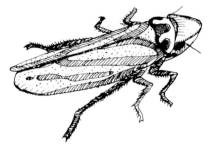

Leafhoppers are small, pale green to greenish white and very active creatures that eat foliage with sucking mouthparts. They are found on the undersides of leaves. Through a hand lens, they appear to have a large head with a somewhat triangular body, the wings coming to a high ridge along their backs. Although they are not usually a serious problem on roses, they can reduce the vigor of badly infested plants.

Leafhoppers overwinter both in the egg stage and as adults. Adults become active early in spring and often mate even before leaves appear. They push their eggs into the midrib of the leaves. The first generation appears about the time leaves become full-size, and they begin feeding by sucking sap from the undersides of the leaves. If disturbed, they will live up to their name and hop from leaf to leaf. If an infested plant is shaken, a small cloud of leafhoppers will be airborne, but they settle quickly, as they are not flyers. Several generations are produced each year, and as each leafhopper grows, it sheds its skin in the molting process. These small white skins cling to the undersides of the leaves, confirming the presence of leafhoppers.

Leafhopper populations vary from year to year. The best general advice for leafhoppers is to keep your plants actively growing. They have little effect on a well-fed, well-watered rose.

Leafhopper

MITES

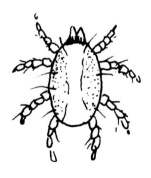

Mites are closely related to spiders. Several types can infest roses. The most common in northern gardens is the European red mite. The two-spotted mite and the spider mite can be pests in the greenhouse. Mites are quite small and you'll need a hand lens to see them. Their presence is indicated by a general yellowing of the leaves and fine web structures on the undersides of the leaves, where they feed. They are sucking insects that destroy the inside tissues of leaves.

Mites spend the winter as small red eggs on branches, around bud scars or in crevices. About the time apple blossoms are opening, the eggs hatch and the first generation begins to feed. If conditions are right, the mites will begin to multiply rapidly. Their entire life cycle can take as little as four days to complete and several generations a year may occur, although the northern gardener is blessed with a shorter, cooler growing season, which helps to limit the number of generations.

Mite

Mites can be thought of as a signal that your roses are not receiving enough water. A well-watered, vigorous rose is rarely affected by mites. Mulching roses will go a long way toward ensuring that your soil stays adequately moist. If the weather is extraordinarily dry, be sure to give your roses a good soaking. If you notice a buildup of mites, wash the foliage. Once off the leaf, mites cannot regain their place on the plant. Mites have numerous predators. Certain species of thrips have a voracious appetite for mites. They eat both the eggs and the larvae. There are also predator mites, which feed on the pest mites. Ladybugs and related insects also enjoy a good meal of mites.

One last note concerns dormant oil. This product can be sprayed on the dormant bush and will smother mite eggs during the early spring. The problem with dormant oil is that it also kills the eggs of predatory mites.

SAWFLIES

Larva of sawfly

Several species of sawfly eat roses. Sawflies are in the larval or caterpillar stage when they do their damage. They are smallish, usually about 1/2 in. (1.3 cm) long, somewhat enlarged at the front and have a characteristic habit when active of holding on to the leaf with their front feet and curling the remainder of their bodies into the air. When resting they remain curled on the underside of the leaf. Some sawflies roll the leaves as they eat them. Others eat all the leaf except the main veins. Populations vary from year to year, but, when dense, sawflies can cause a great deal of damage to rose foliage and are one of the most aggravating pests.

The adult sawfly lays its eggs on the leaves. These hatch out into tiny larvae, which begin feeding immediately. When they reach maturity the larvae fall to the ground, where they spin cocoons around themselves, remaining in the leaf litter until spring, when they emerge with wings and lay eggs to begin the cycle again.

Populations vary so much from year to year that some years sawflies may be no problem at all, while in other years they may strip whole bushes clean. Certain varieties of rose seem to attract sawflies more than others, but no good study on variety susceptibility has been done, to my knowledge. At the first sign of infestation, a thorough hand picking should be done. The more sawflies you pick, the fewer will get a chance to reproduce. A simple but effective technique of lowering sawfly populations is to beat infected rose bushes with a padded stick or to kick them. The caterpillars will drop to the ground. There, away from their habitat, they become easy prey for ground-patrolling birds and insects. Severe infestations can be treated with materials such as rotenone, pyrethrins or insecticidal soap. However, use these as a last resort, as they will disrupt other insect populations. If you have a severe infestation, it would be a good idea to work the soil around the roses deeply or add a thick layer of mulch; this will kill many of the overwintering cocoons by burying them in damp soil. Birds should be encouraged, as they are one of the primary predators of the sawfly.

SPITTLE BUGS

Spittle bugs are also known as froghoppers. They are usually noticeable only when they surround themselves with a protective layer of white foam, which looks just like spit. They have sucking mouthparts that draw sap from the stems of many plants, including roses.

They begin life as eggs, which hatch into small green nymphs. During the year they molt, gaining size as they do so. Eventually they mate and lay eggs in the fall for next year's generation.

Although noticeable, spittle bugs do little harm to roses. Occasionally a larger than normal number may appear on bushes, but these can be easily sprayed off with a garden hose or picked off by hand. I find them interesting and inoffensive and rarely take the time to destroy them.

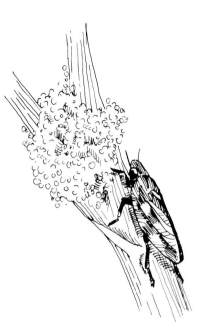

Spittle bug

OTHER PESTS

There are many other insects that attack roses, such as Japanese beetles, chafer beetles and earwigs. Patrol your roses and learn to recognize the presence of such pests. Usually a hand picking will take care of an infestation if caught early. The earwig, a nocturnal species, can be caught in traps made of strips of corrugated cardboard. They crawl into the corrugation at daybreak and can then be disposed of. Solutions to pest problems are often simple. Both the expert and your neighbor may have answers. Magazines and gardening books are mines of information. And remember, if you look with open eyes you may find your own solutions.

DISEASES OF ROSES

Roses have a reputation as troublesome plants that need to be constantly coated with various fungicides to prevent the diseases to which they are prone. In part, this reputation is deserved. Many roses, particularly in the more humid climates, fall victim to rusts, mildews and that most ubiquitous of rose diseases, blackspot. The modern hybrid teas and floribundas are quite susceptible to fungal diseases. The popularity of the hybrid teas, coupled with this weakness, has helped to give the rose its reputation as a difficult subject. The northern rose grower should take heart, however. A good percentage of the super-hardy roses are bred from the more healthy species. With careful planning, you can choose roses that will require little, if any, protection from diseases. At the same time, there are hardy roses that, though prone to some diseases, are so lovely that we cannot bring ourselves to garden without them. So a little advice is in order.

In general fungi, which are among the more serious diseases, are spread in damp conditions. While it is impossible for you to change the weather, you can help discourage fungus. The placement of roses is so important. If your roses are placed in a garden where there is very little air movement, they will take much longer to dry after a rain and will tend to hold the humidity around them. Roses placed where there is good air movement will dry out more quickly and will, therefore, have drier foliage. This will often make the difference between a heavy infestation of fungal disease and a light occurrence or even total absence of disease. Sunlight helps to inhibit fungal growth, and the availability of sun is of great importance in preventing it. Pruning roses to open up the bush will increase both air movement and sunshine within the bush.

Rose varieties differ dramatically in their resistance, or lack of resistance, to disease. If you want to stay away from fungicides, you would be well advised to choose varieties with disease resistance in mind. The descriptions and lists at the back of this book will aid you in this choice.

Cleanliness is crucial in the garden. Be sure to clean up old prunings and any dead branches. Dead branches and stubs left by careless pruning techniques often give diseases like cankers a place to take hold. From there they can move into living tissue, where they can cause severe damage.

BLACKSPOT

Without a doubt, blackspot is the most common scourge of roses. Most varieties are at least partially susceptible, and some varieties can become defoliated if it is not controlled. As its name suggests, the symptoms are black or brown spots, which begin to appear in early summer. The previous year's infected leaves release millions of spores into the air, which settle on the leaves and begin to grow. Blackspot generally shows up first on the older, lower leaves, and can eventually infect the entire shrub.

It is helpful to remove and burn or compost any infected foliage on or under your rose bushes. This will reduce the number of spores the next season. A new layer of mulch each fall will bury overwintering spores and prevent them from dispersing. Keep susceptible varieties pruned to an open shape and try to get as much air movement as possible around the plants. Peter Beales, in his book *Classic Roses*, recommends as a preventive measure using overhead sprinklers every ten days at night for periods of at least five hours. The continual washing removes many of the spores from the leaf surface. Although I have not tried this, it may be worthwhile. If you wish to grow some of the more susceptible varieties, you will need to begin a preventive spray program in mid-spring. Wettable sulfur powder provides reasonably good protection and does not have the toxicity of fungicides such as Captan or Benlate, although it does not have the residual property of these fungicides. Spray after each rain or wet period. Use a few drops of a liquid soap in your sprayer to help spread the sulfur evenly over the foliage. Without a spreader the sulfur will tend to bead and roll off the leaves. An old remedy uses baking soda (sodium bicarbonate) as a preventive spray. Mix 1 oz. (30 g) of baking soda in 10 gallons (40 L) of water and apply after damp periods. I assume the baking soda changes the acidity of the leaf surface, making it an inhospitable place for fungi to grow.

Some wonderful breeding work has been done in the past fifty years to develop blackspot resistance. Some of the most important work has been carried out by Wilhelm Kordes of Germany. Using a particularly resistant seedling, Kordes has bred numerous varieties, including some reasonably hardy modern shrub types, which are quite resistant to blackspot. Felicitas Svejda of Canada has also concentrated much of her efforts on disease resistance, and the results, called the Explorer Series, are nearly all resistant to blackspot. *Rosa rugosa* is a species commonly used in the breeding of hardy roses and is one of the most resistant to blackspot.

CANKER

Cankers usually appear as the result of poor sanitation and pruning. The cankers show up as brown or orange spots on dead wood and then spread to the adjacent live wood. By pruning out dead wood, canker can be almost wholly prevented. Use sharp pruning shears that will not tear wood, and cut cleanly and closely to the nearest live branch. Burn canker when it is found or put it in an actively working compost pile.

CROWN GALL

Crown gall is found on the roots of roses and related plants. It is caused by a bacterium (a microscopic one-celled organism) that is found in nearly all soils and that gains entrance through a mechanical injury or insect damage. The galls are irregular, bulbous growths, which over time can become quite large. There is some debate over how much crown gall harms the plants it infects, but the concensus is that it does affect the vigor and longevity of the plant. Do not use gall-infected plants if you can avoid it. If for some reason you have to use a plant that shows galls, cut off the infected root. A biological control for crown gall is now available. Before planting, the roots are dipped into a solution of water and a bacterium (*Agrobacterium radiobacter*), which inhibits the growth of the crown gall bacterium. This specific bacterium is quite safe to use.

Crown gall is a bacterial infection of roses present in most soils. The bacteria enter through wounds in the roots caused by mechanical or insect injury.

POWDERY MILDEW

Powdery mildew shows up as a grayish-white coating on the surface of infected leaves. It is particularly troublesome in late summer. Susceptible varieties can be severely harmed unless measures are taken.

Mildew, as is the case with so many diseases, tends to show up on stressed plants more than on healthy ones. Roses that are either poorly nourished or overstimulated by heavy feeding of nitrogen fertilizers are particularly prone to mildew. Plants that do not receive enough water are likewise affected. Keep your plant mulched and well fed with compost. This will promote a balanced growth that will help to prevent mildew. Place susceptible varieties in areas where they will get good air circulation. If you are growing a particularly susceptible variety, you may find it necessary to adopt a spray program using wettable sulfur. Bicarbonate of soda can be used as well.

RUST

Rust shows up as orange patches on the undersides of leaves and can, if unchecked, spread to the stems. It shows up in warm, moist weather. It does not seem to be as widespread in the more northern areas. This may reflect a difference in the types of roses grown, or perhaps rust is unable to overwinter in colder temperatures.

The life cycle of rust is much the same as that of blackspot, overwintering on leaves. If you notice rust, immediately remove and burn any infected foliage. Infected leaves should likewise be removed from the ground to prevent re-infection. A new layer of mulch will help prevent dropped leaves from dispersing spores into the air.

VIRUSES

Viruses are mysterious organisms that show up throughout the animal and plant world. Virus-infected roses will show symptoms such as yellowed and streaked leaves. The flowers may tend to be small and few, and foliage may drop prematurely. You cannot cure virus. It is most often spread when infected stock is used for nursery propagation. If you are sure you have a virus-infected rose, and not simply a rose that is suffering from pests, lack of water or nutritional deficiencies, rip it out. Sucking insects such as aphids can spread a virus to healthy plants.

Reading through a section on insects and diseases can be disheartening. Please, do not be discouraged. Our gardens are never sprayed (with the possible exception of a little sulfur on a few blackspot-susceptible varieties), and we have no serious problems. Keep your garden well tended, spend time building healthy soil, choose healthy varieties where possible, and you will be rewarded with healthy roses.

Propagation

ROSE PETALS LITTERED ACROSS THE FLOOR AND THE GENTLE click of pruning shears are some of the sights and sounds that surround me when working at my favorite pastime – propagation. The creation of new plants is one of the great pleasures of the horticultural world and is for me the primary reason for being a nurseryman. Propagation lies at the very base of horticulture. Whether from seed, cuttings, grafting or budding, the result is the same – a new generation of plants. Through centuries of trial and error, propagators have discovered the easiest ways to produce the many plants that gardeners have been interested in growing. A great deal of effort has been devoted to the rose.

Several methods of propagation are used. Each method has its own merits and problems. Some methods work for some roses and not for others. The problem of growing roses in the north throws a curve into the equation, and it is my contention that getting hardy roses on their own roots is a decided advantage. Be that as it may, all the methods described below can be successfully used to produce roses.

If you are curious about how roses are produced, or if you are interested in producing your own plants, the following section describes the various techniques in some detail. If you are not interested in the actual propagation procedures, please feel free to skip this section.

Propagating new plants is one of the pleasures of gardening.

SEEDS

Growing roses from seeds is the oldest form of propagation. As the petals of a rose unfold, the female part of the flower – the pistil – becomes receptive to fertilization by the male pollen. Usually this fertilization occurs between two plants; therefore the seed contains characteristics of both parents and is unique. These differences are usually minor within a species, although occasionally a seedling will differ substantially from the general type.

If you would like to try growing roses from seeds, collect them in the fall when the hips are fully ripe. Test for ripeness by opening the hip. The seeds inside should be turning a deep tan to brown. Immature seeds will appear whitish or very light tan. Once collected, rose seeds, particularly from hardy species, will require a period of cool, damp conditions called stratification. Seed can be planted directly into prepared earth beds or trays in the fall. If you use trays, put these in a place where they will remain near the freezing point till spring. Be sure they are protected from mice, which will make short work of your seeds. Another method is to mix 1 part seed to at least 3 parts of a barely damp, sterile medium such as peat moss. Place the mix into a sealed polyethylene bag. Put this in a refrigerator and keep just above freezing for three or four months. Be careful not to keep fruit in the same refrigerator, as stored fruit gives off ethylene gas, which may injure the seed. Germination should be prompt in warmer temperatures.

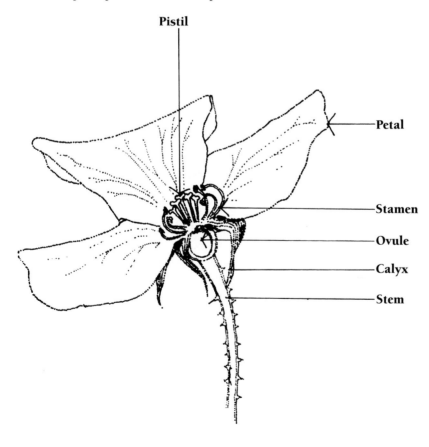

Pistil

Petal

Stamen

Ovule

Calyx

Stem

The petals of a rose attract insects, which transfer pollen formed in sacs at the tips of the stamens to the pistils. Growing through the pistil, the pollen enters the ovule, where fertilization and seed formation take place.

Seeds collected from any rose will produce seedlings that are different from the parent. For this reason, seeds are generally used only for the propagation of species roses and in breeding work.

Rose breeders have a curious but fascinating job. By crossing two varieties with desirable characteristics, they try to create different roses. The technique of breeding is simple, but proper timing and delicate hand work are needed to ensure good results.

To cross two roses, first choose the female or seed parent. This parent must be a fertile variety. Fertile roses form fruit (rosehips). Carefully remove all the petals from the flowers of your seed parent just as they begin to open. With tweezers, gently remove the tops of the stamens, which contain the pollen. Put a paper bag over these emasculated flowers for approximately 24 hours to prevent unwanted pollen from fertilizing them, then examine the pistils of these flowers. When they are slightly sticky, they are receptive. Take pollen which you have gathered from your male parent's stamens and gently brush it on the pistils of the female parent. This is usually done with a fine sable brush. If you are using several different male parents be sure to carefully wash out the brush with alcohol and dry thoroughly each time you change pollen sources. Cover the flower with the paper bag again. After a week or two the fruit will begin to swell if fertilization has been successful. Remove the bags and carefully mark each cluster, noting the male parent used for the cross. Harvest the seed in fall when the fruit turns color. Check to be sure the seeds have turned to a tan or brown color. Unripe seed will be white. Most seedlings you produce will probably be roses of little value, but the dream of creating that special new rose keeps the breeder ever hopeful.

Although few people have the patience for breeding roses, and even fewer have the time and money required for a major breeding program, innumerable varieties have been created by enthusiastic amateurs. Even if you do not create the rose of the century, the process and results can be satisfaction in themselves.

LAYERING

As a rose bush grows, it often sends out underground stems or suckers. By digging these suckers out and cutting them off from the main plant, you can easily create new plants. Among the northern roses, *Rosa rugosa* is well known for its suckering nature, and these suckers are a simple way to produce a few plants from the original. Be careful when taking suckers from a budded or grafted plant. The rootstock will be totally different from the variety on top. A careful examination of the leaves will usually show any differences. Even if a variety does not readily produce suckers, however, the process of layering offers an opportunity to the propagator.

Layering involves bending down a stem and burying it several inches into the soil with the tip protruding. A metal or wooden stake may be required to keep the layer from popping out of the ground. Be sure to keep the layer well covered and damp. Some propagators wound the base

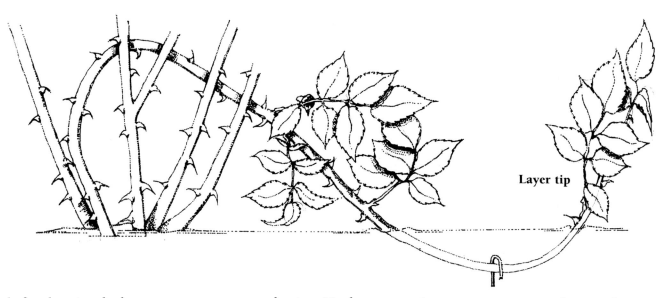

Layer tip

before burying the layer to promote root production. Hard-to-root varieties may also benefit from the application of a rooting hormone such as IBA (indole-3-butyric acid) to the wound.

The buried portion will eventually form roots. If layered in the spring, most layers will have formed enough roots so you can remove them by the fall or early the next spring. A few varieties may require longer periods. When digging these layers be careful not to injure the delicate new roots. To remove from the parent plant, cut the base of the layer cleanly off with snips, and if the top is long, cut it back to only a few buds. Plant and water well.

This technique is easy and reliable, particularly for the home gardener, as it takes no special equipment or structures. The commercial grower faces the problem of producing large numbers of plants. To accomplish this, many growers bud their roses.

Burying a stem underground stimulates roots to form. Later the layer tip, with its new roots, can be severed from the mother plant and planted.

BUDDING

Budding is the preferred technique of most commercial growers. Although it requires some practice to master the art of budding, it is essentially a simple process and can easily be performed by anyone with enough interest and a sharp knife.

Budding is the placing of a bud from the desired variety onto a root-stock. Several rootstocks are in general use today, though most growers in Europe and North America use either *Rosa multiflora* or *Rosa canina*. Thornless varieties of these species are preferred.

The rootstocks are grown for one or two years either in the field or in containers. Budding is usually performed during the period of active growth, which in most northern areas is between late June and mid-August. Prepare the rootstocks by cleaning off any adhering soil. With a sharp, thin-bladed knife, make a T-shaped incision 1 to 2 in. (2.5 to 5 cm) from the soil line; the cuts should slice through the bark, no deeper. Pry back the two corner flaps to insert the bud.

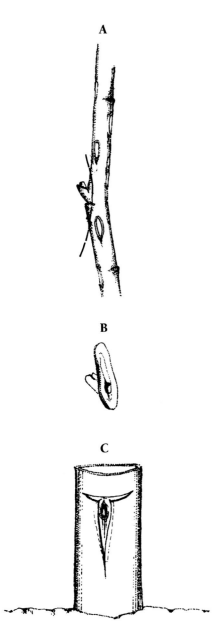

Budding
A Removing a bud of the desired variety.
B The shield bud with inner wood removed ready to insert.
C The bud inserted under the bark ready to be tied in place.

Single buds of the desired variety are cut from stems that are nearly ready to flower. The cut is made just slightly into the woody portion of the stem; the resultant shape is somewhat shield-like. Carefully remove the woody portion under the bud so that only the bark and the bud itself remain. Insert the bud, pointing naturally upward, into the incision.

After positioning, bind the bud to the rootstock by wrapping around it an elastic band or a latex tie especially made for the purpose. This wrapping ensures that there is good contact between the bud and rootstock and prevents air from getting into the wound and drying out the bud before it has a chance to unite with the stock. After a month, remove these ties and examine the bud. If it has taken it will be green and swollen. If not, it will be blackened and dead. Leave the successful plants until either winter or, preferably in colder areas, very early spring, before cutting off the tops of the stocks 3/8 in. (1 cm) above the bud. This cut should slope slightly down and away from the bud. As the bud grows, rub off any suckers from the rootstock. If not removed, these may use up much of the plant's strength.

Budding has several advantages. The use of an established rootstock furnishes the bud with tremendous vigor, and a sizable plant can be produced in a single year. The use of rootstocks also imparts vigor into varieties that, on their own roots, would remain smaller. Perhaps the major advantage, from the nurseryman's point of view, is that a plant can be produced from a single bud. This means that the required number of stock plants, from which the buds are taken, is relatively small.

There are disadvantages as well. A budded plant remains two separate plants. The rootstock is quite different from the top variety. Often the rootstock will send up suckers. The flowers on these suckers will be completely different. A double red rose suddenly has small single white flowers in its midst. Gardeners not familiar with how roses are produced often say, "My rose has gone wild." Though the flowers may be pretty, most gardeners do not want the rootstock suckers, and removing them is a constant problem that must be attended to with budded roses. A second disadvantage is a more serious problem, particularly for growers living in hardiness Zone 4 and colder. The most common rose rootstocks are not reliably hardy that far north. Even though the variety may be perfectly hardy, you may lose your plant if the rootstock suffers winterkill. Without an insulating layer of snow, frost penetrates deeply into the ground and temperatures may fall below what the rootstock can tolerate. This is especially troublesome in areas that do not receive reliable snowcover.

Plant budded roses so that the bud union is a good 2 to 4 in. (5 to 10 cm) below the soil surface. This will prevent light, which will initiate suckering, from reaching the rootstock. As well, it will give the variety a chance to form roots of its own, thereby making the plant less dependent upon the survival of the rootstock. In heavier clay soils, planting deeply may at first reduce the rose's vigor because oxygen levels will be lower, but as roots form on the upper sections, vigor will return. Plants that are pruned heavily will tend to sucker more. The reduction of the top stimulates dormant buds on the rootstock into growth to try to replace the lost leaf area. A gentler pruning regime on budded roses may therefore be advantageous.

GRAFTING

Grafting and budding accomplish the same task. Only the technique differs. Instead of placing a bud under the bark, a section of stem is placed on top of the rootstock.

Grafting is usually done on dormant rootstocks in winter or very early spring. Several different methods are used to join the variety to the rootstock. The most commonly used are the splice graft or, alternatively, the whip-and-tongue graft.

Two things are absolutely necessary to the success of grafting. You must have a razor-sharp, thin-bladed knife and tough fingers. Rose thorns are difficult to deal with at the best of times, but they can be a real nuisance when you're grafting. I find it extremely difficult to graft with gloves on. Grafting requires dexterity, and gloves just get in the way. However, if you have thin leather gloves, you may find them useful. Many rose varieties have thorns that are easily removed by gently pressing them sideways. Your job will be much easier with such roses.

To make a whip-and-tongue graft, cut the rootstock with a sharp blade just above the roots at an angle that leaves the length of the exposed surface about three times the diameter of the stock. Halfway down the cut, and with the blade pointing down the slope, make a second cut. When making this cut raise the blade just slightly from the surface, so that a thin flap is created. This cut should be no longer than one-quarter the length of the exposed surface of the initial cut. Using a section of stem containing one to five buds, make the same sequence of cuts on the bottom of the piece from the desired variety. This piece is referred to as the scion. Slide the scion down onto the rootstock. The thin flaps at the center of each cut should lock the two pieces. Fit them gently and snugly together. If the cuts are flat and the flaps are thin, there should be good surface-to-surface contact. When you fit the graft, it is essential that at least one side of the union have the cambiums aligned. (The cambium is the thin green layer just under the bark.) This is where cell division occurs and therefore where the two sections will knit together. Without proper alignment, the cells will not be able to connect, and the graft will fail. If the scion and rootstock are different sizes, make certain at least one side is aligned.

Once you have locked the two pieces together, bind them tightly with a budding rubber, masking tape or even string. When tying, be careful not to shift the alignment. Once tied, brush on a grafting wax to seal the graft. This will prevent the graft from drying out before healing takes place. Several grafting waxes are available on the market. If you are unable to find a commercial preparation, melted paraffin wax will work. We make up our own mix of 1 part rosin to 2 parts beeswax. This must be heated to be workable. (Rosin, which is the hardened gum of

Whip-and-tongue graft

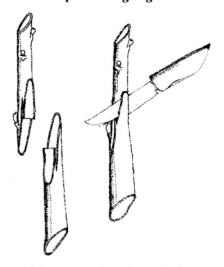

Healthy material, a sharp knife to make flat, clean cuts, and good alignment of the inner bark (cambium) are the essential elements of successful grafting.

Wedge graft

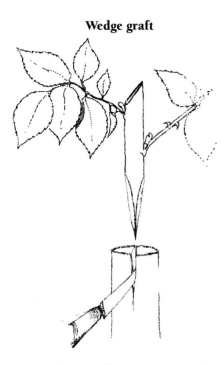

A simple and effective method of grafting, particularly on small material in the greenhouse.

certain pines, is becoming increasingly difficult to find.) Place your grafts in a cool place until you are ready to plant. Be sure that the roots are kept slightly moist.

There is a variation of the grafting process that we have found very useful. This technique is used in the greenhouse, but could be adapted to a coldframe or humidity tent. We collect sticks of both the desired rootstock and the variety in late spring and summer. Only slightly hardened, new wood is used, and this should be vigorous and reasonably thick. First remove the leaves from the rootstock sticks. Cut these sticks into sections 3-4 in. (8-10 cm) long, being sure to keep track of which ends are top and which bottom. Using a sharp knife, make a vertical cut down into the center of the top of a rootstock section. This cut should only be 1/2 in. (1.3 cm) deep. Next cut a section of the variety stick, leaving 2 or 3 leaves on each section. Slice the base of the variety section into a 3/4 in. (2 cm) long wedge. Using the tip of the knife to open the top of the rootstock section slightly, insert the wedged end of the variety into the cut, aligning the cambium layers as you do so. Push the wedge far enough so that it is snug, but not so far that it will split the rootstock section. If properly made, the graft will be snug enough without needing to be tied.

Dip the base of the completed graft into a rooting hormone. We usually use a 0.2% IBA talc powder preparation, but a similar-strength liquid hormone will work. Gently stick the cutting into a rooting medium, which should be clean and perfectly drained. A mixture of 4 parts perlite to 1 part peat works well. Clean sharp sand will work as well. If kept sufficiently moist and warm, this grafted cutting will root within two or three weeks. Once rooted it can be potted up until it is sufficiently acclimatized to be planted outdoors.

Grafting is a reasonably simple and rewarding technique for producing roses. Like budding, it creates plants that are the union of two different varieties, and the problems of suckering and rootstock hardiness are the same. On the whole, grafting is somewhat more reliable than budding when done on rootstocks growing in the field. Newly budded roses can suffer winterkill in areas with very low winter temperatures, especially when there is no snowcover. Grafting is one of the oldest propagating methods for roses, and it is still one of the most dependable.

CUTTINGS

Nearly all varieties of roses can be rooted from cuttings. Some are easy to root, while others are difficult. Most fall in the middle. Yet this simple technique is rarely used by commercial growers because budding and grafting methods are more economically advantageous.

There are two general types of cuttings – softwood and hardwood. The names refer to the condition of the wood when the cuttings are taken. Softwood cuttings are taken in spring and summer, when the wood is actively growing and fairly soft. Hardwood cuttings are taken when the plants are dormant and the wood is quite firm. The vast majority of rose cuttings are softwood. It is my experience that hardwood cutting propagation in the north is usually unsuccessful. In England, where winter temperatures are mild, hardwood cuttings are stuck directly in the ground and usually root by spring. In our cold winters, this technique usually fails, and we confine our work to softwood cuttings. The process of rooting rose cuttings is quite simple. What is needed is an understanding of the environmental requirements necessary to keep the cutting healthy until it is ready to be put out as a rooted plant.

Collect softwood cuttings as soon as the first flower buds form in the late spring or early summer. Cuttings taken from stems that are just about to flower consistently have the highest percentage of rooting. Gather your cuttings when conditions are cool. Morning is a good time, as the stems have not been wilted by the sun. Never let cuttings dry out. Move them quickly into a cool place and sprinkle with water immediately.

Take great care in selecting your cuttings. You will not succeed without healthy cuttings. Cuttings should be collected from well-fed, actively growing and disease-free plants. A healthy cutting has an adequate supply of nutrients in its tissues to sustain it until it roots. Diseases or insects can interfere with the cutting's ability to function properly. Cuttings with insects such as aphids on them can cause havoc in the greenhouse. We soak all cuttings for a few minutes in an insecticidal soap dip before rinsing them. Insecticidal soaps are nontoxic to mammals but kill most insects in short order.

The availability of material and the number of plants you want to produce determine how large a cutting you take. Most roses will form roots on small cuttings with only one or two leaves. If material is available though, larger cuttings are preferable. A cutting 4 to 8 in. (10 to 20 cm) long will make a much stronger plant than a smaller cutting. Cut any flowers or flower buds off the tips. While the cut is still fresh, dip the base of the cuttings in rooting hormone. When using talc preparations of rooting hormone, be sure to dip only the very bottom of the cuttings in the hormone and shake off any excess. Too much hormone can burn them. When using liquid hormone preparations, be sure to dip the base only for as long as recommended. Softwood rose cuttings do not require a strong hormone concentration. Use a 0.2% IBA preparation (#2). Stronger concentrations can burn the cutting.

Stick the cuttings in a rooting medium. A rooting medium serves two purposes. It holds the cutting in place and provides enough moisture around the base to aid the rooting process. An excess of moisture, however, can cause the base to rot. The ideal medium, therefore, has perfect drainage yet holds enough water to keep the cutting moist. I have found that a mixture of 4 parts perlite to 1 part peat moss works well. Most references I have read recommend 1 part perlite or sand to 1 part peat. Our experiences with rooting mediums like these were disastrous. We lost crop after crop from rot. We gradually decreased the peat content until we arrived at the 4 to 1 mix. The roses will root in straight perlite, but once roots form they seem to need some organic material to toughen up. Roots grown in straight perlite do not seem to survive transplanting as well as roots grown in a perlite-peat mixture. Although perlite is an ideal material, if you cannot obtain it, use clean sand. Sand has been the material of choice for centuries. Just be sure it has no organic residues. These organics harbor pathogens, which can cause rotting.

A great deal has been written about the use of fertilizers in rooting mediums. The rooting medium itself is sterile; therefore, when the cutting roots there are no nutrients to absorb, and the cutting essentially feeds off itself. Organic fertilizers such as compost present problems when used in rooting mediums, for they can contain life forms that may feed on the injured portions of the cutting and may eventually rot it. It would seem that fertilizer added to the medium might help to feed the cutting until it can be potted up in a soil mix. However, free nitrogen in the medium before the cutting has rooted promotes the growth of a range of microscopic life forms, some of which will feed on the injured tissues at the base of the cutting and increase the likelihood of rot.

The compromise we have adopted is to use a slow-release form of fertilizer that is activated by moisture and temperature. These fertilizers are made of granules coated by a thin layer that releases the nutrients gradually throughout the growing season. Although not as readily available as the more common fertilizers, slow-release fertilizers can be found in many garden centers and nurseries.

When mixed in small quantities in the rooting medium, a slow-release fertilizer can be very beneficial. When the cuttings are first stuck, the coating around the individual grains of fertilizer prevents any appreciable amount of nutrient from escaping into the medium. When the first roots appear after about two weeks, the levels of fertilizer are sufficient to provide nutrients to the new roots. Before we began using this slow-release formula, many of our cuttings would form roots, then drop their leaves and die. The use of a slow-release fertilizer prevents this, and the cuttings are able to begin growth as soon as roots emerge.

Creating the proper environment for cuttings is critical to the success of the whole operation. What the propagator needs to achieve is a humidity level that is high enough to prevent the cutting from wilting yet not so wet that it will saturate the rooting medium and leach out nutrients from the leaves. Several innovations in propagation equipment have provided commercial growers with systems that create a fog or fog-like environment in the greenhouse. These systems spray a very fine mist that floats in the air and surrounds the cuttings with moisture without soaking the cuttings and medium. The older type of overhead mist nozzles use more water and tend to keep the cuttings so wet that they run with water. This system can be used with success, but it is not as desirable.

Most gardeners do not have fancy systems or greenhouses in which to propagate their cuttings. There is a simple alternative. A small cold-frame structure built on the north side of a building can be a useful propagating facility. By placing it on the north side, it will not receive direct sun, which can heat up the interior and raise temperatures to dangerous levels, thereby drying out the cuttings. During the daylight hours, keep the cuttings slightly damp by occasionally spraying with a hose or a simple set of built-in nozzles. If the coldframe is tight, the humidity can be kept high with only a few mistings a day. Hot days may require more mistings. Once cuttings begin to root, the top of the coldframe can gradually be raised for short periods until the cuttings become acclimated to the drier atmosphere, at which point they can be transplanted.

Temperature is important in determining how speedily your cuttings will root. Reasonably high temperatures will speed the process of cell activity. Once above 88°F (30°C), however, growth slows down. Higher temperatures can be detrimental to the cuttings. Cuttings that have been allowed to dry even for as short a time as 15 minutes may be irreparably damaged. This is why many amateur propagators fail in their attempts to root roses. The process is simple, but constant vigilance is necessary to succeed.

Heat from below can also be an advantage when rooting cuttings. This heat can be provided by hot water pipes or electric resistance cable run in the bed under the cuttings. A constant temperature of 70-77°F (22-25°C) is ideal. We have found that *Rosa rugosa* hybrids respond well to bottom heat, particularly when cuttings are taken early in the growing season.

Once the cuttings have produced several strong roots they should be potted. Move your newly transplanted roses into an area where you can water frequently to help the new plants gradually adjust to the drier atmosphere. Many plants are lost at this stage, and nothing hurts more than to have gone through all the trials of rooting your cuttings only to see them dry up after transplanting. It is also a good idea to partially shade your newly rooted plants to keep temperatures from becoming too high and drying out the leaves. At this point the leaves are "lazy." On their surfaces are small pores, called stomata, which open and close to regulate the amount of water in the leaves. In the high humidity of a greenhouse or coldframe they seem to grow sluggish and do not respond as rapidly to changes in humidity levels. If the plant is put in the hot sun, the stomata stay open, the moisture in the leaves escapes and they dry up. If given several days of slow adjustment after removal from the greenhouse or coldframe, however, the leaves start functioning normally and are ready to face the harsh realities of sun, wind and heat.

At the nursery these plants are moved out into the field to grow for the remainder of the season and through the next year before they are sold. At home you can plant these young roses in their intended site. Be careful to keep them adequately watered. A mulch will help to ensure they do not dry out. Once firmly established in the soil, the rose will need only routine care.

It is my contention that a rose on its own roots is a superior plant, particularly when placed in a northern garden setting. The aggravating problem of rootstock suckering disappears. The problem of incompatibility between the rootstock and the variety is nonexistent. Most important, you need only worry about the hardiness of the variety. Many of

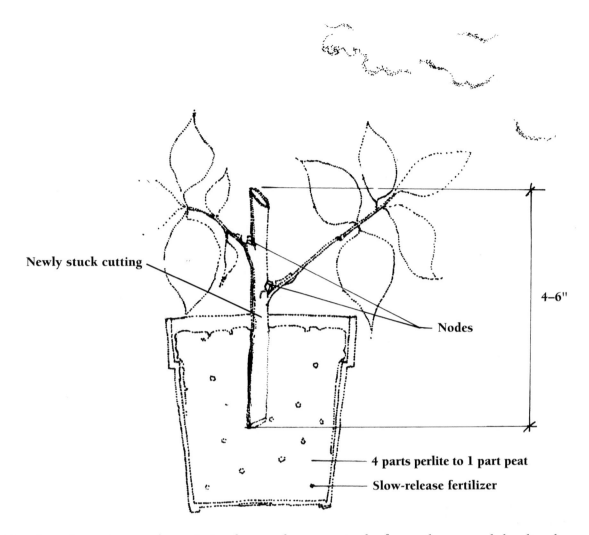

Newly stuck cutting

Nodes

4–6"

4 parts perlite to 1 part peat

Slow-release fertilizer

A well-drained and sterile rooting medium, rooting hormone and high humidity are necessary to root a cutting. It is a simple process, but one requiring unfailing diligence.

the varieties that can be grown in the far north are much hardier than the rootstocks on which they are budded. You are far less likely to lose your rose to winter injury. As well, often the rootstock will influence the hardening off process in the fall. The more tender rootstock will keep the variety growing longer into the fall than it might if it were on its own roots. Another factor that is perhaps overlooked by most rose growers is the rootstock's influence on the variety's vigor. In many cases increased vigor is not an advantage, particularly when you are seeking a rose for a small space. Many dwarf or low-growing roses become far larger plants when pushed by their rootstocks. By propagating roses on their own roots, you can be more certain of their ultimate size. These factors make the time and trouble involved in rooting roses worthwhile.

It is a regrettable fact that roses on their own roots are very difficult to find in the nursery trade. For the northern grower it is worth the search. If you have the inclination and the time, and can put together the facilities, the challenging and rewarding process of rooting roses can let you produce your own. There is no finer feeling than the pleasure of watching the first blossom unfurling on a rose bush that you have helped create.

**Dew accentuates the fluid lines
of Rheinaupark.**

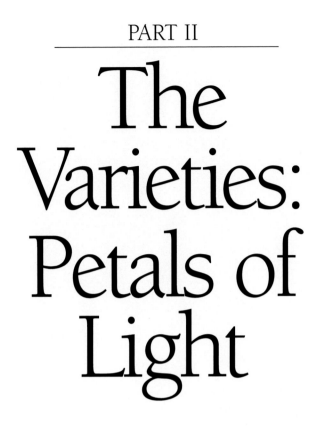

PART II

The Varieties: Petals of Light

**Henry Kelsey is the best red
climbing rose for cold areas.**

6

Climbers

Shrubs growing taller than 6 ft. (1.8 m) and
suitable for tying to supports

AÏCHA

HENRY KELSEY

JOHN CABOT

LEVERKUSEN

WILLIAM BAFFIN

AÏCHA

Parentage: unknown, Rosa spinosissima hybrid.

For me, this rose symbolizes the exciting new generation of hardy roses. When the first blooms on my plants opened, I was intrigued by their distinctive form and dazzled by their sunshine-yellow color. I would visit the plants every day to watch the newest buds unfurl and the older flowers pale to a delicate pastel.

Each flower's immense outer petals cradle five inner petals, which in turn encircle the largest grouping of stamens I have seen in a rose. Its flowers are borne on vigorous and thorny stems, which can be trained to form a spectacular climber, one that is perfectly happy to spend the winter in the chill wind. Although our plants are young, they have performed so well that I have little hesi-tation in recommending this rose for northern growers.

This is also an easy rose to grow, with healthy deep green foliage. It can be propagated with moderate success by cuttings or by budding, layering or using suckers from plants that are on their own roots. The gently arching stems create an admirably shaped bush if you prefer not to use it as a climber, and those with a nose for fragrance will delight in the perfume of this dazzling newcomer.

You may still have a difficult time finding this new rose, but make the effort. Even on a cloudy day the cheerful petals of Aïcha bring a welcome sunshine into the garden, and you will be amply rewarded for the time spent obtaining it.

HENRY KELSEY

Parentage: Rosa kordesii × hardy seedling of complex origin.

Delicate arches hugged by winding branches, clothed in lustrous green foliage and dripping with vivid red roses – Henry Kelsey is a vision of rose heaven.

This recent introduction from Agriculture Canada has long arching canes that can be tied up and used as a climber. If left to grow naturally, Henry Kelsey is a low, arching, somewhat pendulous bush. I have used it as a medium-height ground cover, although it is perhaps a bit sparse for this purpose. When tied up, it makes an admirable climber. A well-grown Henry Kelsey will send up fantastically vigorous long shoots, which in just a few seasons will top an arch or trellis.

Vigor alone makes Henry Kelsey a standout, but the deep red petals, contrasting with the golden yellow stamens, create an irresistible lure. Large clusters appear from early summer until the first frosts. The intense red of the new petals gradually fades to a deep rose as the blooms drop cleanly off the bush.

Henry Kelsey is highly resistant to powdery mildew. Although it is not immune to blackspot, this fungal disease is not a serious threat. This rose can be left on the trellis in Zones 4 and 5 without serious winter injury. It is easy to propagate from softwood cuttings or layering.

Henry Kelsey is the best red climbing rose available for cold areas. It is superior to existing red climbers, and it should be in every collection where such a rose is desired.

JOHN CABOT

Parentage: Rosa kordesii *Wulff* × *(Masquerade* × *Rosa laxa).*

Many years ago I walked up to a display of roses at the Agricultural Research Station near us. I was so enthralled by what I saw that I asked permission to take a few cuttings. Several roses stood out among the many in the group. One in particular, labelled L07, caught my eye. The bush was a powerfully upright yet arching plant covered in symmetrical double blooms that were a deep orchid pink, almost red. Its robust, healthy glow convinced me that here was a rose worth watching. Several years later I read that a new rose called John Cabot had been released, originally grown as seedling L07.

John Cabot has helped to set new standards for hardy roses. Its symmetrical, robust form, coupled with its long blooming season and excellent disease resistance, make it one of the most important new roses for northern gardens. It is also reasonably easy to propagate from softwood cuttings. It is difficult to know whether to call John Cabot a vigorous shrub rose or a climber, because it can be either. Since roses with such vigor and long flowering season are rare, I have decided to include it with the climbers.

LEVERKUSEN

Parentage: Rosa kordesii × *Golden Glow.*

The history of superior hardy roses is in many ways a history of those breeders who have spent many dedicated years developing them. If you take the time to see where many of the hardy roses come from, the name Wilhelm Kordes appears often enough to make you wonder how one man could have found enough time to accomplish such a monumental achievement in a lifetime. Following in his footsteps, his family business has continued a tradition of superlative breeding work. The number of roses released by this firm is staggering, and many remain important. One rose, Leverkusen, is assuming more importance each year.

After seeing the first blooms of this tremendously vigorous bush, I kept my fingers crossed the first winter, hoping that it would survive. A few tips were burnt that winter, but the amount of injury was small. The plant did even better during the second winter. Although we have observed this plant only a few years, I feel confident enough in its merits to include it on our list of recommended hardy roses.

Leverkusen is a testament to the vision of its creator. Kordes realized the importance of producing roses that were not only beautiful but healthy. The foliage of this plant is always glossy and free of blackspot and mildew. The bush is rampantly vigorous, making it a candidate for a climber, at least in Zone 5. Even if not trained, it makes a wonderful hedge or specimen plant.

I have saved the best for last: the flower. Lemon-chiffon buds opening to a creamy, pale yellow create a warm glow to this rose that is enhanced by its informal, semi-double form and delicate scent. A rose in the classic old style. And we can enjoy them all season, for Leverkusen repeats until well into the fall, and is easy to root.

WILLIAM BAFFIN

Parentage: open pollinated seedling of L48 (Rosa kordesii Wulff × complex hardy seedling).

One of my favorite pastimes is watching how people react when they walk through the gate of our garden and look out across the multitude of shrubs, perennials, vines and evergreens that lies before them. In the late summer, as many of the roses and daylilies are waning, most eyes are instantly drawn to a corner where a semi-circular hedge of robust rose bushes grows.

Of all the climbers we have grown William Baffin has impressed us most, not only with its strawberry ice cream flowers but also with its vigor and health. As a bush William Baffin is upright and slightly arching, with a dense, full look – perfect for a tall hedge. As a climber it is unmatched. Your only problem may be to keep its vigor from overfilling the trellis with strong, thick canes. You certainly will not have to worry about fussing over this rose. Unless your winter is truly arctic, you will be able to grow William Baffin. We have never seen an injured bud in our garden. And it's healthy – no blackspot, no mildew, no rust – and easy to root from softwood cuttings.

The loose, carefree blooms of William Baffin are charming. They are certainly not aristocratic. If you are looking for a healthy, ironclad hardy, robust rose that is blanketed by clusters of bloom throughout the entire season, this is the rose for you. William Baffin should assume an important place in the northern garden.

**William Baffin is ideal for a
tall hedge.**

Harison's Yellow is an adaptable rose that survives the frigid temperatures of a northern winter.

7

Tall Shrubs

Shrubs growing up to 6 ft. (1.8 m) or more

ALEXANDER MACKENZIE
BLANC DOUBLE DE COUBERT
CARMENETTA
CHLORIS
CONSTANCE SPRY
F.J. GROOTENDORST
FRÜHLINGSGOLD
GOLDBUSCH
HANSA
HARISON'S YELLOW
JOHN DAVIS
MRS. ANTHONY WATERER
ROBUSTA
SARAH VAN FLEET
SCABROSA
SCHARLACHGLUT
THÉRÈSE BUGNET
WILLIAM LOBB

ALEXANDER MACKENZIE

Parentage: Queen Elizabeth × (Red Dawn × Suzanne o.p.).

Alexander Mackenzie is a well-tailored rose. Its foliage and form create an elegant backdrop for the flowers, which embroider the bush more skillfully than any threads could hope to do. The bush is upright and symmetrically arching.

Tall and tulip-like, the deep raspberry buds open to reveal a classic form with delicately folded petals curling back as the first warm days of summer draw them out. The petals gradually mellow to a deep, warm pink, and exude the fragrance of fresh-picked raspberries. On our hillside they have three successive waves of bloom during the season, the last flowers fading in September's first light frosts. After a wet period you will sometimes find the exterior petals browning, and the odd imperfect petal may appear at the flower's base. Aside from a few stray petals, Alexander Mackenzie is a most gratifying rose to grow.

The most welcome news is that this rose is a remarkably hardy plant. It has impressive resistance to disease, although it does attract leafhoppers and sawflies. The leaves have a waxy sheen that exudes health. The deep reddish new foliage is an added extra of this extraordinary rose, complementing the dark green of the older leaves. It can be layered or propagated from softwood cuttings.

If I told you I know of a rose that is hardy, healthy, beautiful *and* fragrant, wouldn't you be tempted? Alexander Mackenzie is an important new rose.

BLANC DOUBLE DE COUBERT

Parentage: Rosa rugosa × *Sombreuil.*

This large white rose is one of the first that comes to mind when we think of fragrance. Like wines, roses have their degrees of sweetness. Blanc is definitely a sweet port, with a fragrance so strong you can actually overdose by inhaling deeply inside a freshly opening bloom.

The loosely arranged petals, clustered around the yellow center, reflect the wayward vigorous shoots of this bush, which in time, and particularly in groupings, forms an impressive hedge or informal bed. The first bloom resembles a swarm of large white butterflies resting on the deep green foliage and is a sight even for eyes jaded by the many flowers of spring. The blooms do not leave the bush till the nights get their first real chill. Although not as numerous later in the season, Blanc always has a perfumed treat for the garden wanderer.

If you are in search of a delicate, well-mannered rose, look elsewhere. Blanc is a robust grower and a thicket-type bush, sending suckers outward as it grows. This very vigor makes Blanc a valuable plant for stabilizing steep banks or creating hedges and large beds. Softwood cuttings root relatively easily if taken early in the season just before flowering, and suckers can be used.

Unless you live where winter temperatures can freeze spit before it hits the ground, you stand a chance of overwintering Blanc. This adaptable and healthy rose has been one of the most important of the truly hardy roses.

CARMENETTA

Parentage: Rosa glauca (*formerly* Rosa rubrifolia) × Rosa rugosa.

If I lived where there were only fifty frost-free days a year and where winter temperatures routinely plummet to -40° (F or C) or colder, I would be limited to growing only a few of the hardiest varieties. Carmenetta would probably be one of them.

Carmenetta is a seedling of the Red Leafed rose, a species with a lovely arching form and a reddish foliage that gives the plant a warm glow, even when not covered by its star-shaped single pink blooms. The breeder of this rose gently dusted pollen from a *rugosa* rose onto the centers of the flowers on his Red Leafed rose. He carefully saved each seed from this union, then planted and observed each as it grew. After several years one seedling in particular caught his eye most often. It was a robust arching plant with flowers that were noticeably larger than that of its siblings. Nearly ninety years later I grow this same seedling in my garden, and so can you.

The red pigments that run all through this rose also color its bark, so that the deep red new growth colorfully accents the graceful silhouette of Carmenetta in the snow. Those pigments also suffuse the veins of each flower petal, making the entire plant an enormous pink bouquet. Like first romance, Carmenetta does not last as long as we wish, but the experience is enough to make us long for our next affair. The fruit is oval, reddish purple, and Carmenetta is easy to propagate from softwood cuttings.

CHLORIS

Parentage: unknown, Rosa alba *hybrid.*

The search for the thornless rose has a long history, and even today the goal of a first-class thornless rose occupies many a breeder. Some thornless roses are available to growers. The most famous one is the Bourbon rose Zéphirine Drouhin. While hardy by most standards, this rose is not tough enough for the coldest areas. There is a rose, however, that is virtually thornless, exceptionally hardy and exceedingly beautiful. Its name is Chloris.

Chloris is a diaphanous pink that seems nearly transparent. The petals are loosely arranged around an infolded grouping of petals that form a neat button at the center. The scent of the soft, double blooms is exquisite.

This rose is easy to grow and root from softwood cuttings. It is quite vigorous, with long, deep red, erect stems that look as good after the bitter cold winter as they did when the first snow bedded them down. The foliage is of the deepest green and is a picture of health, giving the plant presence even when it's not in bloom. And on top of this, when you go collecting a fresh spray of flowers for your table, the beast will not bite.

CONSTANCE SPRY

Parentage: Belle Isis × Dainty Maid.

I received my first Constance Spry several years ago but did not know it. When my plants began to bloom I was overwhelmed by this rose's unusual, perfect form and superb color. Only it was not the variety I had ordered. Nevertheless, I told the propagators to take cuttings. Several years later I ordered Constance Spry. When it began blooming I immediately suspected that our orphan was the very same rose. Receiving the wrong rose is exasperating for any gardener, but for the nurseryman it represents a real danger, for many of these roses take two years to begin blooming. If they are not caught in time, the wrong rose can be put into the nursery beds and later sold, followed by a very embarrassing period of explanations.

If you are a peony fan, then Constance Spry will be welcome in your garden. Its beautifully formed, round, cupped flowers truly resemble the peony and are large enough to make you stop for a second look to be sure that this is a rose. The flower is a pure, bright pink with a delightful fragrance that has been likened to myrrh, and the foliage is gray-green and abundant.

In warmer climes this rose is used as a climber. Although it suffers some winterkill in our garden, making it a poor climber, it is tough enough to form a very tidy shrub. Spring pruning can make this somewhat sprawling, vigorous plant into a handsome part of the landscape. This was one "mistake" that we are glad to have in our garden.

F.J. GROOTENDORST

Parentage: Rosa rugosa × *Mme. Norbert Levavasseur.*

F.J. Grootendorst has a prolific display of small, soft red flowers, more reminiscent of carnations than roses. Its long season, hardiness and thrusting canes covered in deep green foliage have ensured it a place in the northern garden. This rose has also become an intriguing mystery to me. It has been assumed that Grootendorst was found by a Dr. De Goey from Holland in 1918. Recently, however, I read these lines from *Horticultural Horizons* by Canadian breeder Frank Leith Skinner:

"My first attempt at plant breeding was with roses. Either in 1907 or 1908, I crossed *Rosa rugosa* with one of our wild roses and this success encouraged me to try some other crosses. I used pollen of Mme. Norbert Levavasseur on *Rosa rugosa* and obtained three seedlings, one of which was identical with the variety that was to be brought out about fifteen years later as F.J. Grootendorst. It was not, however, entirely hardy, usually killing back to within a foot of the ground each winter, although it did flower quite freely on the wood that survived.

"I rather liked this rose and thinking it might do well at Ottawa I dug it up, together with some other plants and sent them on to Dr. W.T. Macoun at the Central Experimental Farm, Ottawa. The same day I also sent some plants to Professor F.W. Brodrick at the Manitoba Agricultural College. Both parcels were sent by the same railway from Roblin; no parcel reached Professor Brodrick, and the plants which he should have received were delivered to Dr. Macoun. It was too late by this time to bother about the parcel that had disappeared.

"I wrote to F.J. Grootendorst, Boskoop, Holland, after I had seen the Grootendorst rose and asked if he would care to let me know its parentage as I too was engaged in breeding roses and other plants suitable for our climate. In his reply he stated that his firm had bought the rose with the privilege of naming it, and that it was a chance seedling that had appeared among a batch of *rugosa* seedlings raised by a small grower near Boskoop. Since then I have seen it listed as having been raised in 1918 by Dr. Goey, the result of a cross between *Rosa rugosa* and Mme. Norbert Levavasseur. Mr. Herman Grootendorst told me that they had had this rose before 1914 but had been unable to market it owing to the war. There is, apparently, some doubt as to who did propagate the rose known as F.J. Grootendorst. I definitely raised an identical rose and its parentage was *Rosa rugosa* × Mme. Norbert Levavasseur."

A good story. I will let the historians find the truth. Whatever the verdict, F.J. Grootendorst will remain famous for its beauty and toughness.

FRÜHLINGSGOLD

Parentage: Joanna Hill × Rosa pimpinellifolia *hybrid.*

I was once given a bundle of root pieces of the variety Harison's Yellow by a generous and dynamic lady, who was also a first-class gardener. When the plants began blooming I noticed that one was quite different. Although yellow, it was a larger and paler rose. For many years this orphan remained a mystery to me. Then one day, while reading through Beale's *Classic Roses*, I saw a picture of Frühlingsgold and immediately knew it was my mystery rose.

True to its name, Frühlingsgold ("spring gold") helps to usher in the rose season. Its large semi-double blooms are an ethereal primrose yellow. Our type of soil adds mysterious wisps of pale pink, giving the barest hint of an accent to this soft pastel flower.

The bush is a strong and resourceful plant. As this rose matures, the branches create a pattern of numerous intersecting arcs. Even these stems reflect their flower's color, the green of the new growth being suffused with goldenrod yellow until time fades them gray. The leaflets of Frühlingsgold have edges that fold under, giving the rose's foliage a soft look that becomes a quilted backdrop for the flowers.

Frühlingsgold is often budded or grafted. It can be difficult to root. Use clean, vigorous wood that is setting flower buds, the earlier in summer the better, and stick in high humidity, but do not keep wet. When roots appear, transplant as gently as possible into a good growing medium.

In the garden this rose exhibits uncommon hardiness and the tips seldom suffer from frostbite. It seems to succeed even in rather poor, dry soils, although with care and good soil, you can grow blooms whose delicate pastels will enroll you as a new member of the Frühlingsgold fan club.

GOLDBUSCH

Parentage: unknown, Rosa eglanteria *hybrid.*

Although artists throughout the ages have tried to capture the essence of roses in their works, a bloom from a rose such as Goldbusch relegates all these attempts to the class of pale imitations. We paid very little for our Goldbusch, but this work of art is now among our garden's most cherished possessions.

Goldbusch was bred from the Eglantine or Sweet Briar rose, and its long arching canes reflect its heritage and make it a good candidate for a climber. Like the Sweet Briar, its foliage is sweetly scented. Even more impressive to me is the healthy glow of the medium green leaves. Little if any blackspot or mildew mar the backdrop they provide for the exquisite blooms. This lovely rose is also easy to root from softwood cuttings.

The tight pyramidal buds are a deep honey color with just a hint of orange. They open into a semi-double flower of alluring bright yellow. The fragrance is a fitting asset of this wonderful flower.

It is difficult to find any faults with this captivating rose. It seems quite hardy, although I doubt it will survive in the very coldest sites.

HANSA
Parentage: Rosa rugosa *hybrid.*

Venerable bushes of Hansa grow on innumerable old farmsites throughout the countryside where I live. In the suburbs, younger plants have appeared, taken there by the sons and daughters of those who first planted these roses. For many, this variety represents the term "hardy rose." These long-lived plants form immense mounds, often hollow on the inside from lack of light. Throughout the early summer, they bloom with large mauve-red flowers. It is generally very healthy with no serious insect problems. Its beauty, tenacity, hardiness and ease of propagation have made Hansa common, the highest compliment in horticulture.

One of the most enduring appeals of Hansa is the heady draught of fragrance on a still summer evening. Although you can eat the petals, those after more substance will delight in chewing around the core of a Hansa rose hip. This rose produces a profusion of deep orange-red fruits that are large and meaty, just right for the makers of rosehip tea, those who cherish late autumn color, or the birds.

HARISON'S YELLOW
Parentage: Rosa pimpinellifolia × Rosa foetida persiana.

Of all the colors in roses, yellow is the color that northern growers desire the most, perhaps because it is the most difficult color to obtain in a hardy rose. This fact makes Harison's Yellow a special rose, for it is both deep yellow and incredibly hardy.

Strangely enough, this winter-hardy rose was developed in Texas, quite far from the numbing cold of the north. An amateur rose fancier named Harison crossed the Scotch Briar rose with the Persian Yellow, another hardy yellow rose, and Harison's Yellow was the result. Most people consider this variety the original "yellow rose of Texas," made famous by the well-known song of the same name. Whether in the scorching heat of a Texas summer or in the deep freeze of a northern winter, this adaptable rose has earned a place in the hearts of many.

Harison's Yellow is an early bloomer like its parents. The numerous small buds turn themselves inside out to reveal the sulfur yellow petals hidden within. The delicate branches of this unassuming shrub suddenly become arching sprays of sunshine. This tropical display lasts but a few weeks and we are left with a rather coarse and humble bush for the remainder of the season, but, like the sun, Harison's Yellow can't shine forever, and if it did, we would not appreciate its radiance.

To propagate, take cuttings early in the season from wood just setting flower buds. Keep in high humidity, but not overly wet. When roots appear, carefully transplant into a good growing medium and carefully harden them off to drier conditions. It is most often budded or grafted. Suckers can be used.

JOHN DAVIS

Parentage: Rosa kordesii × (*Red Dawn* × *Suzanne o.p.*).

Occasionally a rose appears that causes an instant buzz in the nursery world. John Davis cuttings were sent to our nursery several years ago and were planted in the display garden. They began blooming even as tiny plants, and by the third year we had people begging for just one plant. Try as I might, I simply could not get this rose from any of the usual sources. They were like us, trying desperately to create as many stock plants as they could. New as it is, John Davis has the makings of a star.

When they unfold, the semi-double blooms of John Davis flatten their outside petals, leaving an attractive tulip-shaped center of the remaining folded petals. They are a deep orchid-pink at this stage. Gradually the center unfolds until the blossom lies open, fading to a lighter shade of pink as it does so. Once in bloom this rose always has flowers, being close to everblooming.

The bush is vigorous but somewhat sprawling, eventually becoming a large, lax shrub. This rose could probably be successfully trained into a medium-sized climber. It is also one of our hardiest new varieties. Our specimens have never winterkilled in the slightest, and I have no doubt that it will prove hardy into the far north. As with so many of the Explorer Series roses, it is also highly disease resistant, although it attracts leafhoppers and sawflies early in the season. It can be propagated from softwood cuttings.

MRS. ANTHONY WATERER

Parentage: Rosa rugosa × *General Jacqueminot.*

It confounds me why this rose is not more popular. It has so many good features and yet remains one of the lesser known *rugosa* roses. If my words of praise encourage you to obtain this rugged and reliable variety, I will consider my efforts worthwhile.

Mrs. Anthony Waterer is an excellent grower. Its vigorous shoots reach upward and gradually arch outward to form a handsome large bush. It is a good specimen on its own or will create a tall and colorful hedge if combined with others. The healthy foliage is seldom damaged by disease and forms a green foil worthy of its blossoms.

The flowers are unusual for a *rugosa* as they are well shaped and a deep and true crimson from center to edge. As the bud unfolds, the outer petals form a circle that delightfully frames the cupped center. Emanating from these bright flowers is as lovely a fragrance as one could wish. Best of all, these richly hued blossoms are produced abundantly throughout the entire season. This rose roots well from softwood cuttings taken early in the season just before flowering.

Mrs. Anthony Waterer was introduced at the end of the last century. Discriminating growers have ensured its survival for nearly one hundred years. Perhaps at last more gardeners will be able to understand what these few growers have always known and give Mrs. Anthony Waterer her long overdue recognition.

ROBUSTA

Parentage: Rosa rugosa × *seedling.*

Fallen petals of a Robusta rose have become a meal for a scavenging beetle. Above, new crimson flowers unfold. Not all roses have this ability to repeatedly generate new flowers. Many, having performed their yearly fertility rite, pass into the summer's heat clothed only in their greenery. Robusta belongs to that elite and much prized group of roses that are remontant, or repeat-blooming.

Although Robusta is simply formed, the size and crimson color ensure that this rose will take a back-seat to no others. It is indeed a robust rose, and easy to root from softwood cuttings. Viciously thorned stems thrust upward from the plant's base to form a tall, vertical shrub, well suited to frame smaller plants. The combination of large, textured dark green foliage and wine-red stems is visually exciting as well. A delicate, fruity fragrance emanates from Robusta, so those who garden for their nose as well as their eyes will not be disappointed.

A 50% winter killback is average with this rose in our garden, but it inevitably makes a spirited come-back, and by mid-July we are tipping our hats to the skilled hands of Wilhelm Kordes for giving us another healthy and incredibly lovely rose.

SARAH VAN FLEET

Parentage: Rosa rugosa × *My Maryland.*

Many people have told me that they don't bother growing shrub roses because the plants don't bloom long enough. This attitude is, sadly, a widely held one, mainly because many of the better varieties are not available to the public. Many of these roses are new in the nursery trade, and it takes many years to get enough out in the landscape to create a demand. Until recently there has been little incentive for the nursery trade to propagate shrub roses. The public seemed uninterested in the shrubs. New trends in gardening, however, have dramatically changed the situation.

Varieties like Sarah Van Fleet will go a long way toward revising people's perception of shrub roses. This plant gives a perpetual show of fragrant, clear pink, semi-double blooms. While not quite as hardy as some of its *rugosa* relatives, Sarah Van Fleet does very well in our garden even in the worst years, killing back only the top half of its vigorous, upright shoots. In warmer areas this rose will form a tall shrub. Under more northern conditions it will stay somewhat smaller, but each year's shoots are remarkably tall. It does suffer from a bit of blackspot on the lower leaves, and I have seen a touch of mildew in damp conditions. I have read that this variety is inclined to rust, although I have not seen any on our plants. Although this makes the plant sound like a mass of disease, we have found it generally quite healthy and easy to root from softwood cuttings.

SCABROSA

Parentage: A selected Rosa rugosa *seedling.*

Although cursed with a most unfortunate name, this wonderful rose is a delight in the garden. Its immense cerise single blooms are its major claim to fame, but I think its most important feature is the bush. Given proper space, this rose will fill a sizable area. It is vigorous and dense with lush, deep green foliage, making it an excellent background plant or a luxuriant hedge. The prolific flowers continue throughout the entire season, making the bush a colorful as well as prominent part of the landscape. In fall, this bush becomes a beacon of yellow, red and golden hues. Large, orange-red hips are sprinkled liberally throughout this iridescent foliage, making Scabrosa one of the most attractive roses at the season's end.

This rose becomes more impressive as it ages. When young, Scabrosa is simply another pretty *rugosa* rose. When older, it commands attention with its impressive stature and floral abundance. It is certainly one of the hardiest roses you can grow, and you never need worry about dragging out the sprayer, as it is virtually immune to disease. It roots well from softwood cuttings taken early in the season, and suckers can be used. Scabrosa is tough, dependable, floriferous and beautiful. It is hard to ask more of a rose.

SCHARLACHGLUT

Parentage: Poinsettia × *Alika (Rosa gallica grandiflora).*

Scharlachglut comes close to the look of crimson crushed velvet. And if ever there were a rose to turn the heads of those who say "I'm not interested in single roses," this is the one. The English translation of "Scharlachglut" is "Scarlet glow" or "Scarlet fire." Neither name can quite capture the intensity of this rose's color.

Part of Scharlachglut's effect lies in its size. It has the largest blossoms in our garden, and, in keeping with this grand design, the bush is also large, with thrusting canes that droop slightly. Although a bit open, the bush forms an adequate background for its flowers. Judicious pruning will help to thicken the bush and improve the overall presence of this rose.

We had few hopes for Scharlachglut when it was first planted, but although it requires some pruning of dead wood each spring, this rose has proved tough. It is generally very healthy, and can be rooted from softwood cuttings. After four years it now commands a prominent place at our garden's entrance, having convinced us that it intends to stay.

THÉRÈSE BUGNET

Parentage: (Rosa acicularis × Rosa kamtchatica) × (Rosa amblyotis × Rosa rugosa plena) × *Betty Bland*.

There are many unsung plant propagators in farflung places who never receive the acclamation they deserve. Georges Bugnet of Legal, Alberta, is such a person. Emigrating from his native France in 1905, Bugnet arrived in a land with rich soil but intensely cold winters. Roses had to withstand temperatures that regularly fell to -40° (F or C) or colder. Using the native roses, as well as roses he imported from such exotic places as the Kamchatka Peninsula in the Soviet Union, Bugnet created some of the hardiest garden roses in existence. One in particular is a rose of uncommon distinction – Thérèse Bugnet.

Thérèse Bugnet is a remarkable rose, not only for its unusual hardiness but for the large and intensely fragrant blossoms that occur so prolifically from late spring to late summer. When this impressive, fountain-like bush first blooms, the foliage is barely visible. Later flushes are less showy, but Thérèse Bugnet is rarely out of bloom during the season. The tissue-paper texture of this soft pink rose has an informal look, yet the plant has lost the wild look of its parents and is sophisticated enough for virtually any garden.

Thérèse Bugnet also gives color to the landscape in winter. The well-balanced silhouette of this vigorous bush is a deep clear red. These same stems have the added advantage of being almost thornless near the flowers, making them much easier to pick for bouquets than many of the shrub roses. This rose is extremely easy to root from softwood cuttings.

WILLIAM LOBB

Parentage: unknown, Rosa centifolia muscosa *hybrid.*

People are slowly awakening to the immense body of plants that has been neglected and that deserves a more important place in the garden. Perhaps with this exciting trend gaining momentum, we will soon see such varieties as William Lobb in more gardens.

William Lobb is the English name of a French rose, Duchesse d'Istrie. To complicate matters, its sensuous purple-crimson blooms inspired the name Old Velvet Moss. Whatever name you prefer, this rose is a welcome addition to the northern garden. Its extreme vigor is matched by its tremendous hardiness. In our garden the long, thorny stems are rarely touched by even the coldest winters, and after a few years of extraordinary growth, the bush becomes an imposing part of any rose bed. For this reason, be sure to give the plant room. As well, you may want to give it some support, as its long stems are somewhat lax and the numerous blossoms, which come in large clusters, weigh the stems down.

This is one of the Moss roses. The interesting soft bristles that cover the buds and upper stems of these roses are quite abundant in William Lobb. The flower itself is very double and well formed with a delightful fragrance. Although only medium in size, the sheer numbers of blooms will create a dazzling display. William Lobb is also fairly easy to root from softwood cuttings.

**Schneezwerg's powerful fragrance
and hardiness are exceptional.**

Semi-vigorous Shrubs

Shrubs growing up to 6 ft. (1.8 m)

AGNES

CELESTIAL

CHARLES DE MILLS

DART'S DASH

HENRI MARTIN

HUNTER

J.P. CONNELL

KAKWA

KARL FÖRSTER

KÖNIGIN VON DÄNEMARK

MAIDEN'S BLUSH

PERSIAN YELLOW

SCHNEEZWERG

SOLEIL D'OR

SUAVEOLENS

AGNES

Parentage: Rosa rugosa × Rosa foetida persiana.

The *rugosa* rose is, without a doubt, the species most utilized by northern growers. Not only are many *rugosas* important garden varieties, but this species has been extensively hybridized to produce some of our most exciting hardy roses. A great deal of work has been done to produce hardy yellow *rugosa* hybrids. Agnes is one of the few successes of these endeavors.

This rose has many attributes that recommend it as deserving a favored place in your garden. The delightful fruity fragrance of this rose is as essential a part of its character as its pastel petals, which subtly shift from apricot to light yellow to ivory. These flowers adorn a bush that is exceptionally hardy, and the crinkled lime green leaves are seldom if ever bothered by disease. Agnes is usually budded or grafted. Suckers can be used. Cuttings should be taken just before flowering early in the season. Avoid overmisting. A humidity tent works well.

Some may find this rose too fragile. Its petals are delicate and will not stand up to heavy wind and rain. This lack of substance can be called a fault, but the loose, carefree blooms of Agnes have an undeniable charm that stiff, more formal flowers can never achieve, a crown for fairies rather than kings.

CELESTIAL

Parentage: unknown, Rosa alba *hybrid.*

Never judge a plant by its name. When you are in the business of selling plants, you realize how much people react to the emotional connotations of names. Give a dog of a plant a catchy name and it will sell . . . for a while. Ultimately, however, a plant's merits become its best advertisement and determine its staying power.

Celestial is a nurseryman's dream come true. For here is a name that conjures up images of heavenly choirs or colorful galaxies floating in space and the flower actually lives up to these visions of ethereal beauty. For this is a rose of the purest pink and the most delicate of textures. This fine and very old double form of the *Rosa alba* has remained popular for centuries.

These (dare I use the word) heavenly smelling roses are set on a very neat bush with bluish-green foliage. Though perhaps not for subarctic areas, most northern gardeners should have no trouble overwintering this carefree and rewarding rose, or propagating it from softwood cuttings.

CHARLES DE MILLS

Parentage: unknown, Rosa gallica *hybrid.*

On a warm July day I noticed a slightly exasperated-looking elderly woman working her way purposefully through the garden. As I approached her to ask if I could help, she looked up and fairly shouted at me, "Don't you have any double roses here?" I pointed out several roses near her that were double. "Oh, not that kind. I mean *really* double." I realized that this lady was looking not for a double rose but for what is called a quartered rose, one with so many petals that, lacking room, the flower seems to fold itself into four equal parts. I led her to the Charles de Mills, and when she saw the large and extravagant blooms, an instant calm spread across her face. "Now *that's* a rose," she lectured me.

Charles de Mills's flowers are a glowing blend of rich red and purple with the edges shading toward the deepest of pinks. Unlike many of the shrub roses, Charles de Mills maintains an elegant cupped form even when fully open, and a bush covered with these large, vibrant flowers forms an elegant centerpiece in any garden. Add to this the flower's intense perfume and it is not surprising that this is one of the most popular of the *Rosa gallicas.*

The deep green foliage is rarely bothered by disease, although the occasional blackspot will show up on older leaves or where air circulation is poor. The bush forms a symmetrical globe with slightly lax stems that are fairly free from thorns. Although it's not for the very coldest of sites, most gardeners should be able to grow this rose, for it is quite hardy. It is also reasonably easy to root from softwood cuttings.

DART'S DASH
Parentage: *unknown*, Rosa rugosa *hybrid*.

This *rugosa* rose is a scaled-down version of the well-known Hansa rose. Its flowers are the same mauve-red color and have the same general petal formation and similar growth habits and foliage, but Dart's Dash flowers for a much longer period and the bush is more compact. A long flowering season is an advantage for any rose, but in modern horticulture small has become beautiful, as people try to fit plants into small-scale urban and suburban sites, and Dart's Dash, with its smaller stature, can be a useful component of such gardens.

This rose's large orange globular hips have enough flesh that the delicate nibbler, chewing around the seed core, can have an enjoyable snack. One of my favorite treats is eating Dart's Dash hips just after the first light frosts have softened them. This culinary pleasure is particularly enjoyable because, at the same time, I can inhale the strong fragrance of the blossoms, which even that late in the season are still gracing this most interesting rose. To propagate Dart's Dash, take softwood cuttings from wood early in the season.

HENRI MARTIN
Parentage: Rosa × centifolia muscosa.

The Moss roses are a most unusual group. They had their beginnings in the seventeenth century, when one of the Cabbage roses underwent a strange mutation. Some of its branches grew odd glandular structures on the flower stems and calyxes that have a remarkable resemblance to moss. This freak rose was cultivated and eventually bred to create new Moss roses with a wide range of flower colors. Although a number of these cultivars are quite hardy and well adapted to northern gardens, Henri Martin has a special place in my garden because of its masses of crimson flowers.

In late spring Henri Martin is a fountain of blossom. Each cluster is carried by rather slender, wiry stems with thorns that are deceptively harmless-looking. The bush is generally upright but somewhat lax and spreading. Even though we need to prune Henri reasonably hard each spring to remove winterkilled stem ends, most of the bush survives, and its ability to spring back is remarkable. The deep orange hips are small and vase-shaped, and Henri Martin is reasonably easy to root.

Moss roses add a distinctive and curious bit of variety to the palette of common roses, and isn't variety the spice that drives most of us to seek yet more plants to fill our overflowing garden beds?

HUNTER

Parentage: Rosa rugosa rubra × *Independence.*

True red is a rare color in the *rugosa* roses, which are usually a reddish purple or mauve. This relative newcomer to the group is a spectacular crimson. Its velvety petals are gently and symmetrically folded into a very alluring fully double form.

The color alone would make this rose interesting, but what makes it important is the intense, dark green, shiny foliage that forms a perfect background for the flowers, its neat and compact growth habit and the fact that this rose is a continuous bloomer.

It is difficult to find any faults with this wonderful rose. The only disappointment for me is that it is not as ironclad as many of the *rugosas*. In our area this rose will kill back slightly, but it bounces back each spring, and we will gladly put up with a little extra pruning to have Hunter grace our garden all summer. To propagate cuttings can be taken early in the season just before flowering.

J.P. CONNELL

Parentage: Arthur Bell × open pollinated seedling of Von Scharnhorst.

For those who look, the rose world has clues that can help to identify the different varieties. Examine the pattern of thorns on a stem of J.P. Connell. You will see a random pattern of short needles, a pattern different from every other rose, much like our fingerprints are unique to each of us. I have already imprinted this rose's thorn pattern in my mind, for I intend to grow this new Canadian rose.

Although prey to blackspot, the disease that haunts nearly all yellow roses, J.P. Connell fills an important niche in the inventory of hardy roses. Wave after wave of symmetrical, fully double and high-centered blooms appear all season. The first year's flowers may appear washed-out; however, as the plant establishes itself, the blossoms become larger, more profuse and colored a rich, creamy yellow. The plant is upright with plentiful rich green foliage and stiff yellow-green stems that hold up their elegant blooms.

With a little extra attention, this valuable introduction can transform a piece of your garden into an exciting showcase for one of the best new hardy yellow roses. Layering may be the best way to propagate J.P. Connell, which is moderately difficult to root.

KAKWA

Parentage: unknown, Rosa pimpinellifolia *hybrid.*

As the late spring nights lose that cool edge and the early spring flowers are reduced to simple greenery, the rose grower's anticipation heightens. The sight of those first unfolding buds is exhilarating and rejuvenating. In our garden it is the Kakwa that first appears. Almost overnight, this reliable and carefree rose becomes blanketed so thickly with blossoms that the foliage is virtually hidden under their delicate weight. This petaled coverlet is creamy white from a distance, but as you approach, the subtle pink tones of these double blooms become apparent. Another wonderful aspect of this early rose is its intense fragrance. I recommend you keep your nose at a slight distance from the flowers. Putting your nose into a Kakwa blossom is a bit like sticking it into a bottle of perfume – overpowering.

The bush is an extremely adaptable one. It will grow even in fairly poor soils and even prefers a lighter, well-drained soil. Although not a large plant, Kakwa will slowly mound upward to form a compact and dense shrub. It is a remarkably tough and hardy plant, easy to root, and will grow for most any northern gardener.

Although few roses have such an effect in bloom, Kakwa soon gives way to the many roses vying for our attentions. It is as if it gives everything it has in one exuberant burst of energy and then collapses to await the raising of the next spring curtain. Some may call it a bit part, but it acts its role with such energy that I would hate to think of the play without it.

KARL FÖRSTER

Parentage: Frau Karl Drushki × Rosa pimpinellifolia altaica.

Some roses have a way of tapping you on the shoulder and saying, "Take a look at me." My first Karl Förster plants sat at the edge of the garden for two years without attracting much attention. Then, in their third spring, they erupted with a display that took us by surprise. Shapely pointed buds by the hundreds unfolded into loose blossoms the color of whipped cream, until the foliage virtually disappeared under this unique petaled topping.

Karl Förster would not let us forget this extravaganza. As a reminder, it continued to bloom throughout the summer and early fall, an amazing feat for a Scotch rose. An added feature of this prolific bloomer is the red color of the new stems. Contrasted against the gray-green leaves, they lend a characteristic look to this relatively new rose.

All these wonderful attributes mean nothing to us if the rose does not perform well in our merciless winters. Karl Förster has passed the test with exceptional honors. It seems to have inherited the toughness of its Scotch rose parent as well as the flowering ability of its hybrid tea parent — a near perfect combination. Karl Förster is often budded or grafted. It can be rooted from softwood cuttings, but requires careful attention just after rooting or it can drop its leaves and die.

KÖNIGIN VON DÄNEMARK

Parentage: unknown, Rosa alba *hybrid.*

The Queen of Denmark is definitely a member of the royal family of older shrub roses. Many rose fanciers have a special place in their hearts and in their gardens for this most attractive and reliable rose. Although not as large as many other shrub roses, its classic flowers are artfully arranged into a well-formed cup shape that contains so many petals they seem to swirl around the button center. The pure pink tone of this rose is deeper than many of the *Rosa alba* group, fading gently to soft pink before the petals drop. The fragrance that emanates from the Queen befits nobility and is one more reason for the continuing popularity of this old rose, which is reasonably easy to root.

Generally, it is a pleasure to prune the *alba* roses because they are not as thorny as most shrub roses, but be sure to put on your gloves for this rose. Its stems, although not as vicious as those of the *rugosa* roses, make you pay for the dismemberment that you inflict on them. The bush is a nicely shaped tall mound clothed in handsome gray-green foliage. Like all *albas*, Königin von Dänemark flowers but once. However, the flowers that crown this distinguished rose are the highlights of a most glorious reign. Long live the Queen.

MAIDEN'S BLUSH

Parentage: unknown, Rosa alba *hybrid.*

There are actually two forms of this popular rose. The most common form is Maiden's Blush Great. The less common is Maiden's Blush Small. The only real difference between the two is the comparative size of the bush and flower. Whichever form, it is difficult to find a rose that creates more response from people than Maiden's Blush. That this rose is still popular after 500 years is a testament to its immense appeal. I can think of no other rose with such an intoxicating aroma, such sensuous color or such perfection of form.

The bush is a moderate size with stiffly erect stems and blue-tinted foliage that shows a bit of blackspot but is otherwise healthy and abundant. Like so many of its *Rosa alba* kin, Maiden's Blush is very hardy. In late spring heavenly scented blossoms of warmest blush pink arrive in great numbers. A good deal of this rose's charm is due to the informally arranged and gently folded petals which, although neatly contained, have an endearing character that must be seen to be understood. When the Maiden's Blush comes into bloom, the rose season becomes complete for us.

This rose, aptly and more sensuously named Cuisse de Nymph (nymph's thighs) in France, will continue to be one of the most popular of the older shrub roses. For me the only disappointment is that it never lasts long enough. Maiden's Blush is generally budded or grafted. It is fairly easy to root, but blackspot can pose a problem under greenhouse conditions, causing the leaves to drop about the time the roots form.

PERSIAN YELLOW

Parentage: Rosa foetida persiana.

Virtually every yellow rose can trace its color back to this double form of *Rosa foetida*. Originally found in southwestern Asia, *Rosa foetida* is shrouded in the mists of ancient history. Around 1837 this double form appeared and was soon introduced into European and North American gardens. Rose breeders continue to use it for its rich, golden color and double form. As well as transmitting its color, Persian Yellow has contributed its susceptibility to blackspot to the genetic "soup" of modern roses. But it's hard to complain about some spots when the alternative is a world without yellow roses.

The flowers of Persian Yellow appear in late spring and continue for three or four weeks. The form is globular. The fragrance is light and unusual, although definitely not fetid, as its Latin name would suggest.

This very hardy bush is generally upright with a tendency to sprawl as it ages. Its branches are somewhat thin and appear a bit wayward. It is not totally ungainly, and as it matures, this rose assumes a fairly full and impressive stature. This is definitely one rose to prune with restraint. Its flowers arise from the old wood, so drastic spring pruning will severely limit your blooms. As well, this rose does not seem to respond well to heavy pruning, and continued aggressive pruning may kill the plant.

Persian Yellow is one of the few varieties that I treat with wettable sulfur. If not treated, it will drop most of its leaves shortly after flowering. If you live in areas with humid summers, blackspot will be a problem you must deal with. Those in drier areas will find Persian Yellow fairly easy to grow, particularly as it is more tolerant of poor, sandy soils than most roses. The rose is very difficult to root from softwood cuttings. Use new wood and avoid overmisting. It is most often budded or grafted.

SCHNEEZWERG

Parentage: Rosa rugosa × *a Polyantha rose.*

From late spring till hard frost this tough and adaptable bush sends forth innumerable small pure white blossoms. As each semi-double bloom opens, a center of deep yellow stamens adds a cheerful accent to the flower.

Schneezwerg's lustrous, healthy foliage amply demonstrates the disease resistance so common to the *rugosa* roses. The density of this bush makes it a good hedge plant. With annual attention to shaping and thinning, a hedge of Schneezwerg can be a valuable addition to your garden.

To all these attributes, add a sweet and powerful fragrance and a hardiness that is virtually unmatched in the rose world. It is no wonder that Schneezwerg remains one of the most popular white *rugosa* roses, one modern breeders use to create new varieties. Schneezwerg gives you all the beauty of a fresh snowfall without the bother of having to shovel it. This rose is easy to root from softwood cuttings taken just before flowering. Suckers can be used.

SOLEIL D'OR

Parentage: Antoine Ducher × Rosa foetida persiana.

I will never forget the first blossom I saw on this rose. I called the entire nursery over to take a look. The combination of colors contained in its petals was like nothing I had ever seen – yellows, oranges, golds and even a reddish tint all blended into a fully double flower. I checked each new flower as it opened. I never grew tired of looking at this fascinating rose.

This is a very special variety in the history of roses. It was the culmination of intense breeding efforts to produce a yellow hybrid tea rose. Luckily for us northerners, the hardy Persian Yellow rose was one of the parents, and this rose inherited its hardiness. It is considered the oldest surviving yellow hybrid tea type, and interestingly for me, is the only hybrid tea I have found hardy in our gardens. Soleil d'Or is usually propagated by budding or grafting.

To grow this distinguished and lovely rose you must, unfortunately, live with the blackspot that invariably will show up on its foliage. If you wish to keep this disease at bay, you will need to spray. Wettable sulfur will work well if used as a preventive spray, and it is reasonably safe to use.

With roses it seems we must live with the pain of thorns and the bane of blackspot if we are to enjoy the beauty and pleasure they bring. It's no wonder that the rose is used as a symbol of love.

SUAVEOLENS

Parentage: unknown, Rosa alba *hybrid.*

In the heart of the Balkan mountains of Bulgaria is a steep valley bordering the Tundza River, which eventually spills into the Black Sea. This exotic valley is noteworthy in the history of rose growing, for this is Kazanlik, where the most famous "attar of roses" is made. In early summer the green valley transforms into a pastel carpet as the millions of roses needed to create this famous perfume come into bloom. The aromatic petals are collected and carefully distilled into a substance so highly prized that it was once available only to the nobility of the world. Very few roses contain enough natural fragrance to make them suitable for the Kazanlik essences. One of these is Kazanlik, a Damask rose named after the town of its origin. Another important variety is the *alba* rose Suaveolens.

Connoisseurs of fragrance should be convinced. Those interested in the beauty of roses will rejoice in the semi-double blooms of nearly pure white surrounding a center of golden yellow stamens. This rose has an informal yet refined look. The bush is quite hardy, healthy and vigorous, and this rose is moderately easy to root. Although not as easy to locate in the nursery trade, this is a rose that you should seek out.

From late spring onward, Stanwell Perpetual produces a regular succession of blush-pink blooms.

9

Low Shrubs

Shrubs growing up to 3 ft. (1 m)

CHAMPLAIN

FRU DAGMAR HASTRUP

HENRY HUDSON

MORDEN RUBY

NEARLY WILD

ROSE DE MAUX

STANWELL PERPETUAL

STRIPED MOSS

CHAMPLAIN

Parentage: Rosa kordesii *Wulff* × Rosa laxa × Rosa spinosissima L.

Champlain is a hardy and ever-blooming rose. Once it begins blooming, only the hard frosts can stop it. Although certainly not an ironclad hardy plant, it is a valuable addition to the northern garden. In our garden we often experience a good deal of dieback with Champlain, but we have never lost a plant, and when on its own roots it is able to spring back even if killed to almost ground level.

Champlain is a rich, velvety deep red. In our garden it is definitely the plant people ask about most. In addition to its sumptuous color, this rose is entirely free of disease. It is exceedingly resistant to blackspot and mildew. What is even more exciting is that under outside growing conditions Champlain is virtually free of aphids. Many roses seem somewhat resistant to these pesky green sap suckers, but Champlain is truly exceptional.

Champlain is not a vigorous rose. It is quite low in stature and makes an excellent bedding rose. In fact, if this variety has a fault, it is that the plant seems all bloom at the expense of foliage. With proper pruning, however, it forms a compact and useful garden subject. It is extremely easy to root, although cuttings are often difficult to obtain in numbers due to lack of growth.

FRU DAGMAR HASTRUP

Parentage: unknown, Rosa rugosa *seedling.*

If there were such a thing as pink spiders that wove cloth, their silken product might resemble the petals of Fru Dagmar Hastrup. The light pink flowers shimmer in the light. They are large and, when opening, resemble chalices. Best of all, they do not stop blooming until freezing temperatures put an end to their prolific beauty. The flowers are intensely fragrant.

This exceedingly hardy rose is a low-growing form and stays fairly compact, becoming more wide than high. It is very well protected by thorns so numerous that there is no smooth stem surface. Both short and somewhat longer thorns are interspersed in this formidable armor. It is a very healthy rose, being nearly immune to blackspot and mildew.

Hips are numerous and large, useful for those growers who enjoy these vitamin-packed fruits.

One of the most endearing qualities of Fru Dagmar Hastrup is its fall foliage. As the daylight hours wane, the green leaves take on a deep maroon tone. The process continues until the foliage changes to deep golden yellow with coppery highlights that seem iridescent. Although I have always enjoyed this rose's blooms in summer, I will never forget the first time I stood transfixed in my garden as the late afternoon sun glanced off the glowing autumn leaves of this petite gem. I still have not found a rose with a more exciting transition into winter. Fru Dagmar Hastrup is fairly easy to root from cuttings, and suckers can be used.

HENRY HUDSON

Parentage: Rosa rugosa *Schneezwerg seedling.*

I have a rare single red peony in my garden. With its ferny foliage, this peony is very beautiful in bloom, but what makes it stand out is the background of snow white Henry Hudson roses, which carpet the ground around it. This low-growing and prolifically blooming plant is another valuable introduction from the Explorer Series of Agriculture Canada.

Henry Hudson has virtually everything you could ask for. Its deep green and copious foliage is free of disease, it is absolutely hardy, its flowers come continuously in wave after wave, it is richly fragrant and its pink-tipped buds open to a sparkling show of white petals. It is truly a northern explorer and an important addition to the list of hardy roses.

As a low bedding plant this rose is unbeatable, for it maintains a density that few roses can boast, creating a carpet of green that shows off its flowers to good advantage. Be forewarned that, like most *rugosas*, Henry Hudson will spread by suckering, so it is best used where this is desired or where it can be contained. It holds onto its spent blooms, so you may want to pick the old flowers for best appearance. Propagating Henry Hudson from softwood cuttings gives variable results. The best results are with cuttings from early season growth just before flowering. Suckers can be used.

MORDEN RUBY

Parentage: Fire King × *(J.W. Fargo* × *Assiniboine).*

Apparently pixies inhabit my garden. Each time a blossom of Morden Ruby opens, it looks as if they have splashed the deep pink petals with cans of red paint, creating a fascinating spotted pattern that should make many an abstract painter envious. I never tire of looking at these distinctive flowers, and the pleasure they give me lets me forgive the plant's weaknesses.

While not altogether hopeless, Morden Ruby is a rather open and rangy plant. I find that a severe pruning job each spring helps to keep the plant a bit denser and, although this is a tough rose by most standards, we do have to prune out a good deal of dead wood in spring, but this coincides with the pruning program we have for this rose anyway. It is also a bit too subject to blackspot for my liking. However, a few sprays of sulfur or a blind eye make this all too common weakness disappear. Morden Ruby has an important point in its favor. The blossoms that I cherish so highly come in several waves throughout the summer, so I can gaze at these fascinating flowers for many months. Morden Ruby is fairly easy to root, but cuttings often drop leaves shortly after rooting due to blackspot infection.

NEARLY WILD

Parentage: unknown, Rosa floribunda *hybrid.*

It is unusual to find a floribunda rose that will survive in our garden. Most die the first winter. Some survive at most a winter or two before they are added to the compost heap. Nearly Wild is different. It has formed a neat, mounded shrub in the garden, and my contacts in places with severe winters, such as Minnesota, tell me it does quite nicely there as well.

The name says it all. The large single pink flowers do remind you of many of the native roses that fill the roadside ditches with their glorious color in those first days of summer. The difference is that with Nearly Wild you can enjoy them until the rose petals are frozen by the first nips of fall. This exceptional hybrid is a nonstop bloomer.

Nearly Wild is actually a fairly civilized plant. The wildness of the plant is in its flowering, not its growth. In a few years it will form a compact plant that is nearly as wide as it is high. As a foundation plant or a low plant in the garden it is ideal.

In the rapidly expanding list of modern hardy rose varieties, Nearly Wild is one that will appeal to those with an eye for simple beauty but an appetite for the luxury of endless bloom, and is easy to root.

ROSE DE MAUX

Parentage: unknown, Rosa centifolia.

Many believe that those of us living in the colder areas are deprived because we cannot grow so many of the beautiful varieties in the rose world. To some extent this is true. We cannot grow the hybrid teas and floribundas, so we are forced to seek out the species and hybrids that will survive in our rigorous climates. Yet this very fact opens up to us a world of roses that those who grow only teas cannot imagine. Roses that can create effects in the garden that are totally unique and exciting. An example of this exhilarating diversity is Rose de Maux.

The flowers of this rose are not large and splashy but are tight, frilly buttons, a classic rose form in miniature, clear pink and very fragrant. The bush is miniature as well, rarely growing more than 2 ft. (60 cm) high.

Rose de Maux is considered a temperamental rose, not growing well in poor soils. We are blessed with excellent soil in our garden and have been pleased with the performance of this gem. However, this fact should be a consideration for those working with marginal soils. Certainly the winter has not been a problem. Rose de Maux has come through our low temperatures unscathed by frost's icy grip, and is also fairly easy to root.

Maux is a rose we can highlight in the garden, one to cherish for its diminutive elegance and its rare beauty.

STANWELL PERPETUAL

Parentage: Rosa × damascena bifera (*Autumn Damask*) × Rosa spinosissima.

It is by listening to the advice of others that we learn. In one of my correspondences with a rose grower, I was told that I had to acquire the Scotch rose hybrid Stanwell Perpetual. My friend assured me that it would soon become one of my favorites. And so it has.

The Scotch rose has been used to hybridize many roses. Its beauty, hardiness and adaptability to poor growing conditions make it a good breeding parent. Unfortunately, the Scotch rose is an early and one-time bloomer, and most of the hybrids of this variety have inherited this trait. There are a few exceptions, and the Stanwell Perpetual is, in my opinion, the very best of them. This rose was a cross with the exotically fragrant and long-blooming Autumn Damask. It inherited the tremendous hardiness and toughness of its Scotch parent and the fragrant double blooms of its Damask parent. Best of all, it inherited the ability of Autumn Damask to flower throughout the season.

The flower is double, with the old-time charm of the Damask rose. Its soft, blush-pink blossoms cover the plant in late spring, and from then on a regular procession of flowers appears on this gracefully arching low bush. The foliage is a very deep green and, aside from a natural purplish discoloration, is unmarred by disease. It is fairly easy to root, but is usually budded or grafted. If on its own roots, it will eventually produce suckers that can be used.

Stanwell Perpetual never fails to make me stop, bend down and smell the roses. It asks very little of us and gives so much. It pays to take advice.

STRIPED MOSS

Parentage: unknown, Rosa centifolia muscosa.

Humans seem to crave the unusual in nature. In the gardening world we raise curious dwarfs, plants with twisted stems and foliage, and trees and shrubs with oddly colored foliage and flowers. So it is that roses such as Striped Moss are still found growing in our gardens, for this is, indeed, an odd rose.

The flowers are double, cupped and open flat. The white petals, streaked with random stripes of deep and lighter pink, create an effect both startling and intriguing. Among the striped roses, Striped Moss is one of the hardiest, reasonably easy to root, and therefore of interest to northern growers; however it is subject to blackspot. It is also blessed with a good fragrance and the interesting fuzziness associated with the Moss roses.

The bush is small, upright, with stems and buds well mossed, and is well suited to an intimate corner in the garden where the sun can warm its branches and give brilliance to the blossoms of this lovable oddity.

Unlike many ground-cover roses,
Charles Albanel creates a floral
carpet until the end of the season.

10

Ground Covers

Procumbent or ground-hugging shrubs

CHARLES ALBANEL

MAX GRAF

ROSA PAULII

CHARLES ALBANEL
Parentage: Rosa rugosa *seedling.*

This rose is very new and virtually unknown in the gardening scene. It is a *rugosa* seedling that is in many ways similar to its relatives, but one that has a special feature that demands attention. It is very dwarfish and spreading and, with time, creates a thick blanket that will smother an embankment or garden bed with its dense foliage and informal, colorful blooms. The height and density of this plant make it one of the most outstanding hardy ground covers available. The new stems are medium green, turning blackish with age, and the branches are quite thorny. The rose hips are medium-sized, orange-red and flattened globular.

The semi-double flowers are a pleasing mauve-red. They begin in early summer and continue until the very end of the season. Many of the more common hardy ground cover roses flower only once, but this new selection from the breeding program at Agriculture Canada creates a living floral carpet throughout the season.

Both the hardiness and disease resistance of this rose are exceptional. It is virtually immune to mildew and blackspot. Given all these attributes, I have no doubt that this variety will become increasingly common in the garden and in public and commercial plantings where masses of low flowering plants are needed. To propagate, take cuttings early in the season just before flowering.

MAX GRAF
Parentage: Rosa rugosa × Rosa wichuraiana.

This rose is vitally important in the historical development of many of our newest and best hardy shrub roses. Discovered in Connecticut by James Bowditch, this rose came to the attention of Wilhelm Kordes of Germany. He saved seed from a chance fruit on his bush and the seedling that resulted had good hardiness and a remarkable resistance to disease. He named it *Rosa kordesii.* Subsequent crosses using this new species resulted in many important hardy, healthy varieties. Later, the breeder Felicitas Svejda of Canada also used these descendants of Max Graf to introduce blackspot resistance into the Explorer Series of roses.

Although not commonly seen in gardens, the original Max Graf can be useful to the northern gardener, for not only is it hardy and healthy, it also has a low branching structure that makes it a good ground cover. Its lax stems stretch outward, bending down from their own weight. As each successive layer covers the previous layers, a fairly dense low bush is created that is attractive and effective.

Because the flower is single and nonrecurrent, we should not dismiss it. Surrounding a prominent center of deep yellow stamens are five petals of clear, satiny pink that are delightfully scented. Even when not in flower, however, the healthy sheen of the leaves and the long, arching, fresh-green branches add beauty and texture to the garden. Max Graf is very easy to root from cuttings and will also layer well.

ROSA PAULII

Parentage: unknown, supposed to be Rosa arvensis × Rosa rugosa.

A fascinating rose and one of the only true creeping roses that can be grown in the north. For me, this rose was an interesting lesson in the differences between budded and own-rooted plants. When I first received Rosa paulii it was budded onto *Rosa multiflora* roots. I grew it the first year and was disappointed that it was not a true ground cover as I had hoped. It seemed to grow upward and then gradually arch outward. I did, however, instruct the propagator to take cuttings. The next summer I was walking through the beds and came upon what looked like sinuous, thorny snakes on the ground. I had never seen a rose like it. I quickly backtracked to the sign and could hardly believe that this was the same plant that I had brought in. The *multiflora* root had caused the plant to thrust upward, whereas these own-rooted plants never left the soil's surface. The two plants, alike in every respect but their roots, behaved in two completely different manners. This difference points to the importance of knowing what kind of plant you have, for their growth pattern can be significantly altered by placing them on a rootstock.

While this rose does not attain any height, it certainly does not lack vigor. It will grow several feet a year and will rapidly fill a good-sized area with its long, snaky shoots. In the early summer the healthy and heavily textured foliage forms large buds, which open to immense pure white single blooms. The narrower than usual petals converge in the center where a sunburst of golden stamens completes the simple beauty of this flower with delicate elegance. The rose's sweet fragrance and colorful display of yellow and orange foliage in the fall help to make up for the fleeting season of this most useful plant. It roots and layers easily.

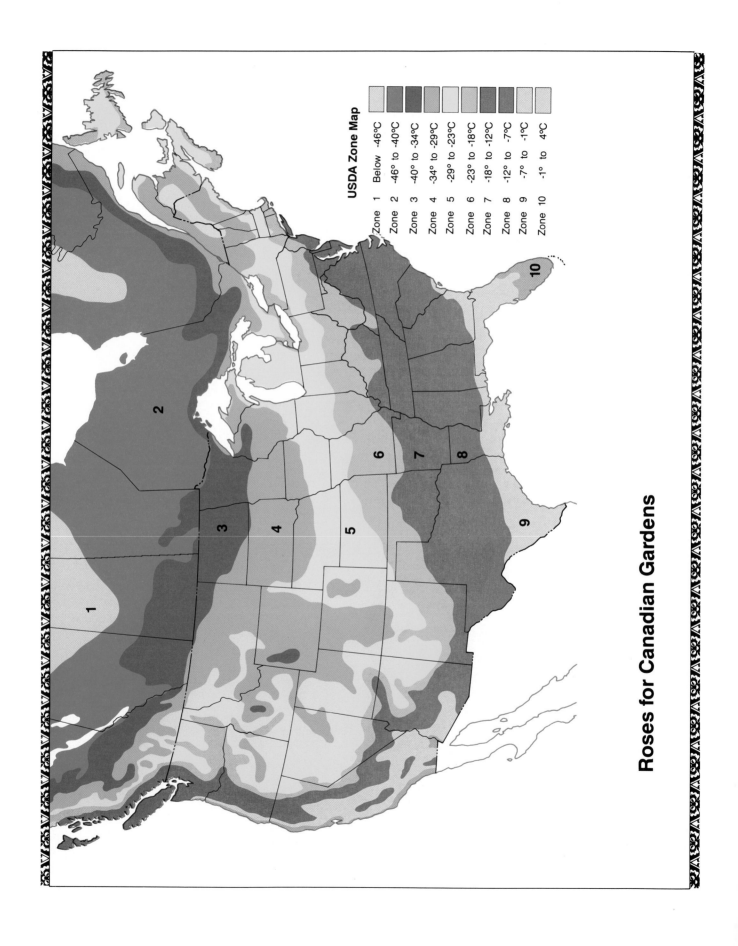

Roses for Canadian Gardens

USDA Zone Map

Zone 1   Below -46°C
Zone 2   -46° to -40°C
Zone 3   -40° to -34°C
Zone 4   -34° to -29°C
Zone 5   -29° to -23°C
Zone 6   -23° to -18°C
Zone 7   -18° to -12°C
Zone 8   -12° to -7°C
Zone 9   -7° to -1°C
Zone 10 -1° to 4°C

List of
Hardy Varieties

The following varieties are those believed sufficiently hardy to be grown in Zones 2 to 5. The varieties chosen are those that are currently available in the nursery trade. There are countless other roses, many of excellent quality and value, but they are either difficult or impossible to obtain. I have relied upon the expertise of others to assign each variety to a species or category. Some roses might just as easily be put in other sections, as they are often the result of interspecific breeding and have characteristics common to both species. The designation of color, form, vigor, fragrance and blooming time are from the results of my own observations and those of others in the field. Some of these are somewhat subjective, and differences may occur according to where a variety is grown and the care given to it. Hardiness designations are based on observation, information from reliable sources and a bit of educated guesswork. These hardiness ratings should be used merely as a guide to assist those choosing suitable roses for their area.

THE VARIETIES	COLOR	FORM	HARDINESS ZONE	VIGOR	FRAGRANCE	SEASON	SUITABILITY FOR HEDGING	DISEASE SUSCEPTIBILITY	BREEDER	ORIGIN	INTRODUCED
ROSA ACICULARIS											
Dornroschen	dp	d	5	sv	ff	r		BS-2	Kordes	Germany	1960
ROSA ALBA											
Amelia	mp	sd	3-4	sv	fff	s	H	BS-1	Vibert	France	1823
Belle Amour	lp	d	3-4	v	ff	s	H	BS-1	seedling	France	c.1940
Blanche de Belgique	w	d	3-4	v	fff	s	H	BS-1	Vibert	France	1817
Blush hip	lp	d	3-4	v	fff	s		BS-1	unknown	UK	1840
Celestial (*Celeste*)	lp	d	3-4	v	fff	s	H	BS-0	unknown	unknown	old
Chloris (*Rosée du Matin*)	lp	d	3-4	v	ff	s	H	BS-0	unknown	unknown	old
Felicité Parmentier	lp	vd	3-4	sv	fff	s	H	BS-1	unknown	unknown	1834

COLOR
w=white or nearly white
p/w=pink and white
pb=pink blend
p/y=pink and yellow
lp=light pink
mp=medium pink
dp=deep pink
mr=medium red
dr=deep red
rb=red blend
m=mauve
mb=mauve blend
ly=light yellow
my=medium yellow
dy=deep yellow
yo=yellow-orange
o=orange
or=orange-red
yo=yellow-orange
c/s=coppery salmon

FORM
s=single
s+=slightly more than single
sd=semi-double
d=double
vd=very double or quartered

HARDINESS ZONE
2 to 5 (see Zone map)

VIGOR
g=ground cover
l=low
sv=semi-vigorous
v=vigorous
cl=climber

FRAGRANCE
f=little or no fragrance
ff=moderate fragrance
fff=exceptional fragrance

SEASON
sp=spring
s=summer
r=repeating
c=continuous bloomer

SUITABILITY FOR HEDGING
H

DISEASE SUSCEPTIBILITY
Blackspot:
BS-0= Immune or so little as to be insignificant.
BS-1= Noticeable but generally affecting fewer than 25% of leaves.
BS-2= Affecting at least 50% of leaves, some defoliation without protection.
BS-3= Affecting most of leaves, heavy defoliation without protection.

Mildew:
M=Varieties that are particularly susceptible to mildew.

Rust:
R= Varieties that are particularly susceptible to rust.

Note: Although roses are subject to several diseases, by far the most important disease of hardy varieties is blackspot. Those in drier climates may not have problems with blackspot, but in more humid areas blackspot can seriously affect many roses. These designations are based on the incidence of blackspot in a moderately humid site. Although you may find the incidence of blackspot either more or less severe than indicated by these ratings, they at least will offer a relative scale of blackspot susceptibility.

THE VARIETIES	COLOR	FORM	HARDINESS ZONE	VIGOR	FRAGRANCE	SEASON	SUITABILITY FOR HEDGING	DISEASE SUSCEPTIBILITY	BREEDER	ORIGIN	INTRODUCED
Jeanne d'Arc	w	d	3-4	v	fff	s	H	BS-1	Vibert	France	1818
Königin von Dänemark (*Queen of Denmark*)	mp	vd	3-4	sv	fff	s	H	BS-0	unknown	unknown	1826
Maiden's Blush Great (*Rosa alba incarnata*)	lp	vd	3-4	sv	fff	s	H	BS-1	unknown	unknown	c.1400
Maiden's Blush Small	lp	vd	3-4	l	fff	s	H	BS-1	Kew Gardens	UK	1797
Mme. Plantier	w	vd	3-4	v	fff	s		BS-1	Plantier	France	1835
Pompon Blanc Parfait	w	vd	3-4	sv	fff	s		BS-1	unknown	unknown	c.1876
Semi-plena	w	sd	3-4	v	fff	s		BS-1	unknown	Europe	c.1500
Suaveolens	w	sd	3-4	v	fff	s		BS-0	unknown	Europe	c.1500
ROSA BLANDA											
Betty Bland	dp	d	2	v	ff	s		BS-1	Skinner	Canada	1926
ROSA CENTIFOLIA											
A Longs Pédoncules	lp	d	4	sv	ff	s		BS-1	Robert	France	1854
Blanche fleur	w	d	4	sv	fff	s		BS-1	Vibert	France	1835
Blush Moss	lp	d	4	sv	fff	s		BS-1	unknown	unknown	c.1844
Bullata (*Lettuce leafed rose*)	dp	d	4	sv	fff	s		BS-1	unknown	unknown	c.1500
Célina	dp	sd	4	sv	ff	s		BS-1	Hardy	France	1855
Common Moss (*Old Pink Moss*), (*Communis*)	mp	d	4	sv	fff	s		BS-1	unknown	France	1696

THE VARIETIES	COLOR	FORM	HARDINESS ZONE	VIGOR	FRAGRANCE	SEASON	SUITABILITY FOR HEDGING	DISEASE SUSCEPTIBILITY	BREEDER	ORIGIN	INTRODUCED
Crested Moss (*R. centifolia cristata*), (*Chapeau de Napoléon*)	dp	d	4	sv	fff	s		BS-1	Vibert	France	1826
Crimson Moss	dr	d	4	sv	ff	s		BS-1	Lee	UK	c.1846
Fantin-Latour	mp	vd	4	sv	fff	s		BS-1	unknown	unknown	?
Henri Martin	mr	d	4	sv	ff	s		BS-1	Laffay	France	1863
Hunslett Moss	dp	d	4	l	fff	s		BS-1	Brooke	UK	1984
Jeanne de Monfort	mp	d	4	sv	fff	s		BS-1	Robert	France	1851
La Noblesse	lp	vd	4	sv	fff	s		BS-1	unknown	unknown	1856
Marie de Blois	mp	d	4	sv	fff	c		BS-1	Robert	France	1852
Mme. William Paul	pb	d	4	l	ff	r		BS-2	Paul	UK	1869
Nuits de Young (*Old Black Moss*)	rb	d	4	sv	ff	s	H	BS-2	Laffay	France	1845
Paul Ricault	dp	vd	4	sv	fff	s		BS-1	Portemer	France	1845

COLOR
w=white or nearly white
p/w=pink and white
pb=pink blend
p/y=pink and yellow
lp=light pink
mp=medium pink
dp=deep pink
mr=medium red
dr=deep red
rb=red blend
m=mauve
mb=mauve blend
ly=light yellow
my=medium yellow
dy=deep yellow
yo=yellow-orange
o=orange
or=orange-red
yo=yellow-orange
c/s=coppery salmon

FORM
s=single
s+=slightly more than single
sd=semi-double
d=double
vd=very double or quartered

HARDINESS ZONE
2 to 5 (see Zone map)

VIGOR
g=ground cover
l=low
sv=semi-vigorous
v=vigorous
cl=climber

FRAGRANCE
f=little or no fragrance
ff=moderate fragrance
fff=exceptional fragrance

SEASON
sp=spring
s=summer
r=repeating
c=continuous bloomer

SUITABILITY FOR HEDGING
H

DISEASE SUSCEPTIBILITY
Blackspot:
BS-0= Immune or so little as to be insignificant.
BS-1= Noticeable but generally affecting fewer than 25% of leaves.
BS-2= Affecting at least 50% of leaves, some defoliation without protection.
BS-3= Affecting most of leaves, heavy defoliation without protection.

Mildew:
M=Varieties that are particularly susceptible to mildew.

Rust:
R= Varieties that are particularly susceptible to rust.

Note: Although roses are subject to several diseases, by far the most important disease of hardy varieties is blackspot. Those in drier climates may not have problems with blackspot, but in more humid areas blackspot can seriously affect many roses. These designations are based on the incidence of blackspot in a moderately humid site. Although you may find the incidence of blackspot either more or less severe than indicated by these ratings, they at least will offer a relative scale of blackspot susceptibility.

THE VARIETIES	COLOR	FORM	HARDINESS ZONE	VIGOR	FRAGRANCE	SEASON	SUITABILITY FOR HEDGING	DISEASE SUSCEPTIBILITY	BREEDER	ORIGIN	INTRODUCED
Quatre Saisons Blanc Mousseaux (*Perpetual White Moss*)	w	d	4	sv	ff	s		BS-1	Laffay	France	*c.*1848
Rose de Maux	mp	vd	4	l	fff	s		BS-2	Sweet	UK	*c.*1789
Souvenir de Pierre Vibert	pb	d	4	sv	ff	r		BS-1	Morseau-Robert	France	1867
Spong	mp	d	4	sv	ff	s	H	BS-1	Spong	France	1805
Striped Moss	p/w	d	4	l	ff	s		BS-2	unknown	unknown	?
The Bishop	m	vd	4	sv	ff	s		BS-1	unknown	unknown	?
Tour de Malakoff (*Black Jack*)	mb	d	4	v	ff	s		BS-1	Soupert & Notting	Luxem.	1856
Violacée	mb	d	4	sv	ff	s		BS-1	Soupert & Notting	Luxem.	1876
White Bath	w	d	4	sv	fff	s		BS-1	Salter	UK	1817
William Lobb (*Old Velvet Moss*)	mb	d	4	v	ff	s		BS-1	Laffay	France	1855
ROSA EGLANTERIA											
Amy Robsart	dp	s	4	v	ff	s	H	BS-3	Penzance	UK	1894
Goldbusch	my	sd	4	v	ff	s	H	BS-1	Kordes	Germany	1954
Greenmantle	r	s	4	v	ff	s	H	BS-3	Penzance	UK	1894
Hebe's Lip (*Rubrotincta*), (*Reine Blanche*)	w	s	4	sv	ff	s	H	BS-2	Paul	UK	1912
Herbstfeuer (*Autumn Fire*)	dr	sd	4	v	f	r	H	BS-1	Kordes	Germany	1961
Julia Mannering	lp	s	4	v	ff	s	H	BS-2	Penzance	UK	1895

THE VARIETIES	COLOR	FORM	HARDINESS ZONE	VIGOR	FRAGRANCE	SEASON	SUITABILITY FOR HEDGING	DISEASE SUSCEPTIBILITY	BREEDER	ORIGIN	INTRODUCED
La Belle Distinguée (*Scarlet Sweetbriar*), (*La Petite Duchesse*)	dr	d	4	sv	f	s	H	BS-2	unknown	unknown	?
Lady Penzance	p/y	s	4	v	ff	s	H	BS-3	Penzance	UK	1894
Lord Penzance	p/y	s	4	v	ff	s	H	BS-3	Penzance	UK	1890
Manning's Blush	w	d	4	sv	ff	s	H	BS-2	unknown	unknown	c.1800
Meg Merrilees'	dr	sd	4	v	ff	s	H	BS-3	Penzance	UK	c.1894
ROSA FOETIDA											
Austrian Copper	or	s	3-4	sv	f	s		BS-3	unknown	Asia	c.1500
Lawrence Johnston	dy	sd	5	cl	ff	r		BS-3	Pernet-Ducher	France	1923
Persian Yellow	dy	d	3-4	sv	f	s		BS-3	unknown	S.W. Asia	1837
Soleil d'Or	yo	d	4-5	sv	fff	r		BS-3	Pernet-Ducher	France	1900

COLOR
w=white or nearly white
p/w=pink and white
pb=pink blend
p/y=pink and yellow
lp=light pink
mp=medium pink
dp=deep pink
mr=medium red
dr=deep red
rb=red blend
m=mauve
mb=mauve blend
ly=light yellow
my=medium yellow
dy=deep yellow
yo=yellow-orange
o=orange
or=orange-red
yo=yellow-orange
c/s=coppery salmon

FORM
s=single
s+=slightly more than single
sd=semi-double
d=double
vd=very double or quartered

HARDINESS ZONE
2 to 5 (see Zone map)

VIGOR
g=ground cover
l=low
sv=semi-vigorous
v=vigorous
cl=climber

FRAGRANCE
f=little or no fragrance
ff=moderate fragrance
fff=exceptional fragrance

SEASON
sp=spring
s=summer
r=repeating
c=continuous bloomer

SUITABILITY FOR HEDGING
H

DISEASE SUSCEPTIBILITY
Blackspot:
BS-0= Immune or so little as to be insignificant.
BS-1= Noticeable but generally affecting fewer than 25% of leaves.
BS-2= Affecting at least 50% of leaves, some defoliation without protection.
BS-3= Affecting most of leaves, heavy defoliation without protection.

Mildew:
M=Varieties that are particularly susceptible to mildew.

Rust:
R= Varieties that are particularly susceptible to rust.

Note: Although roses are subject to several diseases, by far the most important disease of hardy varieties is blackspot. Those in drier climates may not have problems with blackspot, but in more humid areas blackspot can seriously affect many roses. These designations are based on the incidence of blackspot in a moderately humid site. Although you may find the incidence of blackspot either more or less severe than indicated by these ratings, they at least will offer a relative scale of blackspot susceptibility.

THE VARIETIES	COLOR	FORM	HARDINESS ZONE	VIGOR	FRAGRANCE	SEASON	SUITABILITY FOR HEDGING	DISEASE SUSCEPTIBILITY	BREEDER	ORIGIN	INTRODUCED
ROSA GALLICA											
Agatha (*Agathe*)	dp	sd	3-4	sv	ff	s		BS-1	unknown	Europe	?
Alain Blanchard	rb	sd	4	sv	ff	s		BS-1	Vibert	France	1839
Alika (*Gallica grandiflora*)	mr	sd	3-4	v	fff	s		BS-1	Hanson	?	1906
Anaïs Ségalas	rb	d	4	l	fff	s		BS-1	Vibert	France	1837
Antonia d'Ormois	lp	d	4	sv	ff	s		BS-1	Roseraie de l'Hay	France	?
Apothecary's Rose (*Rosa gallica officinalis*)	dp	sd	4	sv	fff	s		BS-1	unknown	unknown	c.1600
Assemblage des Beautés (*Rouge Eblouissante*)	dr	vd	4	sv	ff	s		BS-1	unknown	France	c.1823
Belle de Crécy	mb	d	4	sv	ff	s		BS-1	unknown	unknown	c.1850
Belle Isis	lp	vd	4	l	fff	s		BS-1	Parmentier	Belgium	1845
Camaieux	p/w	vd	4	l	ff	s		BS-1	Vibert	France	1830
Cardinal de Richlieu	mb	vd	4	l	ff	s		BS-1	Laffay	France	1840
Charles de Mills	rb	vd	4	sv	fff	s		BS-1	Roseraie de l'Hay	France	old
Complicata	mp	s	4-5	v	ff	s		BS-1	unknown	unknown	old
Comte de Nanteuil	mb	d	4	sv	ff	s		BS-1	Roeser	France	1834
Comtesse de Lacépède	w	vd	4	sv	ff	s		BS-1	unknown	France	1840
Conditorum	dr	sd	4	sv	fff	s		BS-1	unknown	France	old

THE VARIETIES	COLOR	FORM	HARDINESS ZONE	VIGOR	FRAGRANCE	SEASON	SUITABILITY FOR HEDGING	DISEASE SUSCEPTIBILITY	BREEDER	ORIGIN	INTRODUCED
Cosimo Ridolfi	mb	vd	4	l	ff	s		BS-1	Vibert	France	1842
Cramoisi Picoté	rb	vd	4	l	f	s		BS-1	Vibert	France	1834
D'Agnesseau	dr	vd	4	sv	ff	s		BS-1	Vibert	France	1823
Duc de Fitzjames	mb	vd	4	sv	ff	s		BS-1	unknown	unknown	c.1885
Duc de Guiche	rb	d	4	sv	fff	s		BS-1	Prévost	France	1835
Duchesse d'Angoulême (*Duc d'Angoulême*)	lp	vd	4	sv	fff	s		BS-1	Vibert	France	c.1835
Duchesse de Buccleugh	rb	vd	4	v	ff	s		BS-1	Robert	France	1860
Duchesse de Montebello	lp	vd	4	sv	fff	s		BS-1	Laffay	France	1829
George Vibert	pb	d	4	sv	ff	s		BS-1	Robert	France	1853
Gloire de France	lp	vd	4	l	ff	s		BS-2	unknown	unknown	c.1819
Gros Provins Panaché	mb	d	4	sv	fff	s		BS-1	unknown	unknown	?

COLOR
w=white or nearly white
p/w=pink and white
pb=pink blend
p/y=pink and yellow
lp=light pink
mp=medium pink
dp=deep pink
mr=medium red
dr=deep red
rb=red blend
m=mauve
mb=mauve blend
ly=light yellow
my=medium yellow
dy=deep yellow
yo=yellow-orange
o=orange
or=orange-red
yo=yellow-orange
c/s=coppery salmon

FORM
s=single
s+=slightly more than single
sd=semi-double
d=double
vd=very double or quartered

HARDINESS ZONE
2 to 5 (see Zone map)

VIGOR
g=ground cover
l=low
sv=semi-vigorous
v=vigorous
cl=climber

FRAGRANCE
f=little or no fragrance
ff=moderate fragrance
fff=exceptional fragrance

SEASON
sp=spring
s=summer
r=repeating
c=continuous bloomer

SUITABILITY FOR HEDGING
H

DISEASE SUSCEPTIBILITY
Blackspot:
BS-0= Immune or so little as to be insignificant.
BS-1= Noticeable but generally affecting fewer than 25% of leaves.
BS-2= Affecting at least 50% of leaves, some defoliation without protection.
BS-3= Affecting most of leaves, heavy defoliation without protection.

Mildew:
M=Varieties that are particularly susceptible to mildew.

Rust:
R= Varieties that are particularly susceptible to rust.

Note: Although roses are subject to several diseases, by far the most important disease of hardy varieties is blackspot. Those in drier climates may not have problems with blackspot, but in more humid areas blackspot can seriously affect many roses. These designations are based on the incidence of blackspot in a moderately humid site. Although you may find the incidence of blackspot either more or less severe than indicated by these ratings, they at least will offer a relative scale of blackspot susceptibility.

THE VARIETIES	COLOR	FORM	HARDINESS ZONE	VIGOR	FRAGRANCE	SEASON	SUITABILITY FOR HEDGING	DISEASE SUSCEPTIBILITY	BREEDER	ORIGIN	INTRODUCED
Henri Fouquier	mp	vd	4	l	fff	s		BS-1	unknown	unknown	1854
Hippolyte	mb	vd	4	v	ff	s		BS-1	unknown	unknown	c.1820
Ipsilanté	pb	v	4	sv	fff	s		BS-1	unknown	unknown	1821
James Mason	dr	sd	4	sv	ff	s		BS-1	Beales	UK	1982
Jenny Duval	mb	sd	4	sv	fff	s		BS-1,M	unknown	unknown	c.1750
La Belle Sultane (Violacea)	mb	sd	4	v	ff	s		BS-1	unknown	unknown	1795
La Plus Belle des Ponctuées	pb	vd	4	v	ff	s		BS-1	unknown	unknown	?
Nestor	pb	d	4	sv	ff	s		BS-1	unknown	unknown	c.1846
Oeillet Flamand	pb	vd	4	sv	ff	s		BS-1	Vibert	France	1845
Oeillet Parfait	w	vd	4	v	ff	s		BS-0	Foulard	France	1841
Ombrée Parfaite	pb	vd	4	l	ff	s		BS-1	Vibert	France	1823
Perle de Panachées	p/w	d	4	v	ff	s		BS-1	Vibert	France	1845
Président de Sèze (Mme. Hébert)	pb	vd	4	sv	ff	s		BS-1	unknown	unknown	c.1836
Rosa Mundi (R. gallica versicolor)	p/w	d	4	sv	ff	s		BS-1	unknown	unknown	c.1580
Rose du Maître d'Ecole	dp	v	4	l	ff	s		BS-1	Miellez	France	1840
Sissinghurst Castle (Rose des Maures)	dr	vd	4	l	ff	s		BS-1	unknown	unknown	old
Surpasse Tout	rb	vd	4	sv	ff	s		BS-1	unknown	unknown	c.1832
Tricolore (Reine Marguerite)	dp	vd	4	sv	ff	s		BS-1	Lahaye Père	France	1827
Tricolore de Flandre	pb	vd	4	sv	ff	s		BS-1	Van Houtte	Belgium	1846
Tuscany (Old Velvet Rose)	rb	d	4	sv	ff	s		BS-1	unknown	unknown	?

THE VARIETIES	COLOR	FORM	HARDINESS ZONE	VIGOR	FRAGRANCE	SEASON	SUITABILITY FOR HEDGING	DISEASE SUSCEPTIBILITY	BREEDER	ORIGIN	INTRODUCED
Tuscany Superb	rb	d	4	sv	ff	s		BS-2	Paul	UK	1848
ROSA GLAUCA											
Carmenetta	mp	s	2	v	f	s		BS-0	Ag. Canada	Canada	1923
ROSA MOYESSI											
Eddie's Crimson	dr	d	4	v	f	s		BS-1	Eddie	Canada	1956
Eddie's Jewel	mr	d	4	v	f	r		BS-1	Eddie	Canada	1962
Fred Streeter	dp	s	4	v	f	s		BS-1	Jackman	UK	1951
Geranium	or	s	3-4	v	f	s		BS-0	Royal Hort. Soc.	UK	1938
Highodensis	dp	s	3-4	v	f	s		BS-0	Hillier	UK	1928

COLOR
w=white or nearly white
p/w=pink and white
pb=pink blend
p/y=pink and yellow
lp=light pink
mp=medium pink
dp=deep pink
mr=medium red
dr=deep red
rb=red blend
m=mauve
mb=mauve blend
ly=light yellow
my=medium yellow
dy=deep yellow
yo=yellow-orange
o=orange
or=orange-red
yo=yellow-orange
c/s=coppery salmon

FORM
s=single
s+=slightly more than single
sd=semi-double
d=double
vd=very double or quartered

HARDINESS ZONE
2 to 5 (see Zone map)

VIGOR
g=ground cover
l=low
sv=semi-vigorous
v=vigorous
cl=climber

FRAGRANCE
f=little or no fragrance
ff=moderate fragrance
fff=exceptional fragrance

SEASON
sp=spring
s=summer
r=repeating
c=continuous bloomer

SUITABILITY FOR HEDGING
H

DISEASE SUSCEPTIBILITY
Blackspot:
BS-0= Immune or so little as to be insignificant.
BS-1= Noticeable but generally affecting fewer than 25% of leaves.
BS-2= Affecting at least 50% of leaves, some defoliation without protection.
BS-3= Affecting most of leaves, heavy defoliation without protection.

Mildew:
M=Varieties that are particularly susceptible to mildew.

Rust:
R= Varieties that are particularly susceptible to rust.

Note: Although roses are subject to several diseases, by far the most important disease of hardy varieties is blackspot. Those in drier climates may not have problems with blackspot, but in more humid areas blackspot can seriously affect many roses. These designations are based on the incidence of blackspot in a moderately humid site. Although you may find the incidence of blackspot either more or less severe than indicated by these ratings, they at least will offer a relative scale of blackspot susceptibility.

THE VARIETIES	COLOR	FORM	HARDINESS ZONE	VIGOR	FRAGRANCE	SEASON	SUITABILITY FOR HEDGING	DISEASE SUSCEPTIBILITY	BREEDER	ORIGIN	INTRODUCED
Marguerite Hilling	mp	s+	5	v	f	r		BS-1	Hillier	UK	1959
Nevada	w	s+	5	v	f	r		BS-1	Dot	Spain	1927
ROSA NITIDA											
Aylsham	dp	d	3	l	f	s		BS-0	Wright	Canada	1948
Defender	dp	s+	3	v	fff	s		BS-0	unknown	unknown	?
ROSA RUBRIFOLIA (GLAUCA)											
Carmenetta	mp	s	2	v	f	s		BS-0	Agr. Canada	Canada	1923
ROSA RUGOSA											
Agnes	my	d	3	sv	fff	r	H	BS-0	Saunders	Canada	1922
Amelie Gravereaux	rb	d	3	v	fff	r	H	BS-0	Gravereaux	France	1903
Belle Poitvine	mp	sd	4	sv	ff	r	H	BS-0	Bruant	France	1984
Blanc Double de Coubert	w	sd	2-3	v	fff	r	H	BS-0	Cochet-Cochet	France	1892
Carmen	dr	s	4	sv	ff	r	H	BS-1	Lambert	Germany	1907
Charles Albanel	m	sd	2-3	g	ff	c		BS-0	Svejda	Canada	1982
Conrad Ferdinand Meyer	mp	d	4-5	v	fff	r	H	BS-2,R	Müller	Germany	1899
Culverbrae	dr	vd	4	sv	ff	r	H	BS-0	Gobbee	UK	1973
Dart's Dash	m	sd	2-3	sv	fff	c	H	BS-0,M	unknown	unknown	?

THE VARIETIES	COLOR	FORM	HARDINESS ZONE	VIGOR	FRAGRANCE	SEASON	SUITABILITY FOR HEDGING	DISEASE SUSCEPTIBILITY	BREEDER	ORIGIN	INTRODUCED
David Thompson	dp	d	2-3	sv	ff	c	H	BS-0	Svejda	Canada	1979
Delicata	mp	sd	3	sv	ff	r	H	BS-0	Cooling	?	1898
Dr. Eckener	p/y	sd	5	v	fff	r		BS-1	Berger	Germany	1930
Fimbriata	lp	sd	4	sv	f	r	H	BS-0	Morlet	France	1891
F.J. Grootendorst	mr	d	3-4	v	f	c	H	BS-1	De Goey or Skinner	Holland / Canada	1918 / 1908
Fru Dagmar Hastrup (*Fru Dagmar Hartopp*)	mp	s	2-3	l	fff	c		BS-0	Hastrup	Denmark	1914
George Will	dp	d	2-3	sv	fff	r		BS-1	Skinner	Canada	1939
Grootendorst supreme	dr	d	3-4	v	f	c	H	BS-1	Grootendorst	Holland	1936
Hansa	m	d	3	v	fff	r	H	BS-0	Schaum & Van Tol	Holland	1905

COLOR
w=white or nearly white
p/w=pink and white
pb=pink blend
p/y=pink and yellow
lp=light pink
mp=medium pink
dp=deep pink
mr=medium red
dr=deep red
rb=red blend
m=mauve
mb=mauve blend
ly=light yellow
my=medium yellow
dy=deep yellow
yo=yellow-orange
o=orange
or=orange-red
yo=yellow-orange
c/s=coppery salmon

FORM
s=single
s+=slightly more than single
sd=semi-double
d=double
vd=very double or quartered

HARDINESS ZONE
2 to 5 (see Zone map)

VIGOR
g=ground cover
l=low
sv=semi-vigorous
v=vigorous
cl=climber

FRAGRANCE
f=little or no fragrance
ff=moderate fragrance
fff=exceptional fragrance

SEASON
sp=spring
s=summer
r=repeating
c=continuous bloomer

SUITABILITY FOR HEDGING
H

DISEASE SUSCEPTIBILITY
Blackspot:
BS-0= Immune or so little as to be insignificant.
BS-1= Noticeable but generally affecting fewer than 25% of leaves.
BS-2= Affecting at least 50% of leaves, some defoliation without protection.
BS-3= Affecting most of leaves, heavy defoliation without protection.

Mildew:
M=Varieties that are particularly susceptible to mildew.

Rust:
R= Varieties that are particularly susceptible to rust.

Note: Although roses are subject to several diseases, by far the most important disease of hardy varieties is blackspot. Those in drier climates may not have problems with blackspot, but in more humid areas blackspot can seriously affect many roses. These designations are based on the incidence of blackspot in a moderately humid site. Although you may find the incidence of blackspot either more or less severe than indicated by these ratings, they at least will offer a relative scale of blackspot susceptibility.

THE VARIETIES	COLOR	FORM	HARDINESS ZONE	VIGOR	FRAGRANCE	SEASON	SUITABILITY FOR HEDGING	DISEASE SUSCEPTIBILITY	BREEDER	ORIGIN	INTRODUCED
Henry Hudson	w	d	2-3	l	fff	c		BS-0	Svejda	Canada	1961
Hunter	dr	d	4	sv	fff	c		BS-1	Mattock	UK	1961
Jens Munk	mp	sd	2-3	sv	ff	c	H	BS-0	Svejda	Canada	1974
Lady Curzon	lp	s	4	sv	fff	r		BS-1	Turner	UK	1901
Martin Frobisher	lp	d	3	v	fff	c	H	BS-0	Svejda	Canada	1968
Mary Manners	w	sd	4	v	fff	c	H	BS-1	Leicester Rose Co.	England	1970
Max Graf	dp	s	4	g	f	s		BS-0	Kordes	Germany	1919
Mme. Georges Bruant	w	sd	4	sv	fff	c	H	BS-0	Bruant	France	1887
Mrs. Anthony Waterer	dr	d	3	sv	f	c	H	BS-2	Waterer	UK	1898
Moje Hammarberg	m	d	3	v	fff	r	H	BS-0	Hammarberg	?	1931
Nova Zembla	w	d	5	v	fff	r	H	BS-1,R	Mees	UK	1907
Nyveldt's White	w	s	4	sv	fff	r	H	BS-1	Nyveldt	Holland	1955
Pink Grootendorst	mp	d	3-4	sv	f	c	H	BS-1	Grootendorst	Holland	1923
Rosa paulii	w	s	2-3	g	fff	s		BS-0,M	Paul	UK	1903
Rose à Parfum de l'Hay	dr	d	4	sv	fff	c		BS-1	Gravereaux	France	1901
Roseraie de l'Hay	dr	sd	4	v	fff	c	H	BS-0	Cochet-Cochet	France	1901
Rugosa repens rosea (*Rosa* × *paulii rosea*)	lp	s	2-3	g	fff	s		BS-0	Paul	UK	1912
Ruskin	dr	d	3-4	v	fff	r	H	BS-1	Van Fleet	USA	1928
Sarah Van Fleet	mp	sd	4	sv	fff	c	H	BS-1,R	Van Fleet	USA	1926

THE VARIETIES	COLOR	FORM	HARDINESS ZONE	VIGOR	FRAGRANCE	SEASON	SUITABILITY FOR HEDGING	DISEASE SUSCEPTIBILITY	BREEDER	ORIGIN	INTRODUCED
Scabrosa	m	s	2-3	v	fff	c	H	BS-0	Harkness	UK	1960
Schneelicht	w	s	4	v	ff	r	H	BS-1	Geschwind	Hungary	1894
Schneezwerg (Snow Dwarf)	w	sd	2-3	sv	fff	c	H	BS-0	Lambert	Germany	1912
Sir Thomas Lipton	w	d	3-4	v	fff	c	H	BS-0	Van Fleet	USA	1900
Souvenir de Philemon Cochet	w	d	2-3	v	fff	c	H	BS-0	Cochet-Cochet	France	1899
Thérèse Bugnet	mp	d	2	v	fff	r	H	BS-0,M	Bugnet	Canada	1950
Vanguard	c/s	sd	5	v	fff	r	H	BS-1	Stevens	USA	1932
Wasagaming	mp	d	2-3	sv	ff	s		BS-1	Skinner	Canada	1938
White Grootendorst	w	d	3-4	sv	f	c		BS-1	Eddie	UK	1962
Will Alderman	mp	d	2-3	sv	ff	c		BS-1	Skinner	Canada	1949

COLOR
w=white or nearly white
p/w=pink and white
pb=pink blend
p/y=pink and yellow
lp=light pink
mp=medium pink
dp=deep pink
mr=medium red
dr=deep red
rb=red blend
m=mauve
mb=mauve blend
ly=light yellow
my=medium yellow
dy=deep yellow
yo=yellow-orange
o=orange
or=orange-red
yo=yellow-orange
c/s=coppery salmon

FORM
s=single
s+=slightly more than single
sd=semi-double
d=double
vd=very double or quartered

HARDINESS ZONE
2 to 5 (see Zone map)

VIGOR
g=ground cover
l=low
sv=semi-vigorous
v=vigorous
cl=climber

FRAGRANCE
f=little or no fragrance
ff=moderate fragrance
fff=exceptional fragrance

SEASON
sp=spring
s=summer
r=repeating
c=continuous bloomer

SUITABILITY FOR HEDGING
H

DISEASE SUSCEPTIBILITY
Blackspot:
BS-0= Immune or so little as to be insignificant.
BS-1= Noticeable but generally affecting fewer than 25% of leaves.
BS-2= Affecting at least 50% of leaves, some defoliation without protection.
BS-3= Affecting most of leaves, heavy defoliation without protection.

Mildew:
M=Varieties that are particularly susceptible to mildew.

Rust:
R= Varieties that are particularly susceptible to rust.

Note: Although roses are subject to several diseases, by far the most important disease of hardy varieties is blackspot. Those in drier climates may not have problems with blackspot, but in more humid areas blackspot can seriously affect many roses. These designations are based on the incidence of blackspot in a moderately humid site. Although you may find the incidence of blackspot either more or less severe than indicated by these ratings, they at least will offer a relative scale of blackspot susceptibility.

THE VARIETIES	COLOR	FORM	HARDINESS ZONE	VIGOR	FRAGRANCE	SEASON	SUITABILITY FOR HEDGING	DISEASE SUSCEPTIBILITY	BREEDER	ORIGIN	INTRODUCED
ROSA SETIGERA											
American Pillar	dp	s	5	cl	f	s		BS-0	Van Fleet	USA	1902
Baltimore Belle	lp	d	5	cl	f	s		BS-1	Feast	USA	1843
ROSA SPINOSISSIMA (ROSA PIMPINELLIFOLIA)											
Aïcha	my	s+	3	cl	ff	sp		BS-1	Petersen	Denmark	1966
Altaica	w	s	3	sv	f	sp	H	BS-0		Asia	c.1818
Dr. Merkelely	mp	d	3	l	fff	s		BS-1	Skinner	Canada	c.1925
Doorenbos selection	rb	s	3	l	ff	r		BS-0	Doorenbos?	Germany?	?
Double pink (*Burnet double pink*)	mp	d	3	sv	fff	sp		BS-0	unknown	UK	c.1800s
Double white (*Burnet double white*)	w	d	3	sv	fff	sp		BS-0	unknown	UK	c.1800s
Double yellow (*Old Yellow Scotch*)	my	d	3	sv	ff	sp		BS-1	unknown	UK	c.1800s
Frühlingsanfang	w	s	4-5	v	fff	sp	H	BS-1	Kordes	Germany	1950
Frühlingsduft	ab	sd	4-5	v	fff	sp	H	BS-1	Kordes	Germany	1949
Frühlingsgold	my	s+	4-5	v	fff	sp	H	BS-2	Kordes	Germany	1937
Frühlingsmorgen	dp	s	4-5	v	fff	r	H	BS-1	Kordes	Germany	1942
Frühlingschnee	w	sd	4-5	v	ff	sp	H	BS-1	Kordes	Germany	1954
Frühlingstag	dy	sd	4-5	v	fff	sp	H	BS-1	Kordes	Germany	1949
Gloire de Edzell (*Glory of Edzell*)	mp	s	4	v	ff	sp	H	BS-1	unknown	unknown	?

THE VARIETIES	COLOR	FORM	HARDINESS ZONE	VIGOR	FRAGRANCE	SEASON	SUITABILITY FOR HEDGING	DISEASE SUSCEPTIBILITY	BREEDER	ORIGIN	INTRODUCED
Harison's Salmon	c/s	s	3	sv	ff	sp	H	BS-0	Hamblin	?	1929
Harison's Yellow (*Yellow Rose of Texas*), (*R.* × *Harisonii*)	my	sd	3	sv	f	sp	H	BS-1	Harison	USA	1830
Hazeldean	my	sd	2-3	sv	f	sp	H	BS-1	Wright	Canada	1948
Kakwa	lp	d	3	sv	fff	sp	H	BS-0	Wallace	Canada?	1973
Karl Förster	w	sd	4-5	sv	fff	r		BS-0	Kordes	Germany	1953
Maigold	yo	sd	5	v	fff	s		BS-1	Kordes	Germany	1953
Mary Queen of Scots	mp	s	3	l	ff	sp		BS-1	unknown	UK?	?
Mrs. Colville	rb	s	3	sv	ff	sp		BS-1	unknown	UK?	?
Petite Pink Scotch	mp	s	3	g	ff	sp		BS-1	unknown	UK?	c.1750
Single Cherry	mr	s	3	l	ff	sp		BS-1	unknown	UK?	?

COLOR
w=white or nearly white
p/w=pink and white
pb=pink blend
p/y=pink and yellow
lp=light pink
mp=medium pink
dp=deep pink
mr=medium red
dr=deep red
rb=red blend
m=mauve
mb=mauve blend
ly=light yellow
my=medium yellow
dy=deep yellow
yo=yellow-orange
o=orange
or=orange-red
yo=yellow-orange
c/s=coppery salmon

FORM
s=single
s+=slightly more than single
sd=semi-double
d=double
vd=very double or quartered

HARDINESS ZONE
2 to 5 (see Zone map)

VIGOR
g=ground cover
l=low
sv=semi-vigorous
v=vigorous
cl=climber

FRAGRANCE
f=little or no fragrance
ff=moderate fragrance
fff=exceptional fragrance

SEASON
sp=spring
s=summer
r=repeating
c=continuous bloomer

SUITABILITY FOR HEDGING
H

DISEASE SUSCEPTIBILITY
Blackspot:
BS-0= Immune or so little as to be insignificant.
BS-1= Noticeable but generally affecting fewer than 25% of leaves.
BS-2= Affecting at least 50% of leaves, some defoliation without protection.
BS-3= Affecting most of leaves, heavy defoliation without protection.

Mildew:
M=Varieties that are particularly susceptible to mildew.

Rust:
R= Varieties that are particularly susceptible to rust.

Note: Although roses are subject to several diseases, by far the most important disease of hardy varieties is blackspot. Those in drier climates may not have problems with blackspot, but in more humid areas blackspot can seriously affect many roses. These designations are based on the incidence of blackspot in a moderately humid site. Although you may find the incidence of blackspot either more or less severe than indicated by these ratings, they at least will offer a relative scale of blackspot susceptibility.

THE VARIETIES	COLOR	FORM	HARDINESS ZONE	VIGOR	FRAGRANCE	SEASON	SUITABILITY FOR HEDGING	DISEASE SUSCEPTIBILITY	BREEDER	ORIGIN	INTRODUCED
Stanwell Perpetual	lp	d	3	sv	fff	c	H	BS-0	Lee	UK	1838
Suzanne	lp	vd	3	sv	f	c		BS-1	Skinner	Canada	1949
William III	mb	sd	3	l	fff	s		BS-1	unknown	UK?	?
ROSA SUFFULTA											
Assiniboine	dp	d	3	sv	ff	s		BS-1	Marshall	Canada	1962
Cuthbert Grant	dr	d	3-4	sv	f	c		BS-1	Marshall	Canada	1967
ROSA XANTHINA											
Canary Bird	dy	s	4-5	sv	f	sp		BS-1	?	?	1907
MISCELLANEOUS SHRUBS											
Alexander Mackenzie	mr	d	3-4	v	ff	c	H	BS-0	Svejda	Canada	1985
Adelaide Hoodless	dr	sd	4	l	f	r		BS-2	Marshall	Canada	1972
Birdie Blye	mp	d	4-5	sv	f	r	H	BS-1	Van Fleet	USA	1904
Bonica '82 (Bonica)	lp	d	5	l	f	c	H	BS-1	Meilland	France	1985
Carefree Beauty (*Bucbi*), (*Audace*)	mp	sd	4	sv	f	r		BS-1	Buck	USA	1977
Champlain	dr	sd	4	l	f	c		BS-0	Svejda	Canada	1982
Constance Spry (*Constanze Spry*)	mp	d	4	v	fff	s		BS-0	Austin	UK	1961
Dortmund	dr	s	5	cl	f	r		BS-1	Kordes	Germany	1955

THE VARIETIES	COLOR	FORM	HARDINESS ZONE	VIGOR	FRAGRANCE	SEASON	SUITABILITY FOR HEDGING	DISEASE SUSCEPTIBILITY	BREEDER	ORIGIN	INTRODUCED
Flamingo	mp	sd	5	v	ff	r		BS-1	Howard	USA	1956
Golden Wings	my	s+	5	sv	ff	c		BS-2	Shepherd	USA	1956
Henry Kelsey	dr	sd	4	cl	ff	c		BS-1	Svejda	Canada	1984
John Cabot	mr	d	3	cl	f	c		BS-0	Svejda	Canada	1978
John Davis	mp	d	3	v	ff	c	H	BS-0	Svejda	Canada	1986
John Franklin	mr	sd	4-5	l	f	c		BS-2	Svejda	Canada	1980
J.H. Kern	m	vd	4	l	ff	c		BS-2	Kern?	USA?	?
J.P. Connell	my	d	3-4	sv	ff	r		BS-2	Svejda	Canada	1987
Leverkusen	my	sd	4-5	cl	ff	s	H	BS-0	Kordes	Germany	1954
Marie Bugnet	w	sd	3	v	fff	r	H	BS-1	Bugnet	Canada	1963
Mrs. John McNabb	w	vd	3	sv	ff	r	H	BS-1	Skinner	Canada	1942

COLOR
w=white or nearly white
p/w=pink and white
pb=pink blend
p/y=pink and yellow
lp=light pink
mp=medium pink
dp=deep pink
mr=medium red
dr=deep red
rb=red blend
m=mauve
mb=mauve blend
ly=light yellow
my=medium yellow
dy=deep yellow
yo=yellow-orange
o=orange
or=orange-red
yo=yellow-orange
c/s=coppery salmon

FORM
s=single
s+=slightly more than single
sd=semi-double
d=double
vd=very double or quartered

HARDINESS ZONE
2 to 5 (see Zone map)

VIGOR
g=ground cover
l=low
sv=semi-vigorous
v=vigorous
cl=climber

FRAGRANCE
f=little or no fragrance
ff=moderate fragrance
fff=exceptional fragrance

SEASON
sp=spring
s=summer
r=repeating
c=continuous bloomer

SUITABILITY FOR HEDGING
H

DISEASE SUSCEPTIBILITY
Blackspot:
BS-0= Immune or so little as to be insignificant.
BS-1= Noticeable but generally affecting fewer than 25% of leaves.
BS-2= Affecting at least 50% of leaves, some defoliation without protection.
BS-3= Affecting most of leaves, heavy defoliation without protection.

Mildew:
M=Varieties that are particularly susceptible to mildew.

Rust:
R= Varieties that are particularly susceptible to rust.

Note: Although roses are subject to several diseases, by far the most important disease of hardy varieties is blackspot. Those in drier climates may not have problems with blackspot, but in more humid areas blackspot can seriously affect many roses. These designations are based on the incidence of blackspot in a moderately humid site. Although you may find the incidence of blackspot either more or less severe than indicated by these ratings, they at least will offer a relative scale of blackspot susceptibility.

THE VARIETIES	COLOR	FORM	HARDINESS ZONE	VIGOR	FRAGRANCE	SEASON	SUITABILITY FOR HEDGING	DISEASE SUSCEPTIBILITY	BREEDER	ORIGIN	INTRODUCED
Morden Amorette	mr	d	3-4	l	f	c		BS-2	Marshall	Canada	1977
Morden Blush	w/lp	d	3	l	f	c		BS-2	Collicutt-Marshall	Canada	1988
Morden Cardinette	mr	d	3-4	l	f	c		BS-2	Marshall	Canada	1980
Morden Centennial	mp	d	3	sv	ff	r		BS-1	Marshall	Canada	1980
Morden Fireglow	or	sd	3	l	f	c		BS-2	Collicutt-Marshall	Canada	1989
Morden Ruby	dp	d	3	l	f	c		BS-2	Marshall	Canada	1977
Nearly Wild	mp	s	3-4	l	f	c		BS-1	Brownell	USA	1941
Parkdirector Riggers	dr	s+	5	v	f	c		BS-1	Kordes	Germany	1957
Polstjärnan (*Polestar*), (*The Polar Star*), (*The Wasa Star*), (*The White Star of Finland*), (*Wasastjernan*)	w	s	3	cl	f	s		BS-0	Wasast-Jarnan	Finland	1937
Prairie Dawn	mp	d	3	v	f	s		BS-1	Agr. Canada	Canada	1959
Rheinaupark	dr	sd	5	sv	f	c		BS-2	Kordes	Germany	1983
Robusta	dr	s	4-5	v	f	c		BS-1	Kordes	Germany	1987
Rote Max Graf (*Red Max Graf*), (*Kormax*), (*Kordes' rose*)	dr	s	5	g	f	s		BS-0	Kordes	Germany	1980
Scharlachglut (*Scarlet glow*), (*Scarlet fire*)	dr	s	4-5	v	f	s		BS-1	Kordes	Germany	1952
Shropshire Lass	lp	s+	5	v	ff	s		BS-1	Austin	UK	1968
William Baffin	dp	s+	3	cl	f	c	H	BS-0	Svejda	Canada	1983
Windrush	ly	s+	4	sv	f	r		BS-2	Austin	UK	1985
Zitronenfalter	my	sd	5	sv	ff	r		BS-2	Tantau	Germany	1956

Alexander Mackenzie's foliage and form create an elegant backdrop for the flowers.

Nurseries, Rose Organizations and Source Books

NURSERIES

The following nurseries are known to carry hardy roses and are believed to ship plants. There are doubtless other nurseries that sell hardy roses and the inclusion of these nurseries is in no way an endorsement of their products.

The Antique Rose Emporium
Route 5, Box 143
Brenham, Texas 77833
USA
telephone 409-836-9051
catalog $2.00

Carl Pallek & Son Nurseries
Box 137
Virgil, Ontario L0S 1T0
Canada
telephone 416-468-7262
free catalog, does not ship to USA

Carroll Gardens, Inc.
P.O. Box 310
Westminster, Maryland 21157
USA
telephone 301-848-5422,
301-876-7336, outside
Maryland 800-638-6334

Corn Hill Nursery Ltd.
RR 5, Route 890
Petitcodiac, N.B. E0A 2H0
Canada
telephone 506-756-3635
catalog $2.00

Country Bloomers Nursery
20091 East Chapman Ave.
Orange, California 92669
USA
telephone 714-633-7222

Earl May Seed & Nursery L.P.
Shenandoah, Iowa 51603
USA
telephone 800-831-4193

Forevergreen Farm
70 New Gloucester Road
North Yarmouth, Maine 04021
USA
telephone 207-829-5830
free catalog

Greenmantle Nursery
3010 Ettersburg Road
Garberville, California 95440
USA
telephone 707-986-7504

Gurney Seed & Nursery
110 Capitol Street
Yankton, South Dakota 57079
USA
telephone 605-665-4451

Heritage Rosarium
211 Haviland Mill Road
Brookeville, Maryland 20833
USA
telephone 301-774-2806
catalog $1.00

Heritage Rose Gardens
16831 Mitchell Creek Drive
Fort Bragg, California 95437
USA
telephone 707-964-3748,
707-984-6959

Heritage Rose Group
c/o Miriam Wilkins
925 Galvin Drive
El Cerrito, California 94530
USA
telephone 415-526-6960

High Country Rosarium
1717 Downing at Park Avenue
Denver, Colorado 80218
USA
telephone 303-832-4026

Historical Roses
1657 West Jackson Street
Painesville, Ohio 44077
USA
telephone 216-357-7270

Hortico, Inc.
Robson Road, RR 1
Waterdown, Ontario L0R 2H1
Canada
telephone 416-689-6984
catalog $2.00

Inter-State Nurseries
P.O. Box 10
Louisiana, Missouri 63353-0010
USA
telephone: 314-754-4525
800-325-4180

Jackson & Perkins Co.
2518 South Pacific Highway
P.O. Box 1028
Medford, Oregon 97501
USA
telephone 503-776-2000
800-872-7673 (customer service)
800-292-4769 (to place orders)

Kimbrew-Walter Roses
Route 2 Box 172
Grand Saline, Texas 75140
USA
telephone 214-829-2968

Krider Nurseries
P.O. Box 29
Middlebury, Indiana 46540
USA
telephone 219-825-5714

Lowe's Own Root Roses
6 Sheffield Road
Nashua, New Hampshire 03062
USA
telephone 603-888-2214
catalog $2.00

Morden Nurseries Ltd.
P.O. Box 1270
Morden, Manitoba R0G 1J0
Canada
telephone 204-822-3311

Park Seed Company, Inc.
Cokesbury Road
Greenwood, South Carolina
29647-0001
USA
telephone 803-223-8555
800-845-3369 (out of state)
800-922-6232 (within South
Carolina)

Pickering Nurseries Inc.
670 Kingston Road Hwy. 2
Pickering, Ontario L1V 1A6
Canada
telephone 416-839-2111
catalog $2.00, price list free

Roseberry Gardens
Box 933, Postal Station F
Thunder Bay, Ontario P7C 4X8
Canada
$100.00 minimum order

Rose Hybridizers Association
c/o Larry Peterson
3245 Wheaton Road
Horseheads, New York 14845
USA
telephone 607-562-8592

Roses by Walter LeMire
Highway 3 & Oldcastle Road North
RR 1
Oldcastle, Ontario N0R 1L0
Canada

Roses of Yesterday & Today
802 Brown's Valley Road
Watsonville, California 95076
USA
telephone 408-724-3537
catalog $3.00

Sears McConnell Nurseries
Port Burwell, Ontario N0J 1T0
Canada

Sheridan Nurseries Ltd.
1116 Winston Churchill Boulevard
Oakville, Ontario L6J 4Z2
Canada

The Royal National Rose Society
The Secretary
Chiswell Green
St. Albans, Hertfordshire
England AL2 3NR
telephone (0727) 50461

V. Kraus Nurseries Ltd.
Carlisle, Ontario L0R 1H0
Canada
telephone 416-689-4022

Wayside Gardens
1 Garden Lane
P.O. Box 1
Hodges, South Carolina
29695-0001
USA
telephone 800-845-1124

ROSE ORGANIZATIONS

The American Rose Society
P.O. Box 30,000
Shreveport, Louisiana 71130
USA
membership $25.00 ($23.00
for those over age 65)

The Canadian Rose Society
Anne Graber
10 Fairfax Crescent
Scarborough, Ontario M1L 1Z8
telephone 416-757-8809
Canada
membership $18.00, $20.00
for family

SOURCE BOOKS

There have been innumerable books written on roses. It would be fruitless to list them all as many are out of print, while others have little information on the hardy roses. The following books are valuable for those seeking more information on hardy roses.

Beales, Peter, *Classic Roses*, Holt, Rinehart and Winston, New York, 1985

Beales, Peter, *Twentieth Century Roses*, Harper & Row, Publishers, New York, 1988

Dobson, Beverly, *Combined Rose List*, Beverly R. Dobson, 215 Harriman Road, Irvington, New York 10533, USA (A list of all rose varieties available in commerce.)

Griffiths, Trevor, *The Book of Classic Old Roses*, Penguin Books, USA, 1988

Griffiths, Trevor, *The Book of Old Roses*, Penguin Books, USA, 1987

Krussman,G., *Roses*, Batsford, London, 1982 and Timber Press, Portland, 1981

McFarland, J.H., *Modern Roses 8 and 9*, The McFarland Co. and the American Rose Society; (List of all registered roses, *Modern Roses 9* is an update)

Taylor, Norman, *Taylor's Guide to Old-Fashioned Roses*; (Taylor's Pocket Guides to Gardening series), 1989

Taylor, Norman, *Taylor's Guide to Roses*; (Taylor's Pocket Guides to Gardening series), 1986

Thomas, G.S., *Shrub Roses of Today*, J.M. Dent & Sons, 1974

Thomas, G.S., *The Old Shrub Roses*, J.M. Dent & Sons, 1978

Index

Numbers in italics refer to photographs